# PRAISE FOR *EVOLUTION OF GODDESS*

"Emma Mildon has written an exceptional book with *Evolution of Goddess*. I highly recommend it."
**—Caroline Myss,** *New York Times* bestselling author of *Archetypes* and *Sacred Contracts*

"I'm so excited for all the women this book will be serving as it makes its way into the world."
**—HeatherAsh Amara,** *New York Times* bestselling author of *Warrior Goddess Training*

"*Evolution of Goddess* is a modern-day guide to the feminine.
A must read for spiritual seekers wanting to dive into the rising feminine without
having to read twenty different books! It is a practical guide of the Goddess over time
and the best bit: presented in a way that is easy to understand and a pure joy to read."
**—Rebecca Campbell,** author of *Light Is the New Black* and *Rise Sister Rise*

"With this book, Emma Mildon is giving a voice to the ancient herstories
of our evolution, stories that have been written out of history, and with devastating effects—
whether it's our failing health-care systems, countries in continuous states of war, the repression
of women everywhere, and the ravages of the capitalist system on our environment.
This book is a call to arms for every woman to reclaim the Goddess in her—and in doing so
help to bring about a long overdue reawakening of the Divinely Feminine principal."
**—Ruby Warrington,** founder of *The Numinous* and author of *Material Girl, Mystical World*

"If your inner Goddess is bottled up inside waiting to come out,
this book will guide her to the world and into the light. Emma Mildon's powerful
yet approachable voice makes her the perfect woman to tell this story."
**—Emma Loewe,** editor at mindbodygreen

"The words in *Evolution of Goddess* will speak directly to your soul. The connection I felt to
the content and sentiment was magical; every woman on the planet has to read this book."
**—Taryn Brumfitt,** founder of Body Image Movement and director/creator of the documentary *Embrace*

"*Evolution of Goddess* is a powerful, modern-day invocation [of] the ancient wisdom and practices
of the Goddess. A calling forward of the divine feminine, and a calling out of pseudo-spiritual
propaganda, this book is a no-BS invitation to women everywhere to truly step into their power and
unapologetically reclaim their magic. If you long to live a bolder, more meaningful life, to advocate for
love, and to truly influence positive change in the world, then this is a must read. *Evolution of Goddess*
is the fuel to ignite that fire within and call you forward into the woman you know you can be."
**—Rebecca Van Leeuwen,** founder of Soul Sister Circle

"With her trademark cheek and wicked-but-wise sass, Emma Mildon gives us a divinely feminine read for the modern woman exploring her ancient roots. As a priestess of the Goddess, Emma guides us through the heartfelt connections and collaborations we can all develop with Goddesses from a variety of countries, spiritual beliefs, and practices. Calling upon the powers of Kali Ma, Gaia, Aphrodite, and Demeter has never been presented in such a fresh and fun way."
—**Julie Parker,** priestess and founder of Beautiful You Coaching Academy

"Emma is on a mission to guide us all to happiness, health, and unlimited joy through spiritual understanding and self-awareness. I love this woman and this book. Her message cuts through the clutter and speaks to the soul. Simply transformational."
—**Shannon Kaiser,** bestselling author of *Adventures for Your Soul* and *The Self-Love Experiment*

"A non-cheesey look at femininity with an empowering and unapologetic take on all things Goddess. A must-read for every human wanting to see conscious change in the world."
—**Melissa Ambrosini,** bestselling author and speaker

"A book for anyone with a burning desire to reclaim their Goddess birthright. Emma Mildon plays an important role in helping us remember our forgotten history."
—**Sahara Rose Ketabi,** author of *Idiot's Guide to Ayurveda* and *Eat Feel Fresh*

"*Evolution of Goddess* is a wonderful guide for women to learn how to bring their GODDESS home and Emma's sassy humor makes that all the more enjoyable. A timely book to help raise the feminine vibration, championing women to reach for the light each and every time."
—**Angela Morris,** founder of The Feminine Shift

"*Evolution of Goddess* has done what Emma's first book did—guide me into the spiritual world with the comfort in knowing she is right there with me on the ride. Her wit, her sense of humor, and her realness, backed up with her knowledge make this book like her first—hard to put down!"
—**Makaia Carr,** founder of Motivate Me, blogger, and entrepreneur

ALSO BY EMMA MILDON

*The Soul Searcher's Handbook*

# EVOLUTION OF GODDESS

## A MODERN GIRL'S GUIDE TO ACTIVATING YOUR FEMININE SUPERPOWERS

### EMMA MILDON

**ENLIVEN BOOKS**

—

**ATRIA**

New York  London  Toronto  Sydney  New Delhi

ENLIVEN™
ATRIA

An Imprint of Simon & Schuster, Inc.
1230 Avenue of the Americas
New York, NY 10020

First Enliven Books/Atria Paperback edition July 2018

This publication contains the opinions and ideas of its author. It is intended to provide helpful and informative material on the subjects addressed in the publication. It is sold with the understanding that the author and publisher are not engaged in rendering medical, health, or any other kind of personal professional services in the book. The reader should consult his or her medical, health, or other competent professional before adopting any of the suggestions in this book or drawing inferences from it.

The author and publisher specifically disclaim all responsibility for any liability, loss, or risk, personal or otherwise, which is incurred as a consequence, directly or indirectly, of the use and application of any of the contents of this book.

For information about special discounts for bulk purchases, please contact Simon & Schuster Special Sales at 1-866-506-1949 or business@simonandschuster.com.

The Simon & Schuster Speakers Bureau can bring authors to your live event. For more information or to book an event, contact the Simon & Schuster Speakers Bureau at 1-866-248-3049 or visit our website at www.simonspeakers.com.

*Interior design by Silverglass*

Manufactured in the United States of America

10 9 8 7 6 5 4 3 2 1

Library of Congress Cataloging-in-Publication Data is available.

ISBN 978-1-5011-6406-4
ISBN 978-1-5011-6408-8 (ebook)

# THIS IS FOR ALL THE WOMEN IN THE WORLD FEELING THE SHIFTS. YOU INCLUDED. AND FOR MY MOTHER, FOR YOUR MOTHER, FOR OUR MOTHER EARTH.

*Dedicated to the ultimate self-sacrificing Goddess, my mother,*
*Margaret Helen Mildon. You adopted so much more than my baby being;*
*you eternally imprinted on my soul, and for that, I am forever grateful for getting*
*to spend a small slither of this lifetime with you. The sixteen years we had*
*were most definitely sweet. May you mother lost souls in your next lifetime,*
*like you caught me in this one. Thank you for taking me under your wing,*
*and teaching me with such an open mind and open heart.*
*You gave me a sense of belonging in a world that wanted to mold me into*
*everyone else. Thank you for allowing your gentle parenting to grant me*
*the space to evolve. From letting me buy tarot magazines at the ripe*
*age of five, to allowing me to smother my walls with posters of orcas, crystals,*
*and fairy ornaments. Thank you for never dimming my spirit child and*
*woo-woo weirdness. This is for all the women out there who allow us to embrace*
*our evolutionary journey and ever cheerlead others to be their authentic self.*

# CONTENTS

# NOTE TO READER

Dear Reader,

Truth is, there comes a time when turning a new page in your life is the most liberating and empowering feeling you can experience. It is that sweet moment of fruition, when you realize there's so much more to the book of life. That the power of birthing the life you wish for lays in your hands to turn over, to cast out what doesn't feed your soul, add to your life, help you grow, or consciously challenge you. Keep turning pages, Goddess. You are allowed and encouraged to change.

Love Emma
xox

# INTRODUCTION: RECLAIMING THE GODDESS WITHIN

*"SHE'S ALREADY HAD EVERYTHING SHE NEEDS WITHIN HERSELF.
IT'S THE WORLD THAT CONVINCED HER SHE DID NOT."*
—RUPI KAUR

Zhena made every ounce of my energy feel good. My muse, mentor, and self-appointed mystic mother, Zhena Muzyka is a wonderful mix of gypsy, business warrior, and Goddess. One morning, as we sat in her towering bungalow that overlooked palm trees and rice paddies, she said something profound to me. We had come to Bali to work on this very book together, and as my wise guide it was evident that I, her young grasshopper, needed an inauguration activation. So, she told me: "The only way out, is in." Mind. Blown.

Her wise glare and Goddess presence made it impossible not to listen. She is a woman with gracious authority; she is caring yet commanding, nurturing while being the queen of take-no-shit. She is poised in her power. Beautifully balanced. I admired her energy. I had crossed paths with no one like her. She was as much awake as she was action. She had shown up to her calling a few years prior, when her business-empire-baby had been stripped away from her. She had been confronted with compelling change, like all of us are in our lifetime. You know, the kind of change that leaves you smarter, stronger, but also pissed off.

With transformational learnings, a passion fueled by injustice, and an all-in attitude, she built herself up, brick by conscious brick. Well, book by conscious book. Her call as a publisher was to create conscious content for the world. And not your average run-of-the-mindful-mill-new-age meanderings. Nope, she wasn't wasting her time with the mindless mainstream. Her call was to help foster books calling for spiritual activism. Books that fed people the truth. That cut through the conscious shit. Called for awakened action. She showed up by catching conscious creatives who took heed of their calling to write for the world. She led them. Activating one author after another. Powerfully, and lovingly, nurturing their works to bravely own and walk the sometimes uncomfortable truths they carried on their pages, and sending the calls to conscious action out to the masses. This book and author being one of them.

"No, honey." Zhena removed her glasses to stare down the barrel of my third eye. "No." She shook her head and leaned in toward me. "You are so much more than the girl who writes about evolution. You . . . you write about empowerment."

The hairs on my arms stood up as goose bumps prickled me with an intuitive call to take note. My soul welled up in my eyes. My soul stood to attention in salute. I found no words. All my energy was focused on listening—and trying not to blubber as I told myself to be cool.

"The world doesn't have time for cute. You have permission to step straight into the heart of it all. I mean, you never needed permission, but you have it." Zhena waved her hand at me flippantly as if to gesture, *sure, whatever you need to do to make this happen.* I looked over my shoulder, back out to the rice paddies, and noticed the smoke rising from a fire burning off crops. My eyes stung, gasping for clarity amidst the smoke. Tearing up at the sight.

Her permission came as a revelation to me. I could literally feel a cast-iron vault lift off my chest. My throat chakra cleared itself as I coughed in contemplation alongside the chirping crickets and cicadas. I gulped, digesting her delivery. I felt like I had just stepped out of my Saturn return—blindly bright, hit with conscious clarity.

"Emma, this book isn't just for you, do you get that? It's for them. The women out there who need to know they are powerful spiritual beings beyond measure. The women who are the key to changing the world. The heroines who are currently out there with no swords down the back of their dresses. Give them the f***ing sword."

She was right. You did need to know. We all did. All consciously doing the right thing, and doing nothing at all, at the same time.

Zhena spent her time among scientists, economists, and entrepreneurs. Navigating undiscovered waters, and losing sight of comfortable conscious shores, was second nature to her courageous perception of what change looked like. She walked her evolved conscious talk. Her tribe was the thinkers, the doers.

So the fact that I hadn't thought I had permission, and wasn't fulfilling my calling, probably frustrated the heck out of her. I felt her frustration and passion, so I summoned my energy, responding with the only profound answer I could think of. A flabbergasted, dumbfounded "Woooooooow." Way to play it cool, soul. Face-palm.

She smirked, nodding at me, understanding that I might need a minute to get that I was a messenger—like the Archangel Gabriel, or Gabrielle, to the Goddess movement—charged with letting everyone know the creation of change was before us. My job was to get this message out to you, to all the wise women.

I left her towering Bali bungalow, carrying heavy wings on my spiritual shoulders. The reality that not only I but that we all had a responsibility for being here *was* the reality. Part of me wanted to run out into the streets of Bali, smacking woven baskets off women's heads and crowning them instead with the same realization: That it was time to carry our callings, to find our conscious collectiveness, and to add our contribution to this impending transformation.

I had been seeking enlightenment for years. Countless hours of meditation and endless spiritual odysseys had seen me venture from the depths of Peru to the highest hilltops of New Zealand, from the soul solitude of Spain to the bowing gratitude of Bali. I always thought I was being called to soul search. But it was so much more than that.

## Standing in Your Goddess Power

You know, I often find myself stuck in this rut of wanting to be liked. Wanting to please everyone. I call it my "feminine nature," because I so often see, in myself and other women, how we can get so tangled in shape-shifting ourselves to fit everyone else's demands that we can never truly transform into our full authentic selves. We become people pleasers. Worse, we try to do it all on our own. I get it. I'm equally guilty! Maybe it's in our DNA to want to befriend and tend to others? In fact, we will break our backs and burn out, attempting to love anything and everyone, and trying to be loved by all!

The "self-help/self-love" movement has taught us that we do need to put ourselves first. We have permission to take care of ourselves, to search for ourselves. Our creations and callings included. For most of us, this isn't new or groundbreaking information. But the movement I'm writing about isn't just about self-love. (Although I wholeheartedly acknowledge it will be an important tool for you on this journey.) This book is an evolutionary step beyond learning to love yourself. This is about reclaiming your Goddess within. Why? Because it's time to uncover the feminine face of god (once again), and to stand in your power.

Many of us, me included, have been conditioned to believe we need permission to truly own something—to own our true selves. We don't need an invitation to be real. The truth is: We don't need permission to own the power of what makes us unique, what makes us female. Your emotions, your tears or temper, your love and passion. Our emotions can be wild, untamed, and raging, as they can be loving, nurturing, and consoling. All are powerful feminine energies—and when they are harnessed and directed toward conscious action can be an unstoppable force. So this is your official authorization to awaken into your full-bodied, emotionally activated self. Passion and power included.

## FACT IS, EMPOWER A WOMAN, AND YOU EMPOWER THE WORLD.

The most beautiful thing is going to happen to you in these pages. Empowerment. And then, empowered action. Fact is, empower a woman, and you empower the world. Together we can speak, we can share our voice, we can protect, educate, uplift others, scream, laugh, cry, talk, forgive, and move forward. We can take a knee. Or take a stand. Our feelings can move through us. We can move. More importantly, we can move others.

So, like Zhena's permission, even though she wisely knew I never needed it in the first place, this book is your permission (if you need it). More than permission, it's your push. Your Goddess birthright to create, your instinctive calling to take care of the world, is rightfully re-gifted back to you. That power was always within you. But sometimes we need that challenge, awakening, and activation to understand that power is safe to be harnessed. Harvested. Gathered.

You, along with millions of other mindful women, need to know you are sanctified, blessed, welcomed, applauded, and consciously cheered, to connect and unify with each other. Connected to your true Goddess calling. And connected with like-minded souls. Being supported by other activated Goddesses is essential to your success in changing how the world is. We are not free, until we are all free.

We are stronger together. It is a vital element to you completing your conscious calling. Your tribe makes you accountable. They enlighten and encourage you. After all, many make a movement.

You, me, the woman who blissfully sits next to you on the subway, we have all been in training to become emotionally charged spiritual soldiers. Dropping all guns. Leading with love. Our calling card: *change*. Your calling card.

You, dear one, are that symbol of change. You are the thread that weaves us all together to create the cloak of change draped around your chest. Your bountiful breasts are a symbol of abundant energy, and the fertility to create a new beginning and a new life.

## WHAT IS MORE OF A SYMBOL OF ETERNAL GROWTH AND CHANGE THAN THE GODDESS? THE ETERNAL SPIRAL OF CREATION. COILED LIKE A SERPENT, OUR SHAKTI ENERGY SITS, WAITING TO BE AWAKENED WITHIN ALL OF US.

After all, what is more transformative than the female form? What is more of a symbol of eternal growth and change than the Goddess? The eternal spiral of creation. Coiled like a serpent, our shakti energy sits, waiting to be awakened within all of us. What our bodies and beings were built for. What we were created to do. *Change. Create. Create the change.*

No matter your heritage, religion, background, or opinion, we, as one collective, will take counsel from our Goddess elders, grandmothers, descendants, leaders, and spiritual activists, who are no different from you. Women who all answered the same call. Who all showed up. And who today all live by this ancient awakened acumen.

This book will empower your everyday actions, which will become your offerings to the world. Your everyday thoughts, which will become your prayers and manifestations. Small shifts will become the seed of monumental development and evolved experiences. These pages will support you in every phase of your life—from birth, to "what the hell is this," to death. We are all equally welcomed and worthy, as the moon is to the sky, every flicker to every flame, every drop is to the ocean—together, reunited, gathered together, we are powerful beyond measure. It's time to evolve, as one.

You, sister, are made of the same inner beauty as some of the most guided saints, the most gifted inventors and artists, the bravest of leaders and revolutionaries, and some of the most famed and followed women throughout time. Yeah girl, you have a piece of Mother Teresa, Princess Diana, Joan of Arc, even Queen B in you. We all do. We are, after all, part of the same sacred Goddess-united family now. And you are in the energetic presence of millions of mindful maidens. How should you feel knowing you are in the presence of Goddesses? The answer is a simple one. You should feel good. They should leave you feeling empowered, nurtured, inspired, motivated, bright, bolder, and lighter. The Goddess ethos is: living for love, light, and legacy.

## THE GODDESS ETHOS IS: LIVING FOR LOVE, LIGHT, AND LEGACY.

# ABOUT THE BOOK

*"THE LIFE YOU WANT IS WAITING TO RISE UP TO MEET YOU. . . .*
*WILL YOU ACCEPT IT? DO YOU FEEL WORTHY ENOUGH TO ACCEPT IT?"*
*—OPRAH WINFREY*

My wish for you is that this book becomes a source of Goddess energy and wisdom. You will learn about your Goddess past so you can wake up, listen, and stand in your power. To help you connect, channel, and call upon our Goddess grandmothers who can support you in balance, strength, nurturing, confidence, healing, accomplishment, review, growth, and guidance, and to see you walking in your assured, authentic, and awakened stride.

*THIS IS THE LOST STORY OF OUR FEMININE SPIRITUAL EVOLUTION, A GUIDEBOOK THAT IS GOING TO WALK WITH YOU AS YOU TAKE YOUR JOURNEY FROM WHO YOU THOUGHT YOU WERE TO YOUR TRUE SELF.*

Together, we'll unravel the forgotten umbilical cord that runs through each of us, connecting us with new words that resonate within us; unexplainable knowings; déjà vu; an intuitive pull; a spontaneous curiosity about a land, a people, a past; and unbury forgotten insights, lost or silenced. This is the lost story of our feminine spiritual evolution, a guidebook that is going to walk with you as you take your journey from who you thought you were to your true self. Helping to empower you to take your place in this circle of change. A Goddess game changer.

This book is your journey to discovering all the things the history books, scriptures, and even modern-day Wikipedia left off the list of "important shit you need to know to spiritually evolve and consciously change and heal the world." This book will become a go-to journal for your evolving soul. A source of activation.

We will weave lessons from the elements and the earth itself, collectively connecting to the teachings of our ancient feminine mythology. We will sew in the energetic threads of our conscious cloak, our natural elemental threads, which use our evolutionary archetypes, stories, and modalities—both mystic and modern—to weave it all in as one. So that you can see the beauty and power that comes from stepping into a circle of like-minded soul sisters, with a common purpose, with energy in alignment, and not just with a vision for our near future, but a plan in motion. The energies you once used to let make, break, define, or confine you, will now completely empower you.

You will be called upon to journal, note-take, research, circle, underline, experiment, exercise, and digest new thoughts and approaches to help you connect the dots of your evolution to empowerment. Your story. This book will guide you, inspire you, interact with you, and propel you into a realm of lost wisdom.

Some of the womanly figures will be familiar, some will be new, but you will close the book feeling like you have met a long-lost sisterhood, one not much different from you. Sisters from different times throughout history, from different cultures, from different beliefs, all of whom, like you, were part of a collective consciousness, and stood for change. You will be encouraged to explore the spiritual clues—from your place in the stars, to your interests, to your intrigues, to your inspirations—exposing your true Goddess self.

My wish, for all women, is beyond fighting for equality, it is to *be* equality. In all things, from action to energy. That is the sign of an evolved being.

## YOU ARE STANDING SHOULDER TO SHOULDER GODDESSES; IN LINE WITH THE ENERGY OF FEMININE GIANTS.

My wish is that we may evolve beyond our wildest dreams and become active with conscious purpose. May we all expand beyond any limiting beliefs, anything that distracts or disheartens. None of it matters now. This is about serving your wisdom, spiritual insight, and enlightened empowerment, to serve the whole world with it. And rest assured you won't do it alone. You are standing shoulder to shoulder with Goddesses; in line with the energy of feminine giants. The world and I have been waiting for you to show up. You can only imagine how happy we are to see you.

# MY WISH IS TO HOLD SPACE FOR YOU TO FEEL SAFE WHEN OTHERS ASK YOU TO CONFORM. TO HELP YOU HOLD YOUR BEAUTIFUL GODDESS PRESENCE WHEN PEOPLE ATTEMPT TO SILENCE YOU.

My wish is to hold space for you to feel safe when others ask you to conform. To help you hold your beautiful Goddess presence when people attempt to silence you. To remind you and nudge you when you try to silence yourself. You have space to call in your whole self, and all the fierce and feminine facets that make up you. I've got you.

My wish is to initiate action by inviting like-minded women into circles. Generate Goddess gatherings. Command a conscious callout for change that invites women in, to unify and identify with each other in awakened action. We rise together. Summon your full-embodied empowered self. Every single movement and march has power because every single person showed up on the day. This is your day to show up. That is my wish for you.

In this book, you will learn to:

- ❀ Understand your ever-evolving feminine self on a new profound and powerful level, acknowledging all the Goddess elements that make up you, and all your polarizing beauty.
- ❀ Weave together stories from our Goddess past, from conscious cultures and mythology, that thread together clues of how to best walk forward in today's awakening age.
- ❀ Tap into your evolutionary and elemental archetypes and use them as a guide to navigate a more awakened, mindful, fulfilling life.

## GODDESS GEM, GODDESS (R)EVOLUTIONARY, GODDESS MUSINGS & EVOLUTION EXERCISE

Throughout this book you'll find little gems of wisdom and practices to help spark evolutionary thinking. These are little tools to aid your transformation. Watch for these callouts, for they will help you to create new ways of opening up, swallowing, and digesting new ideas, thoughts, facts, and wisdom that I have woven in between the words of this book for you. I have also added to this transformational tapestry tales of revolutionaries who put the "ess" in Goddess. Some untold, some familiar, they are women who are adding to the world and shaping not just their evolution but helping to shape an ever-changing society. Stories. I share their stories to help you live, to help you live well alongside some of my own thoughts, my "Goddess Musing . . ." These Goddess aha moments and conscious contemplations are nestled between the pages as you journey through this book.

&#10056; Master your elemental modalities and use these transformational tools as an evolving Goddess to strengthen your daily waking life with awakened actions.

&#10056; Allow yourself a sacred space to explore and expand your belief system and challenge your consciousness about life as you know it.

&#10056; Accept a new approach to transforming. Your power is in your response, and this book guides you in responding, Goddess style.

&#10056; Salute the Goddesses before you, both in history and those leading the change today. Sharing with you their Goddess gusto and fem-inspiration.

## UNDERSTANDING THAT TRUE SPIRITUAL EVOLUTION COMES FROM WALKING FORWARD WHILE TURNING INWARD.

### GODDESS MUSING . . .

### BE BOLD, BRIGHT, AND BEAUTIFUL WITHOUT BEING A BITCH ABOUT IT.

Your reactions to situations are going to become defining clues of where you are on the Goddess evolutionary scales of things. So quick thought, when you feel under attack, do you choose fight or flight? Do you punch back, snap back, speak up, and take action? (Your masculine energy.) Or do you retreat, hide, bury your head, and are too indecisive over what you should do, or how you should act? (Your feminine energy.) Or are you somewhere in between? (Ah, balanced energy.) That is where we are headed. I want to ask you to please start to notice your reactions, start minding your Goddess manners and be mindful of your reactions as you read and evolve. Be bold, bright, and beautiful without being a bitch about it. Remember, you can be a Goddess-badass with love, gratitude, humbleness, and grace.

In this book, we will evolve beyond the temple, the mosque, the church while respecting and paying homage to their place in our spiritual evolution. Understanding that true spiritual evolution comes from walking forward while turning inward. And while I'll certainly be your Goddess guide on where to take awakened action and when it's needed, you are going to have to really steer your own evolutionary ship through the transformational voyage of these pages, and at your own natural pace. The power is truly in your hands, beauty.

This book seeks to provide you with straightforward and practical elementary evolutionary life hacks and practices, organized in an easy DIY manner, to help you charge on with your journey in true Goddess fashion, without the fuss or drama. Ain't nobody got time for that.

First, you'll be guided to find your dominant Goddess elemental archetype, which will give you insight into your evolutionary per-

## GODDESS GEM

Make time for inspiring sisters that you dig. I personally love to watch *SuperSoul Sunday*, read Arianna Huffington's blogs or books, or even watch TED Talks on subjects that I have never really given much thought to. Some of them rev me up, some make me rave, and some make me rage. All signs of challenges, of change. Some great books to read about Goddesses you can fangirl on are: *Women Who Run with the Wolves, Warrior Goddess Training, Dakini Power,* and *Stripped*. These scripts hold stories of women exploring their spirituality and evolution, be it through archetype, or an awakening experience. The point is to be conscious of changing, and conscious of what changes. Pay attention to it all. This is the art of true awareness.

sona and support your approach to your awakened walk ahead. Second, you'll activate your Goddess archetype. This archetype will then plug into the core areas of your personal activation, highlighting your mythology, powers, and modalities—all of which will allow you to dive deep into your evolution by supporting you with practical rituals, remedies, stories, and exercises.

## MOON. WATER. EARTH. AIR. SUN. THESE ARE THE FIVE ELEMENTAL ARCHETYPES YOU WILL EXPLORE, LEARN, AND INTEGRATE.

Moon. Water. Earth. Air. Sun. These are the five elemental archetypes you will explore, learn, and integrate. You will learn about the polarizing push and pull of energy: How sun can heat water. How air can carry the warmth of the sun. How moon can pull water. How sun and moon are both important, opposite, but working best when they are in balance. And most importantly, how earth is the ultimate stage, the ground, the space, the evolutionary area for all of these elements to showcase their powers. And you, Goddess, you will be armed with the superpowers needed to charge ahead for transformation.

We will weave these elemental understandings into the lessons of opposites that our ancient mythology teaches us: good vs. bad, right vs. wrong, strong vs. weak, light vs. darkness, and use these (sometime hilarious and often untold) stories as reminders to help us in our day-to-day struggles and triumphs. Connecting all the dots. Synthesizing all the energies. Weaving all the threads of what makes us whole and unique.

# PART I
# YOUR EVOLUTION

# GODDESS WITH A THOUSAND FACES

*"A WISE WOMAN WISHES TO BE NO ONE'S ENEMY;
A WISE WOMAN REFUSES TO BE ANYONE'S VICTIM."*
—MAYA ANGELOU

"Goddess" has many definitions—our old comrade, *The Merriam-Webster Dictionary* defines it well: "A woman whose great charm or beauty arouses adoration."[1] While many of us don't like to be defined by gender-specific terms, we are going to acknowledge all of them, all the labels, from the Goddess to the witch to the bitch, and those elements within each of us. Because, to be fair, there should not be any more of a derogatory connotation behind a strong and powerful bitch as there is behind a genuine and graceful Goddess. All have their place.

A Goddess has many faces. And we can equally be admired for our varying emotions, passions, and integrity in approaching matters dear to our heart. Every emotion is an element of admiration—each part making you one whole—a complete Goddess being. A human being who can cry for another's pain, and fly off the handle in protection of others—after all, we are human.

There are many definitions that mention Goddess in terms of beauty, or Goddess as a deity. For our definition of an admired Goddess, and for the sake of this book, we will define Goddess "beauty" by the quality of one's soul. Our beautifully loving nature, our conscious and caring character, our morals, our awakened actions—our inner beauty. By "deity" we mean we are going to relate this element of the modern Goddess to our divine calling as seen in our service to others, our passion, focus, strength, power, loving drive, and sense of spiritual sovereignty. Our energy in showing up. Service.

## EVOLUTION EXERCISE: SOUL SCRIPTING

Answer these questions like you would a quick-fire session. Try not to let your head interfere; instead, try to channel your soul's account of your experiences, beliefs, life, and its lessons:

• I pride myself on these nine traits:
• Beauty to me is:
• I value these three things in my friendships:
• The part of myself I would most like to work on is:
• What is one of the most inspiring things I tell myself often:

• What are some of the negative self-talk comments I tell myself:
• What three things am I doing to better myself at present:
• What three things would I like to learn to help my spiritual evolution:
• A Goddess to me means:

Right, it's on paper now, soul sister. A soul contract between you and your ever-evolving self; an eternal promise to be your best Goddess self, and what you aspire to become.

AN EVOLVED GODDESS IS SOMEONE WHO HAS A CONSCIOUS COMPREHENSION AND AWARENESS OF LIFE, A BEAUTY IN HER MINDFUL NATURE, AND IS A ROLE MODEL WHO SEEKS TO DRIVE FORWARD CONSCIOUS CHANGE.

So, an evolved Goddess is someone who has a conscious comprehension and awareness of life, a beauty in her mindful nature, and is a role model who seeks to drive forward conscious change. You know Gandhi's saying, "Be the change you wish to see in the world," I think he might have been talking to us evolving Goddesses.

Here is the straight truth about your role: You are an evolving Goddess. A Goddess unites people. She nourishes people's energy, feeds them wisdom, and helps them feel safe and secure in her unified family. She is love. She is education. She is an embodiment of good vibrations. A Goddess doesn't seek out balance; she is balance. When imbalance surrounds her, she seeks to right the wrongs. A Goddess doesn't fight or wait for equality; she is equality.

A GODDESS DOESN'T ASK FOR HER POWER, OR BLAME PEOPLE FOR TAKING HER POWER; SHE OWNS HER POWER, KNOWING IT CAN NEVER BE TAKEN AWAY. HER POWER ISN'T AN EXTERNAL WEAPON. . . . IT IS WITHIN HER. WITHIN YOU.

A Goddess doesn't ask for her power, or blame people for taking her power; she owns her power, knowing it can never be taken away. Her power isn't an external weapon, a yelling cry of "charge," or a stampede of horses. It is within her. Within you. Within all of us. Her power is her emotion and her knowledge. It is a powerful will, a gentle yet demanding daily way, an emotional, and all-encompassing energetic love that is commanding and nurturing. An educated and awakened response to behaving. Behaving with an aura that is bigger than herself. A presence for others.

What a Goddess thinks, does, says, eats, practices, believes in, strives for, and acts on are all reflections of how we choose to live our Goddess lives. Everything blissfully intertwined. Ever on. Ever serving. Be it a simple smile of reassurance to a stranger, supporting someone in need, educating or inspiring others, or simply offering your time and energy for something other than your own needs.

## Starting the Shifts

Dear Goddess.
From the soil to the stars.
Daughters of all mothers, fathers.
Worshippers of truth, love, and peace.
To the nonbelievers.
To you, a believer.
Listen here.

Behold. You, the dreamer of a new future. I bow to you. Truth is that you are a believer that change can happen. That change is a real possibility. And, truth be told, you are the ones who will make it all happen. No doubts about it. And so, start the shifts. The shifts within you, and around you. Here is where we put our backs into it.

### GODDESS GEM

How can we lead and follow from the heart? I like to use these little Goddess guide points to help me curb my ego and use my Goddess passion for collaboration.

- **Be intimate and affectionate with your tribe.** It's a fact, intimacy is not reserved for monogamous relationships; it is a feminine way of connecting and showing you care. So don't think you can't kindly and politely connect with people using touch.
- **Be loving, rain compliments** (I do this every day when I give a compliment to a stranger). Your emotions are a part of your feminine strength, not a weakness.
- **Nurture your tribe, offer support, guidance, and cheerlead those around you.** Do this without any need for it to be returned, just purely to lift up others.
- **Act organically.** When you collaborate with others, allow it to flow. Make sure it is natural, a give and get, without the need to necessarily demand or control the partnership.

# GODDESS (R)EVOLUTIONARY: BARBARA SAVAGE

As soon as I laid eyes on Barbara Savage, founder of the Tribal Trust Foundation, I knew I was in the presence of a powerful soul. Her long gray hair showed me wisdom, and she shared a striking resemblance to eco-queen Jane Goodall. The woman could shape-shift her energy, I swear! One second she would be swimming topless in a pool full of free-spirited Goddesses, the next she would be speaking profoundly about her life-endangering travels to the Congo. Yes, the Congo! She was a wise sage, as much as she was a young vibrant being. I knew this woman would have an interesting story to share, but I never expected it to take my emotions on such a journey!

Her story of how she got called, and showed up, is a worthy one. All of ours are. But this story had to be shared with you.

In her words, she shares her turn of spiritual evolution and the call to activate:

My daily routine started with coffee, meditation, and a run before breakfast. I chose not to engage socially, so evenings were spent praying and journaling. Within two months I had a dream of a man and a message commanding: "Come to Africa." I didn't know who he was at the time. I just saw the distinctive face of an African man and his message was clear. It was such a powerful experience that I immediately got up from my meditation pillow and called an airline to book my flight.

A month later I met the man in my vision, Matuto, in Zimbabwe. He was a traditional spiritual leader, believed to be the Divine Ruler/King of the Shona people. When I told Matuto the story of how I received his spiritual calling, he affirmed that I was telling the truth and explained why he had called me to help. This divinely guided experience opened me to my purpose of helping indigenous people preserve their culture and sharing their wisdom in support of nature and global healing.[2]

When asked what she regrets most, it was simple: She would have showed up earlier. "I would have opened my heart and trusted life earlier. Although I had deep faith in my destiny and courage to follow my dreams, I did not appreciate the divine plan for my journey."

She recalls one of the defining moments when women reached out and asked her to help them rebuild their empowerment:

The inspiration came from the jungle of Chitwan, Nepal, after meeting with the indigenous Tharu people. These original people were displaced and disenfranchised. Young unmarried girls became victims of sex trafficking. The women asked me to help them create a women's craft collective, so they could be empowered. I did not have any money at the time to give them, but I did have friends with money. I formed the Tribal Trust Foundation, a 501(c)(3) nonprofit organization, so my friends could make tax-deductible contributions in support of indigenous causes.[3]

And so, her shift began.

One thing Barbara and I agree on is you. That with you comes great responsibility, great growth, and great power. She shares her wish for you:

My wish is for the next generation of Goddesses to help heal the world (and themselves!) through love, service, and joy. If I could do it, you can too! As an elder Goddess, I have the experience and perspective to know you, the next generation, are here to bring forward an expansion of consciousness. You are the feminine future. This can be achieved in your daily life by nurturing your soul and following your heart every day.[4]

When asked what she could tell you directly, if you had to put down this book and look into her soul, she said: "Know your worth, dream big, and never give up! The world needs you."

When asked what Goddess inspires her, she shared a quote from Maya Angelou: "My mission in life is not merely to survive, but to thrive; and to do so with some passion, some compassion, some humor, and some style. If you don't like something, change it. Try to be a rainbow in someone's cloud."[5]

It seems her mission, Maya's mission, and your mission all share the same silver lining.

## I'M GOING TO GIVE YOU THE TOOLS THAT ALL THE GODDESSES HAVE HAD SINCE THE BEGINNING OF TIME TO ENSURE THAT BRIGHT, BOLD, AND BEAUTIFUL ENERGY OF YOURS IS ARMED WITH EVERYTHING IT NEEDS TO CONTINUE ETERNALLY EVOLVING. THE FIRST BEING: *ACKNOWLEDGMENT.*

You feel the need for change. The inner burning. You question things. You feel emotion. You are passionate. Awake. Ready. Great. I'm going to give you the tools that all the Goddesses have had since the beginning of time to ensure that bright, bold, and beautiful energy of yours is armed with everything it needs to continue eternally evolving. The first being: *acknowledgment.*

## POWERFUL WOMEN DON'T NEED ANOTHER PAIR OF YOGA PANTS; WE NEED A MIC.

You are intelligent. You are intuitive. And you are a powerful spiritual being with a conscious calling. You are a woman who can take some serious awakened action

## GODDESS (R)EVOLUTIONARY: KUAN YIN

Riddle me this, if you get offered a VIP pass to your personal heaven, would you take it, or stay and help those suffering instead? The Buddhist Goddess Kuan Yin opted for helping those who needed her. Yes, she has probably heard your cries too.

Stories of her life have a Cinderella ring to it, with parents who made her work, do chores, and cook and she politely and diligently obliged. Just some context for you. So you can imagine heaven seemed pretty appealing after a lifetime of domestic labor. Unselfishly though, Kuan Yin paused at the gates of the heaven, paralyzed by the sounds of the world and its cries of anguish and suffering. She chose to sacrifice heaven to return to help those in need of her compassion. A true reminder of an unselfish deed. She is a mother to all of us.

It is believed she hears all cries, eases the pain of illness, and stands by people passing over and dealing with grief. She loves all, unconditionally. Now that is a heroine, a Goddess martyr, an evolved Goddess nurturing the needs of others and where many would be bitter, or resentful, she chooses love above all else. She takes responsibility for her contribution to healing and helping those in need.

out into the world. We're being called to elevate our conscious pursuits now, to consciously level out the playing field. It's time to go beyond the mat and engage. Women are the Goddess tribe of now. We are the leaders of the loving army for this awakening arena. We are the ones the world has been waiting for. We are the ones the world is counting on. We are the change. So if you have been asking who is going to save the world, the answer is we are. And if you have been asking when, the answer is now. Powerful women don't need another pair of yoga pants; we need a mic.

What if Gandhi had been a spiritual hermit, hoping for the best? What if Mother Teresa had stayed confined to the sanctuary of her Calcutta Catholic church? What if Reverend Martin Luther King Jr. had opted to stay tucked in his parish and not become the mouthpiece for equality?

I mean, imagine if Elizabeth Gilbert had never kicked down the door to her marriage and career to commence an *Eat, Pray, Love* global soul-searching odyssey, and kept her transformational truth to herself. No. These people stood up, talked, kissed the heads of humanity, talked some more, shared, and kept going until there was resolution, until there was understanding, until there was peace. Their story: They all are the holy heroes and heroines of their time.

Your Goddess story: You are the holy one polishing your marching shoes, giving yourself those last motivational pep talks in the mirror, dusting off each shoulder.

This is the conscious nod to roll out. This is the call to forgivingly fight, ever so diplomatically and divinely, helping to heal the injustices of the world. Voicing for balance. The seekers of right doing. The conscious people who live like they give a crap!

## IT'S TIME TO STOP HIDING. IT'S TIME TO KNOW YOUR POWER, CLAIM YOUR VOICE, AND TIP THE BALANCE BACK TOWARD A FEMININE FUTURE.

It's time to stop hiding. It's time to know your power, claim your voice, and tip the balance back toward a feminine future. To restore balance. It's not about man vs. woman. Rulers vs. religion. Command and conquer. This is about harmony. Unity. Removing what has defined and divided us. It's time to become activated Goddesses.

Understand. These shifts are going to make your earth move. So if you know one thing, know this, that if you hold your Goddess energy, your truthful emotion, in your soul, nothing can shake you. Keep your honest *why* close to your heart. This cannot be taken from you. Know you can move mountains with these tools, which will harness something sleeping in you that will reawaken so naturally. You'll begin to allow your power to show up. Your emotions to fully embody and express your passions and dreams.

### GODDESS MUSING . . .

But how do we win the fight? If you are asking this, then I need to let you in on the secret: *There is no fight.* We were never meant to be fighting each other. The only thing left fighting is the earth—for survival. And fair enough I say. So no, we don't fight. Our job is to protect. There is a difference. So instead of fighting, you stand for something. Instead of battling, you advocate. You educate. What if I advocate for you fully? Energetically, I have your back. And the women you surround yourself with should too. This will feel like family. You'll feel effortlessly bound in a sacred contract. Sharing a familiar sense of safety that you are protected in the very sacred work you are all rolling out in each other's presence. It will seem natural. And you lean on each other. Lift each other. And love each other.

Seek women who don't tell you what you can't be, but show you what you can be. When we surround ourselves with women who get it, we all move forward. Resilient, striking, evolutionary. Passionate Goddesses who take a stand. Because they care. And so do you.

Shift into your truth. Give the world the whole you. The full, truthful, untamed you. Your wild wisdom. Yeah, we say, see me in all my glory. And I see you in all of yours.

Your heart will begin to beat with purpose. You will sing a healing chant of change within. Knowing the shifts have far stronger, longer-reaching roots than what can be seen sprouting from the surface. These three shifts are the seeds of conscious change:

**Shift 1: You show up.**

**Shift 2: Then your power will.**

**Shift 3: And then your tribe will.**

## YOU CAN ACKNOWLEDGE YOUR GODDESS ENERGY WHEN YOU SHIFT BACK INTO IT *AND* WHEN YOU STEP INTO YOUR FULLY EMPOWERED SELF.

In order for us to step into this space and show up as ourselves, and know what to look for in a tribe, we must first understand the true essence of our Goddess energy. You can acknowledge your Goddess energy when you shift back into it *and* when you step into your fully empowered self.

## GODDESS (R)EVOLUTIONARY: THE WOMEN OF STANDING ROCK

After witnessing the Dakota pipeline protests lead by the Native American women of Standing Rock, it is clear the Goddess movement has started, and that it can create real change. These women collectively called global attention to a lifelong fight for water started by their ancient grandmothers, and in doing so inspired action. How? They got the world to listen. They moved as one.

First, the call: They called the conscious troops. They sought support wide and far, and now, almost everybody has heard some mention of the Dakota Pipeline. Second, inspired action: They spread their message across the United States, to anyone who was willing to listen. Finally, the movement: A global story that proves that mindful millennials can move masses in a far more meaningful way than any other time or generation in history.

Will they be successful? We all hope. Did they try? You bet they did. And are they backing down? What the hell are you talking about? Course not. They are protecting the earth. They call for other indigenous woman to rise. They summon us all to think about water, to think about life. They are the change. They are the action. The thing I love about this story the most is what water symbolizes—emotion, cleansing, movement.

**SHIFT 1: YOU SHOW UP**

## DO YOU LIVE IN YOUR DAILY GODDESS POWER? AND WHAT IS GETTING IN YOUR WAY OF SHOWING UP?

Do you show up? Do you live in your daily Goddess power? And what is getting in your way of showing up? It is easy to get distracted, let others suck up our time, to lend our energy to worries, anxieties, and things that don't matter. I'd like to ask myself, a year from now—what mattered more? What I worried about, or what I contributed.

> ## GODDESS GEM
>
> I like to wear an Amazonite crystal around my neck to support me in my quest for truth. As far as crystals go, this bad boy is said to aid courage and help you express your true feelings while helping to rid yourself of judgments. If you want a crystal to help you make evolutionary breakthroughs, then Spectrolite stone in the palm of your hand will aid you in evolutionary aha moments.

I need you to check in with what might be getting in your way of showing up. Is it staying in the relationship that no longer feels right? Is it an energetic addiction to not having the energy in you to change? Is it the risk that lies in the reality of change? Or is it as simple as you just don't know where to start? You wouldn't be the first woman to think, *Lord where do I start?*

**SHIFT 2: YOUR SOURCE OF POWER**

## THE KEY TO YOUR POWER IS SIMPLE: *LOVE.* LOVE IS STRENGTH. YOUR COMPASSION IS COMMANDING. YOUR ABILITY TO HEAL IS HAILING. LET THIS BE YOUR GODDESS ETHOS.

The key to your power is simple: *love.* Love is strength. Your compassion is commanding. Your ability to heal is hailing. Let this be your Goddess ethos. Your evolved etiquette that sees you lead with love, meet opposition with understanding and equality, and fuel your sense of power by your drive to service the world. Help all. Heal all. In all reactions to actions, ask yourself what would a Goddess do?

You know the feeling you get when a stranger offers you a random act of kind-

## EVOLUTION EXERCISE: MIND MAP

Okay, so you have all seen a family tree, right? A map with branches out of it of people related or connected to you. Well, imagine a mind map version—made up of all the branches that make up you.

- Start with a blank piece of paper with your name in the middle of it.
- Then, surrounding your name, write three to six key elements that have made you who you are. This could be your family, friends, experiences, your personality, interests, beliefs, goals, and dreams. You can add more sub-branches as your ideas about yourself begin to flow and grow.
- Don't be afraid to circle key or repeating words, or draw lines to link themes. Doing this will help you unearth new relationships about things that you feel are essential to yourself and your personal growth. You can use different colors for different themes, use images, or even create illustrations to help to graphically map yourself.

ness. When they hold the door open. Pick up something you dropped. And, generally, when beings look after each other. That is all encompassed in you. Male, female, your gender doesn't matter. This is the feminine showing up in all of us. Goddess acts are acts of love and sympathy, empathetic, and universal. Your touch ripples out in a profound way. Your energy is boundless. Your empowerment, once summoned, cannot be taken away. That is the thing about conscious beings—they can never walk backward. The only way they see is forward. Ever evolving with ever-loving awakened action. Demonstrated to all beings, in every waking day. You understand this isn't a belief, it is a way of being. If you take care of those around you and those around you take care of those around them, imagine how much change could occur. If we were each responsible for simply serving our own piece of the change pie. Less overwhelming. More doable.

### SHIFT 3: YOUR GODDESS TRIBE

MOST IMPORTANTLY, YOU WILL KNOW IT'S THE RIGHT COMPANY WHEN YOU LEAVE FEELING BETTER FOR IT. THEY WILL AID YOUR TRANSFORMATION.

Next is your tribe: Your spiritual society, your Goddess council, your soul posse will begin popping up around you. You'll recognize them from like-minded conversation. You'll share passions, interests, and both be curiously stepping out in the same direction. They will feel familiar. Being in their company will feel easy. Most importantly, you will know it's the right company when you leave feeling better for it. They will aid your transformation. You will leave their company feeling inspired, motivated, and energized, rather than drained.

Your Goddess tribe will grow and expand in accordance with your own personal growth and expansion. As with the cycle of all things, old friends may organically fall away making room for the growth of new friendships and relationships. This is all part of your evolutionary shift. Know that you may be surprised with who comes and goes. The key is not to be attached. Allow people to ebb and flow through your life. Acknowledge each like-minded Goddess as they show up, and the lessons they bring you—some hard, some fun. You'll vibe with some movements, not so much with others. That doesn't make one better than the other. Know that every movement has its place.

# KNOW THIS: GODDESS MANIFESTO

*"PEOPLE WITH SELF-RESPECT EXHIBIT A CERTAIN TOUGHNESS, A KIND OF MORAL NERVE; THEY DISPLAY WHAT WAS ONCE CALLED CHARACTER."*
—JOAN DIDION

Know this. You were put on this earth for a purpose. Fact.

Your spirit, your soul, your light, your legacy is calling. Listen.

You are the change that will save this world. Will.

Your power in love is more impactful than anything you can imagine. Love wins.

Your wounds are wisdom.

This love will break down barriers, and create shifts this world has never seen. I promise.

Know this. Your soul is as old as this earth.

Your inheritance of this wisdom and power is your birthright. Not property. Not money. Wisdom. And wisdom is power.

You are not a spectator of life, you are a believer, a dreamer, and most of all, a doer.

Know this. To evolve is to embrace change in all of its shapes and experiences. Like women change in curves, emotion, and knowledge. We change too.

We roll. We weave. We sew. We search. We understand. We rage. We forgive. We grow.

Know this. You are the evolution of a spiritual being. Ever changing.

Your lineage of wisdom and love pulsates through your every action.

You are all-encompassing: the old, the rejuvenating, the new. Each with its lessons.

Your fate was always written in the stars. With god. This is your time. It's you.

This love is rising. You are the dawn of the new age. You.

May the sun kiss your face. May the winds of change carry you. May the moon pull you. May the earth ground you. And may your fire burn bright, evolved one.

This, know this.

# THERE ARE FOUR KEY PILLARS HOLDING YOU UP THAT YOU CAN USE TO RE-GROUND YOURSELF: *YOUR RESPONSIBILITY, YOUR COMPASSION, YOUR SENSE OF UNITY, AND YOUR POWER. THIS IS YOUR FOUNDATION.*

When you doubt. When you get in a mindset of it's too hard, I can't be bothered, and when you feel yourself drifting. When you begin to think you are lost again, there are four key pillars holding you up that you can use to re-ground yourself: *your responsibility, your compassion, your sense of unity, and your power.* This is your foundation. Strong. Rooted to your ancestors, to all mothers and grandmothers. Within this space you carry not just your wisdom, you carry their wisdom. You can lay your heavy head in the lap of Goddesses before and breathe easy. They speak through you, for you. They have you. In their energy you are always home. Safe. Protected. Welcomed.

So remember, and know, that this sense of surging meaning, this sense of home, is rightfully yours to immerse yourself in, own, and nurture. With it comes peace. With it comes power. No one can take this sense of home away from you. Its love drapes you daily.

**Know this, you can start over, every morning.**
**Know that every day you have an opportunity to respond.**
**Be educated, rather than angered.**
**Be wise in your walk, rather than wounded or wicked.**
**Your intellect is the sharpest tool in your Goddess kit. Use it. Wisely.**
**Know your value. Know your worth. Know your contribution. Know this.**

## Pillar 1: Your Responsibility
# WE VOW TO SHOW UP—ENERGETICALLY, EMOTIONALLY, ENTIRELY.

Owning your place, owning your contribution. Understanding that none of us is above another person. That's the illusion that keeps us divided. We take responsibility for all our energy, the good, and the bad. Consciously aware of

both our balanced energy internally and how we contribute to energy externally. We take care of ourselves, we take care of each other, and we take care
of the earth. These are our daily responsible rituals. We vow to show up—
energetically, emotionally, entirely.

## Pillar 2: Your Compassion

### WE VOW TO CARE—FORGIVINGLY, EMPATHICALLY, SYMPATHETICALLY.

Let us be clear, this is not a fight. There are no enemies amongst us. There is always
opportunity for education. Conflict is a call for compassion, not a call to charge.
The Goddess's goal is to never turn her back on something that needs love and
nurturing. (As tempting as this can sometimes be.) Be it physical abandonment or
energetic rejection, we choose to hold our power, our sacred space, no matter the
storm, knowing that healing takes energy, respecting that it isn't always going to be
easy. We vow to care—forgivingly, empathically, sympathetically.

## Pillar 3: Your Unity

### WE VOW TO GATHER—WELCOMING, INVITING, INCLUSIVE.

A Goddess's role is to bring people together. Circles. Covens. Communities.
We cross-pollinate consciousness, and seed new insights. Be it as small as inviting a woman over for a cup of tea, or as large scale as a gathering of hundreds.
Every call consciously counts. It unites us in our reality, in our responsibility,
in our power, and in our conflicts. We can lean on and learn from each other
and create more momentum as one, as a conscious collective. When we unite as
one collective family our energy becomes a force. We greet each other with that
energy and the respect every single one of us rightfully deserves. There are no
queens. There are no servants. We are all of service. We are all one. We vow to
gather—welcoming, inviting, inclusive.

## Pillar 4: Your Power

# WITH OUR INSIGHTS AND CONSCIOUSNESS COMES OUR VOWED RESPONSIBILITY, OUR VOWED COMPASSION, AND OUR VOWED UNITY—WITH THAT COMES POWER.

There are no winners and losers. We seek a win-win. Seeing opportunity in crisis. Believe in yourself, and those around. Celebrate each other's strengths; we do not celebrate when someone fails. It is a shift. With our insights and consciousness comes our vowed responsibility, our vowed compassion, and our vowed unity—with that comes power. The choice to do right. The choice to include. The choice to forgive. The choice to love anyway. This is your power. No matter what has been taken from you, what society has or hasn't allowed you, what labels or beliefs limit you, your choice, your response, your action is your power.

# OUR FEMININE ARCHETYPES
# + NARRATIVES

*"YOU ARE AN INFINITELY COMPLEX HUMAN BEING WITH STORIES AND MYTHS AND DREAMS—*
*AND AMBITIONS OF COSMIC PROPORTIONS. DON'T WASTE TIME UNDERESTIMATING YOURSELF."*
*—CAROLINE MYSS*

There once was a little girl. A Goddess. With her came the birth of everything. She created life from nothing in the fertile womb of her healing energy. Her soul duty, her sole purpose, was to achieve and maintain harmony. She, like you, strove for balance. Growth. Expansion. She was the Goddess of earth. Of all things life.

As time passed, the girl evolved into a woman. A mother. The Goddess was taken for granted, used, abused, and often raped and pillaged for her body, for her goods. Wounded, the woman would rage. Sending punishments to those who caused her harm. Sending her infuriated seas onto the lands of the users. Casting spells of drought on those who so desperately regretted sucking her teat dry. Over time, her fierce reactions of anger and hate began to feel empty. Her purpose for balance had been lost in the fight to reclaim power. So she cried. She too had forgotten her empowerment, her healing nature, and her purpose to create harmony. Swept up in the war of her resources.

Feeling defeated, Earth Goddess looked up to the sky, to the gods. Wiping her tears, she realized the sky smiled down at her. She was not alone. The sky's clouds cried with her. By day the sun stood alongside her. In times of darkness, the intuitive moon guided her. Her sisters, the stars, watched over her. They supported her with tsunami, drought, fire, and quakes. Trying to make a shift in the mindset of the takers. Warning.

Goddess Gaia spoke through nature. She offered herself daily in flowers and food, sacrificing herself to serve the users. Maybe, instead of raging, instead of entering into battle, she would evolve to outsmart the users. She would, simply, sacrifice all of herself, letting them use up her resources, until depleted and gone. And so, Gaia, Mother Earth, the great Earth Goddess, began to offer the users one last evolved choice: to live, or to die.

―――――――

The beauty about this story is you are the one who gets to write the ending. Will you be the heroine who transforms this cautionary tale? You, Goddess, are very much part of this story. So what would a Goddess do?

## IN THESE BEDTIME TALES, MYTHS, LEGENDS, AND FAIRY TALES LIE THE LESSONS AND EXAMPLES OF WHAT A GODDESS WOULD DO.

Fact. You are actually quite well read on the stories of Goddesses, on the awakened feminine archetypes that tell the tales of your evolution. And in these bedtime tales, myths, legends, and fairy tales lie the lessons and examples of what a Goddess would do. As with any story, it differs depending on who is telling it. And the era they are telling it from. But our learning and how we evolve with the idea of Goddess etiquette is largely rooted in these ancient narratives of the feminine journey. These stories have been told to girls globally, from the tales shared by African shamans, to those told around the fire pits of the Americas, to the bunk beds of the Western world.

Our evolution of the story of Goddess isn't woven into ancient religious scripts, theories, or philosophies. No, the Goddess teachings have never been labeled, categorized, or kept for a selected few. They have always been accessible to all. Read globally, in different styles, languages, cultures, and beliefs, but all sharing the same story of the little lost girl who found her way, and became a hero in her own right. To study our evolving Goddess story, we will review many bedtime stories that have been whispered to you before you went to sleep dreaming of tomorrow. How perfectly fitting, right!

From Greek mythology, we have tales of Athena, who wove together wisdom, craft, and war. A Goddess who never fought without a purpose. One of her famous tales is the curse of Medusa, who she turns into a hideous monster as a punishment for Medusa's unevolved vanity and ego. Then there is the Celtic Goddess Morrigan, who represents war, fate, death, and magic. She offered her love to a hero of war and, in his rejection of both her love and feminine sov-

## GODDESS GEM

There are a long list of scholars and evolutionary thinkers to explore: from Carl Jung to Joseph Campbell, Dara Marks, Maureen Murdock, Caroline Myss, and Dr. Clarissa Pinkola Estés. For example, Joseph Campbell's book *The Power of Myth* studies and explores mythology, the universe, and life. Explaining how the themes and symbols of ancient narratives continue to bring meaning to our life experiences of all things—birth, death, love, and war. He said, "I always feel uncomfortable when people speak about ordinary mortals because I've never met an ordinary man, woman or child."[1]

He is right, we share more in common with the gods, Goddesses, heroes, and villains then we may realize. We have all conquered darkness, been tricked, been the trickster, been the victim, and the hero. We've been them all. It is all within us. In you. Like the elements are a part of the earth. Myths are not about you, your ego. They are about you identifying with your higher power, with your true self, and with the world. Helping you to see yourself as another earthly element then identifying where you "fit in."

What I love most about Campbell is how he unapologetically points out that how we see others is really a mirror about our own consciousness, our own evolution. If you see a monster as opposed to seeing a hero, it shows your state of consciousness. Campbell puts it well, "Read myths. They teach you that you can turn inward, and you begin to get the message of the symbols. Read other people's myths, not those of your own religion, because you tend to interpret your own religion in terms of facts, but if you read the other ones, you begin to get the message. Myth helps you to put your mind in touch with this experience of being alive. It tells you what the experience is."[2]

So own the experience of it. The journey. Your progress. The evolution of your life.

ereignty, saw his future doomed. He was to perish without ever understanding the consequences of his unevolved actions.

To the Nordic Goddess Freya, whose balanced approach to work and play—as seen in her symbolic connection to everything from love, beauty, and sex to war and death—revealed a warrior and Goddess aligned. Her story of her love and passion for her husband shows how the power of love and devotion when crossed with obsession and fixation stops one from evolving.

To the Babylonian Goddess Ishtar, who ruled love, fertility, war, and sex. As with many deities, she has different names and connects through various cultures and religions; she was passionate as all hell, noted as being as caring as she was spiteful.

## GODDESS (R)EVOLUTIONARY: CLARISSA PINKOLA ESTÉS

My first stirring with Goddess stories and spiritual archetypes was when I read Dr. Clarissa Pinkola Estés's book *Women Who Run with the Wolves*.[3] A classic on the female psyche. I could see the evolution of our Goddess archetype from what Estés calls The Wolf Woman, The Feral Woman, The Dirty Goddess, The Ugly Duckling.[4]

A Jungian psychoanalyst, Estés heavily influenced my research for this book and writing at large. Along with *Women Who Run with the Wolves*, *Untie the Strong Woman* has changed my view on culture and consciousness. Her work has sent a message to the world about the power of feminine archetypes, helping the world better understand completeness, wholeness, and source. Her stories and teachings helped explain and transform our view on masculine and feminine through gender traits and nature, whether it was the Goddess or the Warrior, the Handmaiden or the Hunter, which moved the collective consciousness to reunify us with both our masculine and feminine sides. A Goddess bowing to her inner warrior. The hunter learning to harness his inner maiden. Removing divisions within society, and ourselves.

With the rise of the Catholic Church many mythical deities were turned into demons, such as seeing Ishtar become wrongfully associated with rules, lust, serpents, and black magic. Although really Ishtar was neither pure good, nor pure evil, she symbolizes emotional passion in all its magic and tragedy.

To the Vedic Goddess Maya, who was also associated with magic and illusion. Maya represents the state of delusion, something that can be transformed with transcending knowledge. She asks us, What is true? What is real?

## The Birth of Shakti

The story of the Hindu Goddess Durga is one I feel we can all relate to—her story is the birth of shakti, of the feminine. This was a time where the world was split in conflict, the gods had fallen from the heavens, the demons had risen out of the underworld, and they all walked the earth. The demons, representing suffering, conflict, greed, and corruption, were about to win the world.

Feeling confused, anxious, overwhelmed, the gods united. Each hoping the other would have the answers, and the energy to solve the problem. Suddenly, they realized: *feminine*. We are fighting using only the masculine, and so they called upon the Goddess form to be created. Shakti, the coiling energy of creation unique to feminine was born with Goddess Durga, who appeared riding a tiger.

## STRONG, BIG, BOLD, HAIRY BETWEEN HER LEGS, AND BEAMING A NEW LOVING LIGHT THAT THE WORLD HAD NEVER SEEN. . . . DURGA ENTERS THE BATTLE TO SLAY THE DEMONS.

Strong, big, bold, hairy between her legs, and beaming a new loving light that the world had never seen. Riding her tiger, armed with brilliant white light, receptive to the call, Durga enters the battle to slay the demons. With grace, she slays. In between confronting demons and relaxing deep into her empowering truth— re-rooting herself to love and reconnecting to her purpose—gives her no patience for the tired and restless tormenting games of demons.

She slays the separation they weave of winners and losers, segregation, suffering, conflict, and greed. Her power lays in her loving truth, her ebb and flow of energy, between action and reflection. She uses her shakti energy, of never-ending feminine love, to feed her crusade to rid the world of conflicts that divide us, that polarize us, that weaken us. "Shakti" is an Eastern Hindu term, which literally means creative and divine energy tied to all things life and creation, be it Mother Earth, the universe, or your own feminine wisdom.

I like to call shakti your inner Warrior Goddess; I imagine my personal shakti energy is like a superwoman alter-awakened-ego: she sprays white cleansing pure light like Spider-man sprays webs, smashes the ground she walks on, graciously obliterating bad vibes like the Hulk. She even has a streak of perfectly balanced villain sass to her, an inner energy that pulses through every action, desire, witty comeback, and heart flutter. She is in all of us. Durga/shakti, like you, faced a strikingly, if not eerily similar story, to the one you and I share today. For this reason, I share an affinity with the Goddess Durga, and I want you to call on her energy, and this story, when you face people who confront you with conflict in your day, to remember how powerful your feminine love is, and your power to relax deep into your truth. It has, after all, saved the world once before!

## EACH GODDESS STORY TELLS A VERY REAL LESSON: THAT WOMEN ARE MAGIC. THAT WOMEN HAVE THE POWER TO REMOVE THE ILLUSION THAT WE ARE ALL SEPARATE FROM EACH OTHER.

## GODDESS GEM

If archetypes are your thang, then I could not more highly recommend exploring Caroline Myss's books *Sacred Contracts* and *Archetypes*. Shifting to more mainstream archetypes, such as The Intellectual, The Artist/Creative, The Athlete, The Queen/Executive, The Caregiver, The Fashionista even![5] Even better for the modern Goddess, check out the work of Cristina Carlino, who has an online quiz you can jump to and do right now, archetypese.com. There are also Jungian archetype tests you can take online as well. A must for any goddess quiz junkie or archetype addict!

Together, each Goddess story tells a very real lesson: That women are magic. That women have the power to remove the illusion that we are all separate from each other. That women can take on the underworld, conquer the demons, which represent conflict and suffering. Women can be the voice of justice.

No matter the country, culture, story, or script, there are many similarities between the stories of Goddesses throughout time. From ancient folklore to mythology to pioneering psychoanalyst Carl Jung's stories of the female archetypes. Personas and traits that are seen in characters throughout all time and all tales. From the hero, caregiver, sovereign, lover, explorer, to rebel, we begin to become familiar and comfortable with "types" of human beings, and naturally begin to ingrain the evolutionary type of person we want to be. The story of the winner, the loser, the good, the bad, the trickster, the saint becomes part of our subconscious steps in the direction we evolve. And when you meet an archetype you recognize you may fall victim to archetyping them (dangerously close to labeling) in accordance with your subconscious coding. Seeing the person taking endless selfies as the mirror, Mirror Vain Enchantress, when they might actually be nice as pie!

Globally our stories of history, mythology, archetypes, characters, even bedtime tales begin to build a collective unconsciousness—we all subconsciously already know these tales of morality from our upbringing, they already exist in our evolution, be it your favorite fairy tale or Disney flick. All these tales share stories of resilience, reflection, rejuvenation, and reward.

Essentially, all these stories from our modern childhood hold elements of each Goddess archetype, some more than others. Companies like Pixar and Disney are superb at carrying the Goddess stories to future generations: Ariel, the rebellious Water Goddess who was brave enough to ask why; Pocahontas, the Earth Goddess who used love to unify divided worlds; Rapunzel, also rebellious; Moana, also rebellious. . . . In today's world, we can use their stories as inspiring models that you don't have to live by conventional rules. If you believe there is a better way, there probably is.

Take note of characters from your childhood or that strike a spiritual chord with you today that may have played a role in your Goddess DNA. Personally, I think Carl Jung was onto something, pointing out how much impact stories have in the foundation of building up a Goddess.

All stories—whether myth, legend, or documented archive—can seem like overdramatic supernatural battles between giants, gods, or Goddesses. But really, these stories are no different from real tribulations throughout our time and lives. These stories reflect our spiritual evolution. Our mythology mirrors our movement. These tales tell of our transformation as a species, and as beings.

What is the key to the feminine journey? What can we take away from studying all our Goddess stories from the beginning of time to where we stand now? Like our journey, the narrative of Goddess also shares a transformational arc. And as some of us may experience in our lifetime, being served the same lesson over and over, and over again, these stories we have read over, and over, and over again, mirror our quest to expand, learn, and grow as spiritual beings.

Many before us have seen this connection in stories. The narratives are simple, they all reflect a woman's journey in life. A psycho-spiritual quest we all experience as women no matter what era we journey and evolve through. Yes, the elements of the story are relative to the time, be it the regal Greek and Roman themes of ancient mythology, the domesticated maidens seen in an earlier century's stories, or in today's self-empowered Disney and Pixar feminine stories, which don't necessarily rely on a Prince Charming to save them when they are in distress.

## WHILE WE COULD FLIP OUR LID ABOUT THE FEMALE BEING A DOMESTICATED GODDESS IN SNOW WHITE, WE CAN INSTEAD ACKNOWLEDGE THE UNDERLYING LESSON IN HER ENDLESS QUEST TO OFFER EVERYONE LOVE AND KINDNESS.

If you remove any judgments you may have toward the time and place of the women in the tales, you can instead note the underlying significance and message. While we could flip our lid about the female being a domesticated Goddess in Snow White, we can instead acknowledge the underlying lesson in her endless quest to offer everyone love and kindness, even if the people she offers it to don't believe they are capable of it themselves. She believes in the good heart of an evil queen and a brokenhearted woodsman. Her actions, whether they are domesticated caretaking or nurturing, are acts of love and compassion. The Snow White narrative embodies the Goddess ethos of living for love, light, and legacy.

Goddess archetypes could be misconceived as being stereotypes—the dreaded category we are aiming to step out of, not into! Not so. As with all things, we Goddesses will evolve from child to woman to mother to grandmother. Maiden to Mother to Crone. Archetypes can be defined as "an example of a person," and in a more positive light, a "good example of a person"—in our case we will stick to Goddess archetypes we can relate to, aiding our spiritual evolution. A type of woman who is greatly admired. A Goddess.

## GODDESS (R)EVOLUTIONARY: MALALA YOUSAFZAI

It is worth exploring this transformational arc or archetype through a tale of today, which one day I am sure will become legend. This is the tale of Malala Yousafzai.

The young schoolgirl from Pakistan felt it was unjust the way her society suppressed so many rights for women in the Islamic state, so she decided to speak out. Creating a blog, under a pen name, Malala wrote about the right of education for all, the right of expression for all. One day, as the young girl rode the bus home from school with her girlfriends, she was confronted with the reality of her society. A gunman, asking for her by name, then holding a gun to her head. One final attempt to suppress and silence. Shot. Malala began a harrowing and healing journey. Not just physically demanding, with reconstructive surgery, but also a pilgrimage. Traveling to London to be healed, and spark-

ing a call for change amongst her peers in Pakistan. The call was heard on a global scale.

Malala stayed gracious, understanding, at peace, and in her feminine power, throughout the healing of the attack, and instead of bidding war, vowed to honor the momentum of the change, to never stop standing up for what everyone in this world should be rightfully entitled to. Today, Malala is a renowned women's activist, creating educational opportunities for women less fortunate, speaking up about the change still needed in the world, and being the brave inspiration to so many women too scared to stand up for their rights. Today she is a Goddess of universal human rights. She leads peacefully, and loves everybody. A girl with a gun to her head, and so many justified reasons to be angry, and she rises above the hate. Now that is courage, wisdom, compassion, and evolved existence at its finest.

# TIMELINE BY THE STARS

*"WHEN WE ARE AFRAID, WHEN IT HURTS TOO MUCH*
*WE LIKE TO TELL OURSELVES STORIES OF POWER."*
—STARHAWK

No, it hasn't always been like this. As expected with evolution, shit has changed. Matriarchy was once a real thing. And while the conflict and confrontation of the patriarchy of today may make some of us feel that a female-led society would be better, it is important to note that, as with all things—dark and light, good and bad—the winning combination is balance, not one or the other. There are no winners and losers; simply put, we all lose if we don't awaken and unite. So let's drop the us-versus-them mindset and all get on the same page here.

To unravel our history and understand the source of our feminine energy—where it was, where it has gone, and where we are now—we must first appreciate the journey of how we evolved to get to this point. Life and our history have many cycles and phases. You yourself will change and become different depending on your age and experiences. Seeing changes from biological and spiritual to environmental will affect your view of the world and your contribution to it.

YOU WILL EXPERIENCE THE TRIPLE GODDESS—MAIDEN, MOTHER, AND CRONE. THESE PHASES ARE SYMBOLIC TO NOT JUST YOUR OWN LIFE, BUT LIFE AS A WHOLE. BIRTH, LIFE, AND DEATH. AS WOMEN, IT IS IMPORTANT TO UNDERSTAND *YOU ARE THE CYCLE.*

In your own personal Goddess lifetime, you will experience the triple Goddess—Maiden, Mother, and Crone. These phases are symbolic to not just your own life, but life as a whole. Birth, life, and death. As women, it is important to understand *you are the cycle*. Be it in the giving of life. Be it in rejuvenating life. Be it in the emotional pattern of your menstrual cycle! And, as with all things, our evolution throughout time has seen cycles of change and transformation.

As a global collective, you could say our energy has been swayed to masculine for the last two millennia. When we look back at the leaders, inventors, world and business managers, even gods, especially in the Western world, the majority of positions of influence have sat with men. But although our world, as we have always known it, has been patriarchal, know that it hasn't always been this way. And, more important, know that it does not have to be this way.

Over hundreds of years, global worship shifted from Goddess deities and gods, to gods, and then, in many cases, to simply a god. The evolution from worshipping a woman pregnant with the world to a man nailed and tortured, seems a fateful reality when looking at the current tortured lands of Mother Earth. A Judeo-Christian dogma was enforced when new lands were conquered—through a combination of war, migration, and colonization—in this masculine reign, from the Pacific Islands to South America. The Eastern cultures, such as Asia and India, continued to keep a more balanced masculine and feminine energy, seeing Goddess figureheads continue to be popular figures in society throughout history and today.

However, the Western world, claiming the Judeo-Christian ideology, was transformed to one father-like godhead, and thus, patriarchy was born. The feminine face of god, our Goddesses, were repressed and denied, and women became oppressed, losing our rights, our voice, and our leadership and powers.

So how did we lose the matriarch, the Goddess? Well, beyond enforcement through patriarchal conquest and power, when we study the true meaning behind our gods we can hear many untold or lost stories, which once heard may change how we look at ev-

## GODDESS GEM

**The Goddess serpent and snake from ancient Greece to India was the symbol of life, energy, healing, and movement between the spirit worlds, with its ability to transform or change its skin. The Goddess bird from ancient Egypt to Europe represented water, movement, emotion, and healing. The bee Goddess from Greek to Hindu mythology was symbolic of the priestesses and female workers, healers, using honey as medicine, and the responsibility of pollination, spreading wisdom and insight.**

**The cow Goddess from the Minoans to the Baganda tribes of Uganda represents all things life, from their production of milk to their horns, which represented the shape of the female reproductive organs, and to the crescent moon. Female cows were rarely killed for meat or leather.**

erything. And will change how we move ahead. Many stories that, when translated, show that translation and interpretation may have played a big role in where the Goddess got dropped off. Take the first line of a book that has sparked debate for centuries, the Hebrew Bible, with the common translation being, "In the beginning God created . . ." yet when we look at this line in Hebrew, found in the Zohar, spiritual text of the Jewish Kabbalah, the same line reads, "In wisdom Elohim creates. . . ."[1] *Elohim* is a Hebrew word made of both masculine and feminine in unity. *El* is Hebrew for God and is masculine. *Eloah* is Hebrew for Goddess and is feminine.[2] So essentially, we could also interpret this first line as, "In wisdom Gods and Goddesses create. . . ."[3]

The story of antagonistic gods, such as the Greek Olympic gods and Goddesses who were always bickering and competing for attention (with a balance of both male and female characteristics) has evolved with various interpretations and debates over time to leave us with the one god many of us are familiar with today. In fact, many gods/Goddesses shared both male and female traits from Shiva in India, to the Aztec deities, even angels. So, in the beginning, we were not just created equal, we were all one, unified, and in perfect balance. At least that is what the scripts would tell us. (Or not tell us.)

In writing this book, I became engrossed by the research of Marija Gimbutas, a Lithuanian-American archaeologist who devoted her life and love to the study of Goddesses throughout cultures and time and explaining what she found in her books, *The Goddesses and Gods of Old Europe* and *The Language of the Goddesses*. She discovered the connection between a five-thousand-year-old spiritual war against the feminine divine and the rise of the masculine reign. Her Neolithic and Bronze Age pre-Christian studies and findings rewrote the missing parts of history patriarchy had omitted or dismissed. From her studies of original settlers of Old Europe where she unearthed burial sites and ancient worship totems, she discovered that we indeed started from an ideal society, where men and women operated in balance. Sharing power in society. Worship was widely to female deities—promoting nonviolence, equality, and nature. Her studies reveal the shift from matriarch to patriarch is tied to our Western time of war, war, war, the shift away from the feminine with the Indo-Europeans who saw the balance unravel in a downward spiral of all things Goddess.[4]

From Gimbutas's work, we are reminded that from women the world was gifted medicine, agriculture, art, mathematics, and, in many cultures, they were even considered ancient timekeepers. Marking the months to the moon, and their menstrual cycles. Their voice was equally as valued as men's.

# BY REAWAKENING THE STORIES OF GODDESS-TEACHINGS WE UNVEIL THE FEMALE FACE OF GOD.

Unearthing the truth buried in the depths of our history, and our stories, from archetype to archaeology, helps us to remember and acknowledge what was erased and forgotten. Reacquainting us with the truth that creation never was just a man's job, a woman was always present, always needed. With god comes Goddess. By re-awakening the stories of Goddess-teachings we unveil the female face of god. Un-earthing a world that worshipped women in all forms, and in all levels of society.

It is interesting that in many Amazonian tribes the women, while being very much the nurturers, cooks, and child bearers, are also considered to have the most important job out of anyone in the tribe. Their voice is equal, heard, and very much needed. You see, the men will hunt, claim victory over land, and harvest, until there is nothing more to hunt, kill, or capture. The women's role is to tell the men when enough is enough, to help keep the balance of rebirth, the cycle of life, seasons, and growth continuing. The call to stop and consider their actions, from the feminine voices of the tribe, is important to ensure that animals and the earth could repopulate. The ancient elder-women kept earth in order.

With our ancient ancestors also came the birth of a natural spirituality that acknowledged and honored the moon, the stars, the elements of fire, earth, air, and water. This pagan and nature-based belief system united the feminine with all things life, universe, creation, and earth. With it came birth, life, the taking of life, and rejuvenation, an all-encompassing spiral—from life and death to rebirth—of eternal creation. This was reflected in everything to do with the seasons, to the harvest, to the cycle of life and death. As within nature, earth's creatures were also symbols of the feminine divine. During the time of the ancient Goddess, animal talismans were a unified symbol of the role of Goddess.

So, how did the horns of cows and the new moon, once so sacred, become scorned as horns of the devil or witchcraft?

Back in the fifteenth century, witch hunts and burnings persecuted women like you and me for wanting to be considered spiritual, rather than abiding to one label of religion. More so if they were sexual, using their sexual energy for anything other than procreation. If they used this energy to empower other women, this was bewitchment. I for one would have been charged and burned at the stake, and this book would have been considered sorcery! Sexual and spiritual, I'm guilty as charged. Although the only thing I will bewitch you with is a belief in yourself and knowing you can achieve anything.

## GODDESS MUSING . . .

**The Goddess narrative is always weaved with nature, and throughout scripts and stories it is not uncommon for a Goddess to share a connection with a specific animal. From fairy tale to pagans to indigenous cultures, animal totems have long been connected with signs of experiences, emotions, and an emblem of a person's personality or traits—much like an archetype. Feel free to skip to the chapters in Part IV, "Earth Goddess," to see the different meanings behind various animal totems.**

These gender labels, whether it be witch or whore, cute or bossy, are still damaging today. And while the witch hunts are a big part of our history, it is important to know that conscious, spiritual, sexual, and intuitive women weren't originally seen as bad, or evil, or weird, and certainty not as witches, in the times prior to our Judeo-Christian reign. In fact, in some eras of our ancient ancestry, the priestess was both sexual and spiritual, seen in temples, and equally respected for her spirituality and sensuality. Both were seen as powerful ways to heal and connect with those who needed her love, compassion, and guidance. There was nothing dirty or sinister about it. The sexual energy of a woman was unifying and soothing. Not seen as a power held over a man, and not necessarily just for male company, but seen as unconditional love. Label-less love.

Energy, consciousness, wisdom, and curiosity—especially where all things spirituality, sexuality, and evolutionary were concerned—were a threat to the status quo. Wisdom after all is powerful. There has been a definite leading of masculine energy throughout the past few thousand years, and today we see what many in the New Age realm are calling the "rise of feminine," which I think is important to see as more of a rise to balance, than an overthrow of masculinity.

Energetically this isn't "throw a sack over the head of masculine energy, bind its hands, and shove it in the back of our evolutionary car trunk." More of a "Yo, masculine energy, let's take a drive together and pick a road-trip playlist that vibes with everyone." Less about spiritual and energetic duality, and more about unity.

This shift in our spiritual evolution was predicted to kick off in 2012 and has been mentioned by the Aztecs, Hindus, Yogi Bhajan, even Nostradamus, who said,

"A new law will emerge in the new world of America. At a time when Syria, Judea, and Palestine are significant: The great barbarian empire of patriarchy that men have created will decay during the time that the feminine spirit is completing its cycle."[5] It is believed the "new law" is the energetic shift, and the "new world" is America. Whether you call it the "Aquarian Age," the "shift," or the "new dawn," one thing is consistent: Spirituality is shifting.

When it comes to astrology, especially the shifting nature of all things earth and stars, a very interesting shift was predicted to commence from 2012. Calculated by Mayans over two thousand years ago, December 21, 2012, was noted as the date of the commencement of the Great Cycle, something that was also noted in ancient Egypt, and what astrologists call the Age of Aquarius. As you may spot in the Goddess Timeline on page 38. Following 2012, a gradual shift, with evolutionary growing pains, started to heighten, frustrate, and change as we moved from the masculine Piscean reign, which ruled for over two thousand years—with the masculine energy of controlled religion, the actions of dictators, and the advancement of self-promotion and selfish reasons.

Today, in the Age of Aquarius, we have seen the collaboration of the Eastern and the Western worlds through trade and business, technology evolve before our eyes, and a rise in spirituality with ashrams, temples, monasteries, even yoga festivals, merging New Age thoughts and spiritualism into mainstream society. You only have to walk down the street in NYC to see a yoga studio, organic food store, psychic, vegan burger joint, and bustling bar, all in one block!

---

Our evolution has been an emotional journey. While researching this book, I came across many scriptures, movements, and milestones for us human beings, throughout history and mythology, and noticed many themes in countries, cultures, and communities where there was a connection to an awakening, the birth of consciousness, of equality, and of balance—where there was still a devotion to or acknowledgment of the Goddess. I wanted to synthesize and show you what I had unearthed, in an easily digestible way, to help you transcend and connect to our whole journey as female evolvers in all of its empowering and emotional revelations. So, it only seemed right that a sacred spiral, symbolizing all things Goddess, should be used to highlight some key timeline milestones that sung out to me. See what you are drawn to, what you connect with. Can you visualize the journey, and your part in it? What stories come off the pages for you?

I have bound time together in zodiac eras, referencing astrological years every 2,160 zodiac years. Today we celebrate the new year on the first day of January; in ancient times, it was celebrated on the day that day and night were equally balanced, usually sitting on the twenty-first of March. This is the first day of spring and brings with it new life. These dates vary, with many astrologers sharing different insights into when exactly these astrological ages fall, due to different approaches in making the calculations (there are many variations of this depending on what astrology you use, so I welcome you to explore the astrology workings that best resonate with you), but regardless, they give you an idea of what star energies might have been guiding us at the time of these big evolutionary movements. And, no matter what astrology you explore, there are similar windows of time showing us that, no matter what date you accept, we are in the midst of some big changes. Every person will be affected by this shift in energy, whether they are conscious of it or not.

This history download is in real down-to-earth Goddess lingo, so you can focus more on taking in the download and embracing that evolutionary "aha," than wasting energy on trying to decode those huge multisyllabic historical terms. You and I can both agree, ain't nobody got time to google unnecessary show pony words. We are all here because we need change, fast! Not an ego-induced history lesson. So this powwow is a straight-shooting journey through the story of time, like never before. A fast and fancy-free account of our spiritual evolution based on the stars.

## Evolutionary Timeline

This timeline differs from anything you may have ever seen before. This timeline acknowledges and references your spiritual evolution, and conscious change, documenting the energy and motion behind every major undertaking in time, a conscious overview of every defining action since the dawn of time to where you are now. This conscious chronology in energy and motion is not linear, nor is the time as per the stars. Like us, like the seasons, like the cycles of life, energy moves in spirals, swirls, cycles, and circles—often overlapping and crossing over as it ebbs and flows.

This is your vortex, your window to where you have come from as per the stars and our evolution as spiritual beings. While the symbol of Goddess is the spiral,

## THE AGE OF AQUARIUS

Mayan Calendar / Egyptian Cycle of the
Phoenix begins AD 2012 (also believed
to be from November 11, 2011)

## THE AGE OF PISCES

ca. 6 BC to AD 2000 (Some
believe ending in 2012)

## THE AGE OF LEO

ca. 10,006 BC to 8006 BC

## THE AGE OF ARIES

ca. 2006 BC to 6 BC (Some
believe to be the age of Christ)

## THE AGE OF CANCER

ca. 8006 BC to 6006 BC

## CREATION

Birth

## THE AGE OF GEMINI

ca. 6006 BC to 4006 BC

## THE AGE OF TAURUS

ca. 4006 BC to 2006 BC

representing life, creation, and fertility, you may argue this spiral is more symbolic of the downward spiral variety. This is why this timeline is done in celestial circles of time representing the feminine, rather than a linear recording of battles and empires. Gone are the days of a history of revolution, and here is the day of the story of our evolution. The facts that failed to make our feminine history files.

## CREATION: BIRTH

Whatever you believe—Big Bang = earth; god; Adam and Eve = humankind; ape; or even the collaboration of the god Prometheus who created man from mud with the Goddess Athena gifting man a soul—somehow it all started. Because, well, here we are! Many cultures believe the world started from darkness, from swirling and spiraling chaos (there's that spiral and Goddess symbol again). The Egyptian's believe the god Atum, also known as Ptah, mated with the darkness of his shadow to create life.

Some say Eve was born from Adam's rib. Jews, Christians, and Muslims all have faith in an Adam and Eve beginning. We could be here all day if you want to discuss all the different thoughts around how the world started, so, whatever you believe, one thing we can all agree on is that it was something chaotic. (In Greek mythology, the Goddess of creation is even called Khaos, believed to be the first being born from darkness and night. Fitting name, huh?)

Regardless of what exactly went down and however chaotic, we can all agree in some scientific way or spiritual form that the evolutionary seed was planted. Since, after all, we all exist. And so, it began . . . Stone Age, to Sapiens, to the Silicone Age. What an almighty bang!

Starting in the Stone Age and the first stories of our evolution in a time of survival, where all efforts went into hunting, gathering, or running for your goddamn life, we also see stories of entities that begin to evolve with us. Spirits, fairies, demons even—and in the stories these entities seem weak. Symbolically it is told in folklore that iron kills fairies, the symbol of command and conquer. The weapon of man. As we learn to grow and farm foods, even on a basic level, our gods and Goddesses grow with us. With temples and artwork starting to record gods who seem to be growing in power, so did our belief in them. With the birth of gods came the birth of spiritual storytelling. Scriptures and tales, from etchings on walls to the most sacred of bound books, all started with the understanding that with story comes belief. Understanding. Transformation. From the most holy to propaganda,

## EVOLUTION EXERCISE: YOUR GODDESS TIMELINE

Let's take a state of the Goddess nation from the world pre you, to your birth, and all the magical, disastrous, and divinely gifted spiritual growth spurts you have had this lifetime.

- Start from your conception. (If this has you scratching your head, subtract nine months from your birthday.) Who are your parents, why do you think you picked them, what are the key things they have taught you, and what is your family dynamic?
- What is one of your first memories, how old were you, why do you think you remember this memory, why is it significant?
- Big life events—this is so unique to you, it could be anything from your first boyfriend, to shifting house, to graduation, losing your virginity, or becoming a mother. Influential souls you have crossed paths with, parents and your honest take on friends, teachers, and lovers. Lay it all out on the Goddess table. Look at the events, how and when they happened, why they would have happened, and access the meaning you have associated with that lesson. Is it creating a limiting belief, or has it helped you evolve? It really is one or the other. Take some time to actually zoom out and digest your life.

- Are there any reoccurring life lessons coming up? Are there themes in timings, every few years, every five years?
- Take a moment to have a bird's- or third-eye view of your life, your lessons, the mountains you have conquered, the hillsides you may have tripped and slid down face-first.
- Evaluate how all of these weird and wonderful bleeps on the timeline of you have built toward your evolution. More important, and in the theme of all things evolving, if you see a pattern, change it. If you see a block, shift it. Use your life road map as an opportunity to redirect yourself through the magical mayhem that is your life.

tales have largely shaped our reality of our history. Whether fictional, or fact, these stories are still widely discussed today. Adam and Eve, ape, aquatic ape, Big Bang, the heavens. . . .

### THE AGE OF LEO: CA. 10,006 BC TO 8006 BC

Known as the Golden Age—that stems from Greek mythology—a time widely referenced and recorded because of its ability to inspire art and scripts that set it in time through its tales. The vibe was peaceful, focused on harmony, and people not having to toil and break their backs because the earth just provided. There was a natural order, an organic flow of things in life. This is when a natural religion was in order, one that honored the land and worked with its cycles.

Settlements were established from Denmark to Jordan, and it was an era of hunting and gathering. Clothes were provided from the skin of animals, huts made from trees, food from hunting and the first recorded crops. Wall paintings of hunting life dated to this time were found in Africa.

The Goddess, mother world, and the fertility of earth were widely associated with a feminine energy. The Cat Goddess was widely seen as a Goddess talisman, with the lion, sphinx, and cat worshipped during this era. Seen in the sphinxes in Egypt still standing today. The Cat Goddess and the zodiac Leo shared similarities, with the zodiac linked to the fire sign, and the cat being associated with the sun. The Egyptians were not the only ones to worship the cat; in Norse mythology, there was Freya, the Goddess of earth whose chariot was pulled by two giant kittens. The climate heating up throughout the age of the fire sign caused the melting of many of the glaciers.

**THE AGE OF CANCER: CA. 8006 BC TO 6006 BC**

Known as the Age of Great Mother, or the birth of humanity. We see the birth of Earth Goddesses, and wine was invented—I think that is important to note. Matriarchy ruled. With Cancer being ruled by moon energy, we see a lot of Sun Goddesses transition to Moon Goddesses in mythology. Religion at the time showcased female deities, with many cultures worshipping pregnant female figures. We see the domestication of animals and farming from Iraq to China. Walls were built for homes, and the Wall of Jericho, still the oldest city wall ever discovered, believed to be constructed to guard the city from floods.

There was a rise in awareness of the natural elements of Mother Nature, what she could give in terms of fertile earth to grow crops for food, and the weather of her destruction, hence her worship and appreciation. Think of the power your mother has over you as a child: to feed, nourish, and even punish when you misbehave. Civilization respected mama earth, and rightfully so!

**THE AGE OF GEMINI: CA. 6006 BC TO 4006 BC**

The birth of the Bronze Age was the age of duality, as seen in the twins of Gemini. This was reflected in ancient literature, storytelling, multiple gods, and narratives that share the tales of both loser and victor. It was a time of expression, communication, trade, and the recording of mythology. The first Minoan scripts were created as well as Egyptian hieroglyphics. There was also a global construction of temples. It was the era of the creation of the calendar by both the Mayans and Egyptians.

Gemini symbolizes balance, female and male, dark and light. This is also why many stories and religions began to discuss the duality of good and evil. And the polarity of masculine and feminine began to create a sway between Goddess and god worship. With the rise of literature and storytelling also came a rise in science and mathematics. It was a time of knowledge, differences in thought, language, and expression.

### THE AGE OF TAURUS: CA. 4006 BC TO 2006 BC

Taurus, another feminine sign, signified an age of agriculture and structure. It brought with it the energies of earth and work. Bulls and cows were widely worshipped across many cultures; the cow was seen in many Goddesses and temples, from Egypt to India. Stonehenge was built. The pyramids were built. Egyptians created their first dam to help better manage the great floods. The birth of the Iron Age was largely dominated by Egypt and Babylonia, where women owned land and were equal to men. This era is also believed to be the time of the destruction of Atlantis. This was also the era when chariot warfare commenced. We saw the shift of many populations migrating to new lands because of the chariot.

In Africa, horned Goddesses were found dating back to this era, representing the self-fertilization of Goddess and earth. In Greek mythology Selene and Artemis, Moon Goddesses, were represented by a crescent moon crown, also by cow horns. Kings and queens at the time wore horns to amplify their power as rulers. The end of the age of Taurus was seen with the exodus of the Israelites from Egypt.

### THE AGE OF ARIES: CA. 2006 BC TO 6 BC (SOME BELIEVE THIS TO BE THE AGE OF CHRIST)

This was the age of war, adventure, and expansion of empires—the age of the warrior. A time to command and conquer, of animal sacrifice and combat, of quest and discovery. A surge in initiative and a rise in the arts, science, and new philosophy. The ram and sheep were worshipped by the Assyrians, Greeks, and Romans, and depicted in many religions of the time. Some of the most ancient scripts were written: the Indian Vedas, believed to be completed by 1200 BC; the old book of *Alchemy*; and parts of the Hebrew Bible. As dynasties expanded over China, Chinese characters are also recorded to vary and evolve. Other books are harder to date, such as The Tibetan Book of the Dead, believed to date back to 1240 BC. The earliest reference to the I Ching (Book of Changes) was in approximately 700 BC.

Some of the biggest thinkers of all time also graced this age, such as Plato, Socrates, and Aristotle. Throughout the ancient civilizations symbols of a unified god/Goddess joined both female and male in one. These dually gendered figures have been found everywhere, from the Aztec to the Indian cultures. Even angels were mutually balanced genders said to just "be," and not be one specific gender. Christ—the lamb of god—was also noted to have been born as the Age of Aries came to a close, bringing a rise in Christianity, accompanied by the symbol of the fish, which represents the age Christ led in, Pisces, the next zodiac era.

## THE AGE OF PISCES: CA. 6 BC TO AD 2000 (SOME BELIEVE ENDING IN 2012)

We see the biggest shifts in Western civiliza-

## GODDESS (R)EVOLUTIONARY: JOAN DIDION

Joan Didion is the epitome of a Goddess, and someone to admire from an evolutionary standpoint. She famously said, "Life changes in an instance.[6] The award-winning author and journalist wrote on all things moral throughout the chaos of the civil rights movement and American history. She told the story of changing times—be it in society, in age, and in death. Her essays and observations were perfect, indirect, and complicated. They urged the world to take note of what "united" really meant.

It wasn't anything political, it wasn't anything racial, it was in fact her personal story that touched the world most deep. *The Year of Magical Thinking*, her story about the death of her husband and daughter, is witness to how words and wounds can transform into wisdom. Her stories have shaped and shifted views and opinions of society, as well of herself.

tion in a time of the gods, or god, that truly shattered the status quo and created a new world order. We see division in beliefs from religion to ethics to race. And command and conquer shifts to control and divide.

To put it in perspective, the era started with the fall of Rome. This was a time of development, innovation, invention, and progression. It was a time of faith, charity, and sacrifice. Pisces's dark side, seen in its two fish swimming in opposite directions, represents the deception and silent suffering that was also endured during this era. This was also the era when we see the rise of the Virgin Mary story, reflecting the age of nurturing and protecting, the life force that comes with all things mother. We see the creation of churches, symbolic of the womb of the Virgin Mother. These churches resembled a similar sacred, safe, quiet sanctuary away from the world, protected by mother energy, like a baby would experience inside the mother. In this time, we saw a shift for equality,

## GODDESS GEM

**The Age of Aquarius is associated with the crystal amethyst, as the stone of peace and balance. It is said to hold vibrational subtle energies that supports spirituality, raises hope, lifts spirits, and brings peace, stability, and strength to the wearer. I personally dig amethysts and find it an essential stone to wear or keep on me when my feminine and masculine energies are bickering.**

and a fight for balance, globally, for a unified universe. We had witch hunts; slavery; women's rights, civil rights, and gay rights movements; and a constant fight for liberation for all.

Women earned the right to vote, there were the first female prime ministers (mainly from Goddess-worshipping cultures like Sri Lanka, India, and Israel). There was even a movement called the Goddess movement in this era. The International Council of Thirteen Indigenous Grandmothers was created in this time, uniting all four corners of the globe, bringing together wise elders and medicine women, representing a global alliance of prayer, education, and healing for the earth. A unity between the divided and segmented elements of society began to form, seeing minorities and those treated unjustly by society come together as one. There was also a rise in terrorism, the fight for natural resources and climate change threats, and humanity was forced to confront its approach to life and how to live well, peacefully, with each other and nature.

### THE AGE OF AQUARIUS: MAYAN CALENDAR/EGYPTIAN CYCLE OF THE PHOENIX BEGINS AD 2012 (ALSO BELIEVED TO BE FROM NOVEMBER 11, 2011)

Believed to be the age of raising collective consciousness. Aquarius is connected to all things energy, technology, travel, democracy, freedom, liberation, humanitarianism, idealism, philanthropy, nervous disorders, perseverance, humanity, and nonconformity. The next two thousand years look to be illuminating, inventive, and innovative. This is a time to call for a better world with higher morals from every person, which needs the nurturing and loving energy of the fertile femininity to align with Mother Earth.

As with many cultures, men may be the "leaders," however, they look to women for guidance: when to stop hunting or depleting the earth's natural resources. Leaders will be called upon to lead with a balanced, gracious energy, seeking new technology, new sources of energy—the resources war will stop. This era will seek to be in balance. And now, the call for both balance in humanity, and a return to balance in nature, will be up front and center. Everyone will be called to contribute to a better society. This is also a time where the truth will come out. The fog will lift from the world. It is the age of equality. And here we are, ready for conscious change.

---

So, what does this Goddess Age of Aquarius have in store for us? Netflix subscriptions and iPhone 22s for everybody! Jokes aside, we will use our technology with consciousness, using it to aid in our efforts to heal the earth and the earth's energy and resources. We will shift our view from being victims of each other's decisions to being the creators of a conscious future, making collective decisions to benefit all rather than a few. Feminine traits in both men and women will be embraced, and we will see a return to sacred feminine teachings continue to emerge. Growing curiosity about all things moon to mindfulness.

You, awakened soul, are proof of all the above. The rise in Goddess reading, books by Elizabeth Gilbert calling for writers to grab their pens, stand up, speak out, and share their messages with the world. Authors such as Gabrielle Bernstein, Rebecca Campbell (who wrote *Rise Sister Rise*[7] at the same time I was writing this book, how is that for Goddess alignments!), Shonda Rhimes, and even this book in those hot little Goddess hands of yours, have all been divinely curated and purposefully delivered to you to help you play your part in this conscious awakening and Goddess shift, to create some real change when the world needs it.

Fact is, whether you vibe with the Mayan, Hindu, astrological view, or discount the whole lot as an eyebrow raised, question mark, maybeeeeeeee inflection load of humbug, you have to admit that in terms of Goddess empowerment, the rise of the heroine in pop culture, women in power as board members, even running for president of the United States, becoming prime minister of Great Britain, are all clues that there is momentum toward a balance of energy on a global scale. Well, a start nonetheless! You just have to check your Instagram feed to scroll the #girlboss #squadgoals movement. Ironically, when writing this paragraph this quote came up on my feed, how divinely orchestrated for you: "We need women who are so strong they can be gentle, so educated they can be humble, so fierce they can be compassionate, so passionate they can be rational, and so disciplined they can be free," by Kavita Ramdas.[8] It really is true—our technology can support the spread of consciousness.

# EVOLUTION EXERCISE: GODDESS MAPPING

**INTUITION MAP LAYER**
Grab a map and mark the countries you have an unexplained affinity with. People might always tell you that you look like someone from this country; you might have an unexplained fascination with the language and the culture. You might love their food. Have always wanted to travel there. Love the myths and legends from this culture. Or quite simply always had a connection with their people, their traditions, religions, or rituals.

**DNA MAP LAYER**
Then, using a different-color pen on the same map, mark the countries you know you have a biological connection with. For those of you with grandparents, parents, or relatives, ask about their origins and jot them down on the map. Should you be eager for more, or are like me and need some help in the DNA department, order a DNA ancestry kit and mark down where you have bloodlines. Any interesting connections or observations? Don't throw a Goddess tantrum if there are no connected dots for you at this stage—we still have past life regressions up our sleeve, which will be the third layer to dotting your goddess map journey. . . .

**PAST LIFE MAP LAYER**
Now, in yet another color, I want you to mark where you have had past lives. This can be quite a difficult ask for some people; so, should it not resonate, feel free to skip this layer. You can visit a past life hypnotist, past life regressionist, or try a past life meditation online and see if you get transported back to a forgotten lifetime. Something else, which can be a clue to help trigger a past life regression experience, take note of any birthmarks or scars you have. These are often connected to wounds or trauma you have also received in past lives. Simply google "past life regression meditation" and try to find one with a voice that resonates with you. Plug in your earbuds and allow yourself to visualize where in the world and in what time you showed up. If you have an experience, add it to your map.

## THE SAYING "THE FUTURE IS FEMALE" IS WRONG. . . . THE TRUTH IS, "THE FUTURE IS FEMININE." THERE IS A DIFFERENCE.

I raise you a new thought. The saying "the future is female" is wrong. Hear me out, sister. This, like everything that was out of balance with patriarchy, is flawed, in the same swing of imbalance from female to male, to male to female. The truth is, "the future is feminine." There is a difference.

How is feminine different? Because as with all labels, categorizations divide us.

Evolving means being all-encompassing rather than exclusive. Men are just as capable of being feminine as females are. Therefore, this change isn't solely to be championed by females. But championed by those in tune with and embracing all things feminine. A balanced approach to both masculine and feminine energy. Not one or the other. Remember from the Goddess Manifesto: *Unity is a source of our power.*

———

So here we are. At the age of the Goddesses' return. Leaving the Piscean Age (New Age) where, as a world, we have been focused on hierarchy and patriarchy, and who holds the keys to power. The feminine is widely and rapidly becoming accepted and rejoiced. Our question for this age isn't: *To be or not to be?* It is: *To do with love or not with love?* As a society, we are focused on being successful, being accepted, being happy with the driving energy of the Pisces age, and we find ourselves looking for something to believe in, a way of life, and a way of being.

Now, with the Age of Aquarius (Serve Age) we already have and understand the importance of being, and want to now evolve into the new era of equality in doing. The balancing age. This is the time to open, release, surrender, reset, and embrace your beautiful, strong, gentle, loving, and potent feminine. The beautifully balanced feminine future. You, with your big questions, inquisitive souls, and persistent urge to help and heal everyone and everything, are the Goddesses our world has been patiently wasting and waiting for. Your arrival to awakening, to evolving, couldn't be more timely.

## AWAKENED ACCOMPLISHMENT IS A VERY REAL REALITY, THANKS TO YOU! THE FUTURE IS YOU, IT IS FEMININE, AND IT IS INCREDIBLY BRIGHT.

As women, you are the ones who have the wisdom. It is up to you to help create equality and balance on a global scale. We are the ones who got this privilege. Now, what are we going to do with it? You've been taken through thousands of years to understand your full potential and your alignment with the stars, so what can you do today? Awakened accomplishment is a very real reality, thanks to you! The future is you, it is feminine, and it is incredibly bright.

# 5

# WHICH GODDESS ARCHETYPE ARE YOU?

*"THE PSYCHES AND SOULS OF WOMEN ALSO HAVE THEIR OWN CYCLES AND SEASONS OF DOING AND SOLITUDE, RUNNING AND STAYING, BEING INVOLVED AND BEING REMOVED."*
—CLARISSA PINKOLA ESTÉS

Becoming more aware of what Goddess archetype you are currently in can be transformative in understanding all your many Goddess aspects. Both acknowledging your journey to evolve and what may lay ahead.

## The Triple Goddess and Phases

Traditionally, many pagan women have identified with the three phases, or the triple Goddess, of womanhood: the Maiden (pre-sex), the Mother (from pregnancy to menopause), the Crone (from menopause). From womb to tomb.

### MAIDEN PHASE

This phase doesn't necessarily mean you have to be a virgin in the physical sense, it is more a life cycle you are in that surrounds you with feelings of anticipation, self-confidence, curiosity, and in-dependence, where you are inspired to create art, have experiences and new beginnings. This combination of energy and action means the Maiden is not afraid to express herself. While youthful in energy, she is intelligent and tactful, like a huntress. She knows instinctively when to strike, and when to let nature takes it course. This phase is all about enhancement, expansion, and female principle. The Maiden represents new beginnings, the season of spring, the hunt, nature, movement, and change. She is responsible for only herself and her actions, focused on discovery and joyful living.

Examples of Maiden Goddesses: Artemis, Brigid, Chalchiuhtlicue, Diana, Freya, Hebe, Persephone, Parvati, Rhiannon . . . to name a few.

### MOTHER PHASE

The phase is the fruition of a Maiden into a Mother, an awakened adult; the shift to become the nurturer, the caregiver, the protector. She accepts her responsibilities in life, is disciplined, and her purpose is simple: love and harmony. You don't necessarily have to be a Mother to enter this phase of balance, self-understanding, responsibility, and self-discipline. The Mother has a meaningful purpose of wanting the best for all her creations, be it physical children, business or artistic pursuits, or those around her. The Mother represents fruition, the season of summer, maturity, knowledge, and self-awareness. She is responsible for those around her, focused on nurture and support.

Examples of Mother Goddesses: Aphrodite, Bast (also referred to as Bastet), Ceres, Frigg, Gaia, Hera, Isis, Juno, Mary, Venus, Yemoja . . . to name a few.

## CRONE PHASE

Here we have the completion of a Mother into a Crone—a matriarch, teacher, elder—the shift to Wise Woman, the height of spiritual power. She is the end of the cycle of life, what many people fear: death. She guides others in understanding that without death there isn't transformation and rebirth. She is both the past and the present. Showing you the journey of your evolution from birth, to learning, to completion. The Crone represents justice, the season of winter, balance, wisdom, and deep understanding. She is responsible for magic, guidance, and completion. She cares for all things living, those that come, and those that go.

Examples of Crone Goddesses: Black Annis, Hecate, Grandmother Spider, Kali, Morrigan, Sedna, Xochiquetzal . . . to name a few.

---

Today, with modern Goddesses waiting longer to have children, and women living longer than our ancestors did, it has been suggested a fourth phase of life touches modern Goddesses—the Queen. As with any categorization, these ancient archetypes have been limiting to women in some regards, dependent on the label of the archetype. Spiritual feminists see these categories as examples of how a patriarchal society

## GODDESS GEM

Within any phase—the Maiden, Mother, or Crone—there are elemental energies that will influence your experiences and how you handle yourself in these phases of life. These elements will help define your Goddess personality, or archetype—give guidance to how you react, behave, process, and shift through each phase. The following pages are going to lead you to your Goddess archetype, and we will look at how each one travels through the phases, so you can dive deep into your Goddess roots to aid you in truly understanding not just the experiences but the empowering emotions that come with these experiences.

treats women. A Crone is cast aside—a hag, old and stripped of any association of being of much worth. Today, we see women approaching menopause vibrant with their remaining energy, embodying their feminine power, and very much embracing life. Seeing the modern Goddess reclaim the power of all phases of her life. Crone and the end included. Doubling down on her triple Goddess energy.

## NEITHER A LIGHT NOR A DARK LESSON IS MORE JUSTIFIED THAN THE OTHER, NEITHER IS MORE POWERFUL, BOTH EQUAL IN THEIR OPPORTUNITY TO GIFT YOU NEW INSIGHT, NEW LEVELS OF COMPASSION, AND A NEW MEANING TO LOVE.

As you shift through these spirals and phases of life, each will need different guidance and insight. Growth here comes from not only profound, brave, and new experiences, learning new wisdom, or embodying your truth, but also equally from the dark side of phases including grief, loss, anguish, betrayal, greed, and experiencing life's hardships. Neither a light nor a dark lesson is more justified than the other, neither is more powerful, both equal in their opportunity to gift you new insight, new levels of compassion, and a new meaning to love. All empowering your Goddess.

As with the transformational arc, the journey of the heroine and Goddess, we know that the Goddess can decide to be a wounded victim, pointing blame, angry, bitter. Or the Goddess can choose understanding, growth, expansion, and self-development. Is it hard? Totally. Girl needs some help. We all do, trust me. So, rest assured, I am not going to leave you at an evolutionary crossroad with no tools to arm you with, Goddess.

This phase in your evolutionary knowledge expansion is about tapping into where you are at, in an energetic sense, and gifting you the tools (not rules) to help you walk with grace. This, this is the stuff our schools need to be teaching our sisters. These are the essentials to living without wanting to head-butt-high-heel-throttle those who hurt you on your path 101. Truth is, this book is your Goddess go-to when you experience transitions, shifts, spiritual growing pains, and find your soul feeling the stretch marks of evolution.

So, to help craft a modern Goddess script for your evolutionary road, I have chosen to look at archetypes differently, evolving them, you could say. (You know, again taking a new approach from conscious conventionalism.) Honoring the grandmothers of the Goddess movement before us who studied Goddess archetypes of their time: from famous historians, archaeologists, authors, scholars, and spiritualists much like yourself. I am choosing to shine light on new conscious choices for women in our modern age, not to place judgment on the old archetypes or elements, more so to learn from them and move forward with the new.

This process took me two years of creating a reference system that attributed modern Goddess elemental archetypes that wove together traditional traits, ancient teachings from Goddess movements: from Wiccan to the Vedas, Tao Te Ching and the Shu Ching to periodic elementals, and the elemental philosophy seen in astrology, numerology, ritual, and medicine, translating and scribing scripts and synthesizing all their wisdom. No easy feat. But totally worth the journey, as in doing so I unearthed new elements about myself I had never explored. And for you, I invite you to experience a new look into the realm of archetype and elemental influence.

You and I will look through a new age, modern-day lens at the situation at hand, walking with the wisdom of our grandmothers and ancestors in our transformational tunics. Energetically connected. Unified. When one hurts, we all hurt. When one loves, we all love. From here on in, ladies, we walk together.

Similar to our approach to history, which saw us split up time in our Goddess history into energy, seen in the circles of zodiac eras, we are going to split up our Goddess archetypes into their organic energies. Natural energies, the elements. Mother Nature, Goddess of all, in all her aspects.

# USING THE NATURAL INFLUENCE OF MOON, WATER, EARTH, AIR, AND SUN TO GUIDE YOU, WE COMBINE GODDESS TEACHINGS FROM ALL RELIGIONS AND CULTURES TO GIVE YOU A WIDER EVOLUTIONARY PERSPECTIVE.

Using the natural influence of moon, water, earth, air, and sun to guide you, we combine Goddess teachings from all religions and cultures to give you a wider evolutionary perspective. Traditionally, the four elements are always used and referenced; however, where Goddess is concerned, my intuition, and the guides working with me in scribing this book—and the studies I felt aligned with across paganism, Buddhism, and Indian philosophy—lead me to feel passionately that the fifth element be moon. Moon, after all, is a powerful element of the Goddess, and there is a reason why so many awakening women today are looking to the moon for guidance. New time, new energy, new element.

# Finding Your Goddess Element + Archetype

**Moon**

**Water**

**Earth**

**Air**

**Sun**

Finding your dominant evolutionary archetypical element is a tool, not a rule. I ask you to follow your Goddess intuition. Go with what feels right. Understand that these will evolve, much like you. Respect your right to ebb and flow between all and every element as you enter and exit the new and old phases of life. As with the menstrual cycle, and the ups and downs we experience every month, these elements might change from day to day, monthly, yearly.

The point is that you can use these natural forces to help fuel your new approach to leading with love in the modern world. You can harness Mother Nature's elements to help steer your soul's course and cradle you in times of challenge or when confronting change. So let's get you connected with the element of your evolutionary Goddess archetype.

You have two options. Flick straight to the element that resonates most with you. Are you drawn to earth and being in nature? Does the idea of being in or around water calm and soothe you? Do you crave the sun?

Or, explore your current state by deep-diving into your current mood, feelings, desires, and wishes with this quick and simple quiz that I developed after researching and studying the common threads and traits of the elements and their influence on us.

This quiz is a fusion of those studies, and it aims to give you insights into your key elemental forces. When taking the quiz, go with your intuition and listen to your body, heart, mind, and inner Goddess—all of it. Under each life area, choose the answer that best suits your nature today, right now. We want to find your real-time Goddess element, so try to stay present and follow your soul.

## CONNECTING

You love to be in the company of others; often called a social butterfly, you find connection being surrounded by people and their energy. You love being in the company of people; like the Goddess Ilmatar, you feel lonely when you only have clouds to count instead of chatter. (Air)

You connect through emotion, stories, experiences. Opening yourself up when others open up to you. This helps your healing flow like the running water also enjoyed by your fellow Goddess Anuket. (Water)

You are in your element when you can connect to your intuition. Exploring your dreams, spirituality, higher planes, and a deeper meaning to living. You share a love for spirituality like Goddess Selene, drawn to the moon and heavens. (Moon)

You find purpose and connection through contribution. You are at your best when busy or leading a cause; with it you find balance like the Goddess Sekhmet. When you lack purpose in life, you can find yourself in destructive patterns. (Sun)

You love to create and express yourself, whether it be with your hands, voice, or emotions. You connect by creating. You have a whole Gaia, Mother, Creation Goddess vibe going on. (Earth)

## FEELING

You are incredibly sympathetic to others, deeply in touch with your emotions and the energy around you. You can often seem calm on the surface, but underneath you could be raging and moody given the wrong conditions. Like the Goddess Yemoja, you are talented at comforting others who are anxious being in new waters. (Water)

Like Goddess Durga, you aren't afraid to cut out what doesn't serve you. You are down-to-earth with your emotions, and are not afraid to cast out people and things that no longer serve you in life organically, cutting yourself free from old habits or experiences. (Earth)

There is beauty in your chaos, like the Goddess Khaos. You are innovative, inventive, intuitive, inquisitive—constantly asking questions about love and life. Your intelligence is part of your deep ability to feel out and understand experiences logically rather than emotionally. (Air)

You can get easily frustrated and short tempered with slow or, in your eyes, less "evolved" beings. A bit of a Medusa who turned a slow coach into stone! You are, however, passionate and full in your approach to life. (Sun)

You are incredibly sensitive and extremely instinctive in your emotion and energy. You can often feel out people, environments, and see the truth behind all experiences. Like Goddess Mawu, you seek out the wisdom in everything. (Moon)

## CHANNELING

Goddess Amaterasu. You are welcoming and naturally kind to others. You like to step up, help, and often choose to rise up to a challenge. (Sun)

Goddess Sheela-na-Gigs. You are playful and flirtatious with life. You have a tendency to fly by the seat of your pants, or skirt. You are adventurous and rebellious at times. (Air)

Goddess Oshun. You are a natural caregiver, a nurturer, and often get hurt and upset when the same level of love and compassion isn't shown to you when you need it. (Water)

Goddess Kali. You have no tolerance for ego, and often find yourself being quite cutthroat in cutting people out of your life who don't align with your values. (Earth)

Goddess Hera. You can be mistaken for being moody; in truth, you are just suspiciously observant (which at times is intuitively justified). You are not easily fooled or tricked. You look out for yourself first and foremost. (Moon)

## ACKNOWLEDGING

Goddess Rhiannon shares your love for all things quiet, like having nights in. You move through phases in coming to terms with everything from the highs and lows of life. Often needing to retreat, regroup, rejuvenate, before rejoining the world with your lesson in hand. (Moon)

You have a whole mother of the gods vibe going on, like Goddess Aditi, you are in charge. You can be bold, instinctive, brave, and generous in your lessons in life, and often like to lead by example. (Sun)

You use your wit and your desire to constantly explore and travel, to approach life with a sense of freedom and free-spirited fun. You love to spread your wings like the Goddess Eos. (Air)

You like the DIY life; like the Goddess Nu Gua, you are not afraid to get your hands dirty and work with your experiences. You have a practical and responsible approach to learning and experiencing life. (Earth)

You are good at absorbing a situation for what it is, seeing each emotion rise and fall, and riding out experiences, letting them consume and flow through you. You can conquer your feelings when you tame your thoughts; like the Goddess Benten you have a knack for taming unruly behavior. (Water)

## HEALING

You are almost snake-like, shedding skin and rejuvenating yourself like the Goddess Renenutet. You have a tendency to bounce back quickly and see the nourishment and lessons in hardships. You take life as it comes. (Earth)

You heal by purging, be it through a wave of emotion, detoxing, purifying, or simply diving into the heart of the matter. Like the Goddess Gaṅgā, you are happiest when you are touching water and releasing any fears or sins. (Water)

You need to feel you can fully express yourself to completely heal. You don't like to leave things unsaid, always with the positive intent in mind to restore happiness, like the Goddess Hathor. (Air)

You heal in cycles. You are not afraid to sit in the darkness of a situation until the time is right to release and let go fully. Like the Goddess Juno, who guards the full moon and heavenly light, you give hope for new beginnings and new cycles. (Moon)

Like the Goddess Astraea you are a star. You know you enjoy the burn of busy; however, you are equally aware you may burn out. You fear boredom, which can be evolving as much as it is destructive. (Sun)

## BEING

You are happiest in stability, centered, deeply rooted in your own space or sanctuary. Like the Goddess Selu, you know when it is time to sprout growth, time to be still, and time to reap the harvest. (Earth)

You are spontaneous, imaginative, energetic, and, day to day, very optimistic about life and your approach to it. But be careful, underneath a fire could be brewing like the Volcano Goddess Pele. (Sun)

You are at your best when you are free to be, do, go wherever you please. You have a Goddess Saranya, who seeks freedom in life, to escape it all, energy about you. No restrictions, obligations, or responsibilities. (Air)

Goddess Hina is always immersed in her passions, and so are you. You are in your element when you fully submerge yourself in something, be it an experience, a project, or a job. (Water)

It seems both you and Goddess Luna love a good Goddess get-together in sacred spaces. You are happiest when in ritual, ceremony, or in your sacred space. You enjoy like-minded souls, and often find yourself learning from those like you. (Moon)

## ACTING

You are led by your gut. Like the Goddess Phoebe you have a sixth sense about your experiences, which sees you observe others differently than most. You have a primal approach to living, which often makes you seem quirky, awkward, or eccentric. Insightful and prophetic in your words, there is clarity in your actions. (Moon)

You often let sparks fly when you are excited about something. Like the Goddess Brigid, you are the life of the party or business. You are not afraid to take charge and lead. Your warmth welcomes others to your cause. (Sun)

You have a solid ethical structure, strong in your beliefs. Deeply rooted to what you believe to be right or wrong. You know strongly what you stand for. You are naturally seen as a mother figure, a mother to all like the Goddess Fjorgyn. (Earth)

You have a tendency to act out of emotion, at times hastily. Ruled by your heart, you are similar to the Goddess Ran, who was obsessed with catching men and love. This can see you crash hard onto experiences, or recede from them altogether. You can run hot and cold. (Water)

You are a messenger like the Goddess Arce. You learn, connect, and grow through deep conversation. You love language and words, and you use your words wisely. (Air)

### CHANGING

You are easily influenced by others, and care deeply about others and their journey. You can be clumsy and resistant toward change at first, but swallow your lessons and let them change you more deeply than most. Like Goddess Mazu, you are happiest when you can forecast change. (Water)

Like the Goddess Ceres, you enjoy your own personal self-love rituals. You have a good handle on stress, benefiting most from fruitful experiences that challenge you to grow and expand. However, you enjoy your own space in times of change. (Earth)

Change to you is an eternal cycle, a never-ending thread of transition. You embrace all phases of the journey, dark, light, and full beam. Like the Goddess Kuan Yin, you are ever grateful for every lesson and opportunity to grow, and are compassionate to all your teachers in life. (Moon)

You love change. Like the Goddess Bast, you are a lioness and take charge and adapt when called upon. In fact, you thrive on change. You take it all in your stride, often looking for the positive lessons in every experience. (Sun)

Like the season spring and the Goddess Brigid, you blossom and grow naturally, no matter your environment. You are agile and transition easily, almost effortlessly. You have a go-with-the-flow nature that sees you take flight while some would fight. (Air)

## FAQs

**Q:** Okay, I've taken the quiz, now what?

**A:** Tally up each element. The element you scored most highly in is your dominant archetype. Go and explore the chapters that focus on that element first.

**Q:** What if I have more than one dominant element?

**A:** It is not uncommon to get two or even three higher-ranking elements, as one element usually complements the other. Like moon speaks to water. And sun speaks to moon. Explore all your dominant elements and go to the key element that resonates most for you at this moment in time.

**Q:** What about my lowest scoring element? Should I be worried?

**A:** Not at all. Embrace the ones that you are high in rather than worry about your lower elements. Know that as you grow and evolve you will draw from different elements in different experiences and phases of life. Your elements will change. Truth is, there is no right or top answers here.

---

It is important to know that all the elements are equal but different. Like men and women are equal but different. We hold unique superpowers and weaknesses.

Below is a brief teaser about each element. You can further explore your element archetype(s) in the corresponding chapters that follow.

# Moon Archetype

**Moon = Empowered Insight**

You hold intuitive feminine energy, which often sees you shift from dark places of retreat, into light phases of celebration. You are a deep, sensitive, emotional being who looks for insight and intention in your experiences. You, Goddess, are highly spiritual and are in a space of higher-self evolutionary expansion.

# Water Archetype

**Water = Empowered Emotion**

You are in a place of emotional evolutionary expansion. Experiences and their emotional lessons are flooding you, washing out old beliefs and cleansing your soul. This can be a transformational space, but can also feel like turmoil with the tides pushing and pulling you into a new phase of your life. You are a force now. Powerful. Healing for you, and for those around you.

# Earth Archetype

**Earth = Empowered Creativity**

You have a solid sense of who you are now, and feel grounded in what you stand for. You are in growth mode, expressive and creative. This is a space of sprouting new ideas and blossoming. Your seeds of emotions are growing; your insight and passions are coming to fruition. You are harvesting your emotion and insight.

# Air Archetype

**Air = Empowered Community**

You are highly connected at this time. You crave company, collective experiences, and are very much a messenger for others, so finding like-minded souls and conscious company will serve you and the world around you in this phase. You are creating community, creating belonging, and spreading your thoughts and emotions now. Carrying the seeds of change in the air around you.

# Sun Archetype

**Sun = Empowered Action**

You are powered with the yang of man and the feminine emotion of healing—with this comes great accomplishment and success. You are energized, motivated, and fueled to lead the change. Being able to work on a project, execute your passions, and share your emotions are important during this time of glow and growth.

———

Remember, you are forever changing, transforming, shifting, and so too will your element archetype. It is always interesting to retake the quiz as you learn and grow so you have the tools you need for any of those emotional or spiritual growing pains and big shifts in life. You'll also notice that some elements compliment or work with others, so explore those other elements too as they come up for you in your natural progression in this book. Learning about all the archetypes will give you a wider understanding of your whole evolutionary journey, providing all the elemental skill sets rather than just the ones you need now.

# PART II
# MOON GODDESS

# 6

# MOON MYTHOLOGY + POWERS

"THE MOON DOES NOT FIGHT. IT ATTACKS NO ONE. IT DOES NOT WORRY. IT DOES NOT TRY TO CRUSH OTHERS. . . . THE MOON IS FAITHFUL TO ITS NATURE AND ITS POWER IS NEVER DIMINISHED."
—DENG MING-DAO

Like many women, you come from a long line of moon gazers. In moon comes emotion and intuition. Moon is a feminine energy element, while sun is masculine. The balance of sun to moon, and the phases from full to new moon, bring with them profound energy related to development, expansion, spirituality, intuition, and deep insight and learning. Moon power can be emotional, sensitive, dark, and rejuvenating as it gives you the energy to translate and transform lessons into jewels of wisdom. What is most powerful about the moon is that its essence and energy lie as equally in its light as they do in its darkness, helping the Goddess become whole, in understanding and being, in all the phases of her evolutionary cycle.

Moon energy can be harnessed at any time of night, and is best channeled in dreams, meditation, ceremony, and ritual. By aligning with the moon's phases, you can allow moon energy to reinvent, recharge, realign, or rebirth you with every cycle of expansion. The Goddess sister of moon energy is water, hugely impacted by the moon in the ebb and flow of its tides. These two elements are also powerfully transformative energies. Think of water as the soul mate for moon.

## MOON ENERGY IS ANCIENT, AND WITH IT COMES OUR ELDERS' INSIGHTS. THE SILVER LINING TO EVERY LESSON, A CLARITY OF CONSCIOUSNESS THAT CAN BE A GIFT IN THE DARKEST OF PASSAGES.

Moon energy is ancient, and with it comes our elders' insights. The silver lining to every lesson, a clarity of consciousness that can be a gift in the darkest of passages. Its energy shifts through you from idea, emotion, energy, to evolution. Like the phases of a triple Goddess in a life, the moon will shift through phases in a cycle, which when walked through with awakened awareness can create positive and profound progress. This energy comes from the west, like a sunset over the ocean. It signifies an end of a cycle, a digested lesson that will no longer repeat in your life.

The Moon Goddess energy can be seen as a celebration of change. A transformation ceremony. An awakened acknowledgment that a fresh cycle is on the horizon. You are in the stages of cleansing away the old in preparation for new wisdom to wash up on your shores. You are highly intuitive, almost magical, in harnessing moon power.

Like the innovators and inventors of the world, you see with great clarity and envision new creations that others wouldn't dream possible. You are forward thinking, and are more able to shine light into unexplored realms than most people. You birth new ideas and creation freely and effortlessly when you are in this power. Fertile with creativity.

You are effortlessly guided by your spirituality, and ideas and expression seem to flow through you. This power can almost seem to "switch off" as you move through your evolutionary growth cycles. Your power comes from trusting that this expression will never leave you, and your creative connection will always return. The fear that you have creative blocks and the frustrations that rise when you fight against the cycles is what will disempower you. Something to be conscious of.

## Moon Mythology

LEGENDARY STORIES OF WOMEN AND THE MOON GRACE NEARLY EVERY SCRIPT IN RELIGION AND MYTHOLOGY FROM ANCIENT GREECE, ASIA, TO THE BOTTOM OF THE PACIFIC.

The moon is our guiding light even in the darkest of nights. Our intuition, which knows and sees all. Can you imagine the things the moon has witnessed throughout time. Our moon is the ultimate Goddess symbol of time, change, and evolution. Legendary stories of women and the moon grace nearly every script in religion and mythology from Ancient Greece, Asia, to the bottom of the Pacific. The stories of women who didn't settle for the sky, and shot for the moon instead, Goddesses drawn to all things mystic and mystery. Pulled, like you and I.

Not surprisingly, all moon stories share a common thread of all things insight, intuition, and feminine weaved into tales of (sometimes bizarre) transformational growth. Like you, these Goddesses aren't always perfect, they faced challenges, they have strengths and weaknesses, but they all share empowered evolutionary takeaways that us modern Goddesses could learn from. Each Moon Goddess evolving in her own pace, phase, and period.

**AEGA (GREEK GODDESS)**

This Moon Goddess was the daughter of Gaia, Mother Earth, and of Helios, the Sun. There are many tales of this Goddess, known for her beauty and as a symbol of divine power symbolized in the breastplate of the priestesses of the Goddess Athena. It is believed she rests in the sky as the constellation Capella.

**AINE (CELTIC GODDESS)**

Believed to light up the darkness, Aine means "light." She is the Goddess of love, growth, cattle (Goddess totem), and light in life, and is celebrated for bringing summer, wealth, and sovereignty. Her most interesting tale was defeating the king of Munster who tried to rape Aine, only to have her bite his ear off! Hear, hear! In those times in Ireland a "blemished" person in nobility could be stripped of their crown, which she made sure he was.

**ANAHITA (PERSIAN GODDESS)**

Anahita meaning "pure," she was the Goddess of Venus, rivers, and the moon. Her energy flowed like a river, filled by intuition and love, she brought cleansing and fertile flow to those around her.

**ANUNIT (BABYLONIAN GODDESS), ALSO SEE ISHTAR**

Later evolving into Goddess Ishtar, Anunit was the Goddess of the moon and battle. She represents powerful endings and rebirth. Today she is recognized in the evening star. Ishtar is one of my personal favorite Goddess energies, because she isn't afraid to defend what she believes in; she also signals rebirth, I think of her as an Evolution Goddess.

### ARTEMIS (GREEK GODDESS), ALSO SEE SELENE AND PHOEBE

The famed Moon Goddess who is renowned as a huntress; Goddess of all things nature and birth. The crescent moon is her symbol, reflected in Selene's crescent crown.

### BENDIS (THRACIAN GODDESS)

An ancient moon huntress, much like Artemis, she was celebrated with nighttime torch races on horseback, festivals, and cult-like ceremonies. She had an entourage of satyrs, goat-like men, who would dance around her.

### CHANDI (INDIAN GODDESS)

The female opposite of the male Hindu Lord Chandra, lord of the moon. These two lovers were believed to job share and take turns one month on, one month off becoming the moon. Now that is true balance and partnership!

### CERRIDWEN (CELTIC GODDESS)

A Crone Goddess, she was famed for her wisdom, magic, and cauldron. The waning moon was linked to her energy and reflects her power of transformative rebirth and creative inspiration. She is believed to be the patron Goddess of witches and wizards.

### CH'ANG-O (CHINESE GODDESS)

Hands down, this is the best name for a Goddess. Ch'ang-O lived on the moon and is still celebrated on the full moon of August, the eighth month, symbolizing abundance, birth, and fertility.

### COYOLXAUHQUI (AZTEC GODDESS)

This Goddess of all things moon and Milky Way was famously killed by her brother, who was the god of war. There are many versions of the sibling rivalry, and scholars still can't agree on who really was the victor—the sun, the son, or the moon and star sisters.

### DIANA (ROMAN GODDESS)

While Diana was the Goddess of all things moon, she could also be considered an Earth Goddess, believed to speak with animals and nature. She also had a virgin reputation in Roman religion, vowing to never marry. Girl was a total woodland Disney-princess type, pure, and singing along with bluebirds was her jam. Diana later took over the Moon Goddess role from the Roman Goddess Luna.

### EOS (GREEK/ROMAN GODDESS), ALSO KNOWN AS AURORA

One of my favorites, this is the winged Goddess of the dawn. Also a Titaness, this soul sister rose with the skies each morning as the moon set. Her sister and brother were god and Goddess of the sun and moon.

### EPONA (ROMAN/CELTIC GODDESS)

Her signature was the beating sound of her horses as she rode west to escape the rays of the rising sun. As a Goddess, she guards the night and delivers your dreams. She is a Goddess of great magic, fertility, and feminine divinity.

### HECATE (GREEK GODDESS)

A true triple Goddess, she is often depicted with torches and in triple form. She is the Goddess of magic, ghosts, and crossroads to other realms. She has a long-standing connection to witchcraft. She is rumored to be a priestess, or a Goddess of the stars, while her triple form has largely been linked to the new, full, and half moons.

### HINA (AUSTRONESIAN GODDESS)

Meaning matriarch, Hina is found from Southeast Asia and across Polynesia in the forms Ina, Sina, Tina, and Hina. In Polynesia, Hina is mother. In Hawaiian mythology Hina is a sexy, smart, and savvy woman desired by men and all of god's creatures. As many of us can relate to, Hina gets over living in the crowd, and retreats to the moon.

## GODDESS GEM

The triple Goddess is a well-known Goddess symbol represented by the triple moon symbolizing the Maiden, Mother, and Crone as the waxing, full, and waning moon. The waxing moon represents creation, birth, and inspiration, and the energy of the Maiden in every Goddess—young and of vibrant energy. Then the full moon, which represents fruition and harvest, is the energy of the Mother Goddess. It represents the phases of our feminine energy, magic, and psychic abilities. Finishing with the waning moon representing completion and endings, the energy of the wiser Crone in all of us.

### ISHTAR (BABYLONIAN GODDESS), ALSO SEE ANUNIT

Rumored to be either the daughter of the moon, or mother of the moon, Ishtar also has links to Anunit, believed to be the evening star and Goddess of battle, fertility, and rebirth.

### ISIS (EGYPTIAN GODDESS)

A Goddess who has her balance in check! Girl was not only a deity of the moon, but equally of the sun and was widely worshipped as an ideal mother and wife. She was also the patron for all things nature, magic, and creation. Isis is still widely worshipped today in the Goddess movement.

### IX CHEL (MAYAN GODDESS)

This Central American moon deity was the Goddess of birth. Her snakes symbolized life, rebirth, and health. She had a crush on the sun god who never really vibed back. She would follow him across the sky, ever chasing, and as a result the weather on earth got unbearable. She was so in love, she failed to see the destruction she was causing. Eventually, she captured his attention not with her beauty, but with her craft of weaving cloth, sparking a love affair with the sun god.

### IZANAMI (JAPANESE GODDESS)

I don't know about you, but I could instantly see a resemblance to "tsunami." This moon deity could control water in masses, pushing and pulling the tides, moving fish, and creating ocean destruction.

### JUNO (ROMAN GODDESS)

This moon deity guarded the new moon. Her worship was largely led by hopeful women looking to marry and conceive a child. She is the Goddess of fertility.

## GODDESS GEM

There is a long line of menstrual mythology across different Goddess eras. The Hindus believe that Great Mother created life and the cosmos from her feminine substances of curd or clot. Believing woman have this on a smaller scale (although cramp-wise, some woman would argue there was a cosmos wanting to explode out) in their monthly cycles. South Americans believe all life is served from moon blood. Even some of the most famous gods from the Norse Odin and Thor, to Asian Kali-Maya, to Celtic kings, all reached eternal life and supremacy after bathing in or drinking the menstrual blood of a giantess or Goddess. It is believed that a woman's blood, much like the moon, is the energy that gives life to all things. And as mythology would point out, sometimes the red sovereignty of a Goddess equals eternal life! Bottoms up, ladies.

## KUAN YIN (CHINESE BUDDHIST GODDESS)

Still worshipped by feminist pagans today, this Goddess is of the moon—compassion, forgiveness, love, and healing. Of all the Goddesses, she is one of the most renowned and celebrated. Her Goddess energy is echoed in stories like *Cinderella* and *Snow White*.

## LUNA (ROMAN GODDESS)

Latin for moon, her Goddess name also forms the base of the word "lunatic." Proving to empower the cycles of life and all the emotions within each cycle. Her energy encompasses magic, creativity, femininity, water, and safe passage. Her temple was draped in white and silver, and she was worshipped on the thirty-first of March with Goddesses bringing her offerings of white birds, milk, honey, fruit, wine, and perfume. Which is pretty much what every Goddess should have on her birthday wish list.

## MAWU (AFRICAN GODDESS)

She is the creator of earth and life. Partnering with her brother, who rules the sun, Mawu ruled the night skies and the moon. In her moon energy comes wisdom and knowledge. She is believed to give the breath of life, which is wisdom.

## NOTT (NORDIC GODDESS)

Known as the Goddess of the night, she rode a beautiful horse that had a frosty mane, said to deliver brisk air and frosty dew to the earth each morning. Those are the mornings you know she has ridden over you during the night. Frosty calling card!

## PHOEBE (GREEK GODDESS), ALSO SEE ARTEMIS AND SELENE

Her name means "shining and radiant," and she is also referenced as Selene and Artemis. Although there is a lot of confusion around Phoebe, as her grandmother was Artemis, who was also often called Phoebe. She was believed to be psychic, predicting future outcomes, observant of moon energies, and is referenced heavily for her prophetic powers.

## RHIANNON (CELTIC GODDESS)

Fleetwood Mac's "Rhiannon" comes to mind instantly. This Goddess of fertility can also bring with her death. She is the power of all things moon and night—a night queen. Her themes are that of movement: symbolized by her white horses, she is a leader, messenger, and fertility Goddess.

**SELENE (GREEK GODDESS), ALSO SEE ARTEMIS AND PHOEBE**
With a moon crown that could be mistaken for cow horns or even devil horns, Selene rode a moon chariot across the skies—a huntress of the heavens. She also goes by the name of Artemis. Her name means "light." And she went down in history mostly for her affair with a mortal, renowned as a chick with mad passion. Respect!

## The Keys to Activating Moon Archetype's Power

**Intuition, checking in on your feelings**

**Time, space**

**Being conscious of your phases**

**Ceremony and ritual**

**Growth in cycles**

**Mindful intentions**

**Digestion and reflection**

**Contemplation and revelation**

**Expansion**

**Deep spiritual awareness**

**Emotion**

**Healing and development**

**In synchronicity**

**Luminosity**

**Balance**

**Clarity**

**Fertility**

## The Power of Our Cycle

We are all given the birds and bees (feel free to also check out Goddess animal totems in the earth modalities chapter) yarn from either a very uncomfortable sweaty-lipped parent or a banana-holding sex-ed nurse. But how many of us are taught about our menstruation cycles, and what days we can get pregnant, what the deal is with all the goo (sorry, but you need to know this stuff), and see, this is my point—we are brought up to believe it is taboo, and to stay locked quietly behind cubicle doors in the loo. Well poo-poo to that, we are upping the woo-woo and talking about the goo, okay?

Now, don't get me wrong, I am a spiritualist, but that doesn't mean I am going to be chanting around a totem with my moon cup come that time of the month. (I have tried it and have mad respect for woman who make that work for them.) Personally, I am more of an organic tampon kinda gal. So, this chant isn't going to be off the scale in terms of let's go à la natural ladies. Let's keep it spiritually insightful, evolutionarily interesting, and focus on our fertility and femininity instead of all things blood and gore.

For our ancestors, "Aunt Flo's" visits were a time of creative, spiritual, sexual, emotional, mental, and physical transformation. The monthly cycle was seen as a gift that empowered women to renew themselves each month because it was a symbol of their fertility. In many ancient myths and religions, when we look back across thousands of years, the power of rebirth and blessing has been linked to the womb—and story lines of drinking blood from a chalice for instance pay homage to this.

Today, menstruation is mostly seen as a hassle, something that gets in the way of our everyday life, which is ironic as it is such a powerful cycle, a symbol of fertility, that creates life. So, when and how did it all change?

You may not be aware of this, but your ancestors used to retreat during their menstrual cycle. It's true! They were cast out of society, deemed as "dirty" and

## EVOLUTION EXERCISE: YOUR PERSONAL RED TENT

Rest assured this moon cycle ritual isn't going to end with me asking you to drink your own blood for immortality. So chill. Instead, this exercise is about reclaiming the feminine power coiled within you and honoring the sacred time of your menstruation. So, retreat like your ancestors did under the moon creating your very own Red Tent vibe. Rest into your intuition. This can be done through meditation, a tea ceremony, or a soothing aromatherapy and Epsom salt bath. Light candles, play soothing music, and pamper yourself.

Goddess tools for menstruation include crystals like malachite, moonstone, rose quartz, and lapis lazuli. Place them in your pockets, or around you. Teas with cinnamon, ginger, peppermint, chamomile, or basil all support cramps and ease bloating. And if you feel so inclined, gentle exercise as a ritual can help increase blood flow to the reproductive organs and relieve stress, like gentle yoga or a walk in nature.

## EVOLUTION EXERCISE: SCRIBING YOUR OWN MOON MYTH

It's time to scribe your own piece of "herstory," tell the tale of your transformation. Journal down a story of heartbreak, of hardship, or overcoming obstacles, and try to pinpoint the moments you hit triple Goddess mode. The waxing moon moment you started a new journey or had a new beginning, the full moon moment when it all came to fruition, and the waning moment when you got dealt an evolutionary lesson. Acknowledge the phases in the journey, and your wise takeaway from your own personal Moon Goddess experience. Take this as an evolutionary aha memento, so you can recognize more of those moments as you move forward in life.

unable to prepare food. It is also true that women who spend time together will bleed at the same time (something I am sure you have experienced), so they would sync and retreat for three days to a red tent, moon lodge, or blood temple to rest, shunned from society where they could spend time only in female company talking, nurturing, and supporting each other, and resting away from chores and family responsibilities. (So, shunned or not, it had its perks!) During this time, many of the women would have visions through dreams and meditations, most reportedly happening on their third day of bleeding. They would share these visions with the whole community of women. These visions from the red tent were considered sacred and divinely sent, and used to guide the community.

Today, Western society has evolved in its thinking when it comes to periods being taboo, dirty, evil, bad, or shameful. In fact, today the effects of menstruation are almost ignored. Society and advertisements now tell us that we can play tennis, go for a swim, or be the life of a party "confidently" with glossy packaged sanitary products. While the red tent was a place of outcast, it was also a place for quiet and inward reflection—the concept of a sacred space—to connect, relax, recharge, and tap into our intuition and dreams. While it might not be a good idea to ring in sick every time you have your monthly visit, it is worth creating a sacred space for yourself during this time. Go easy on yourself. Surround yourself with people who make you feel better for being in their company. Honor your need to retreat.

# MOON EVOLUTION ESSENTIALS

## "CHANGE IS INEVITABLE, BUT TRANSFORMATION IS BY CONSCIOUS CHOICE."
### —HEATHERASH AMARA

Hera, also known as Juno—the Goddess of women, marriage, union, and birth—oversees heaven and earth in mythology. The seer of all. I like to think of her as the moon, observer of all things earth to stars. This Goddess is the sort that has her eyebrows and lashes on fleek, even on her third eye. Like the all-seeing eye of a female's intuition.

Even her man Zeus was cautious of her hawk eye, with his wife renowned for intuitively and purposefully seeking out the truth of her husband's philandering and having a hot temper for those who crossed her—gods and mortals alike. She would often feud with Zeus over his roaming sexual endeavors and affairs that resulted in illegitimate children, including Heracles, one of the biggest heroes of Greek mythology. She would be consumed by anger and jealousy, and would often punish the women involved with her husband, even their children.

Hera famously sent two snakes (a Goddess totem, the serpent symbolizes fertility, femininity, and renewal) to kill Heracles as a baby, a symbol of her husband's deceit and infidelity. When the child strangled both snakes to death, the attack instead was the start of his rise to fame—a powerful tale of Hera's fertility, and a story of the symbol of renewal being strangled by the demons of her marriage. A telling tale of how our emotions can be the core of our empowerment, or root of our destruction.

Okay, I agree it is a big call to send snakes to take out a baby, but it is symbolic of all our inner hurts surfacing in times of despair and heartbreak. Admittedly her sense of justice went out the door when her heart was involved. She was a patron of protection for married women, something she clearly took seriously. While she was beautiful, these green-eyed monster moments often make her seem ugly or cow-headed in stories. Ugly in her stubbornness and hurt.

Still, Hera knew how to take care of number one, with an annual self-love ritual that included bathing, relaxation, and a magically restored virginity. Yes, a hymen rejuvenation. Rebirthing herself to chaste regardless of the countless men she had bed. (With her husband's wandering eye, could you blame her?) This ritual or re-newal and rebirth was an act of Hera harnessing her feminine power, and claiming control of her womanhood. While Hera isn't a Moon Goddess in mythology per se, her phases in life, lunatic behavior, and constant rebirth make her the perfect personification of a Goddess with moon pulls, like we all have. Let's be honest, we can all relate to a hormonal Hera, am I right, ladies?

Hera isn't just remembered for her monumental meltdowns, mortals still bathe statues of the Goddess to restore her virtues before big events or celebrations as a sign of respect. See, self-love equals self-respect and self-empowerment. So hymen high five for this supreme Goddess who was by no means perfect (no one is, right?), and who was at times a misguided heroine in emotional hurt and honesty. Her Goddess totems of tiaras, the seasons, the Milky Way, pearls, silver, cows, peacocks, and even lapis lazuli crystals all in regal blues and silvers that promote communication, hon-esty, truth—all vital components in both a marriage and a Goddess.

Essential Goddess elements in all of us get drawn to the surface with the ever-changing moon overseeing us in all things love, life, and war. Hera reminds us: our emotion, behavior, experiences, phases, and journey as women are all part of our evolution and empowerment whether they hurt, help, heal, or simply result in hurtling snakes at others.

## Moon Archetype Personality

WITH MOON AS YOUR ARCHETYPE YOU ARE INDEED ONE HELL OF A VISIONARY. A DIVINE MESSENGER. A CONSCIOUS CREATIVE.

A wonderfully powerful archetype that sees you more spiritually in tune than most. Yeah, girl! You live by your spirit. You most definitely have highly intuitive ten-dencies and are often accused of daydreaming too much about ideals. There is a reason why the moon watches over us all while we dream: she is a powerful vision-ary aid, and with moon as your archetype you are indeed one hell of a visionary. A divine messenger. A conscious creative. You are regularly gifted sacred, guided insights into next steps on your evolutionary journey. When you are clear in your direction, the path unfolds in front of you in the most magical way. Evolution can be effortless, and equally impossible.

Ruled by the power of duality, the Moon Archetype is one of the most evolved of the archetypes should you learn to master the spiritual sweet spot of balance, learning to live with darkness and light, and harness the power of each when nec-essary. This archetype is constantly gifted powerfully confronting challenges and rewarding creative bursts, which makes it a master of the evolutionary journey should it not be consumed by its brightness or dullness. Powerfully playing in the push and pull of lessons and mastery.

## ASSOCIATED ELEMENTS

Moon element is largely connected to her sister elements: water and sun. These two elemental chapters are worth exploring for the Moon Archetype because in God-dess mythology the Moon Goddess often evolves from a place of sun, or vice versa. Most commonly, the moon becomes the sun's refuge and sanctuary.

Moon Archetypes are incredibly cyclic beings that experience many phases in their evolutionary journey. This is why water and sun are essential in helping the moon element move through her phases, shining light when the Moon Archetype might be experiencing the dark side of her moon (sun), and also influencing her highs and lows of the tide of emotions (water) that come with the Moon Archetype.

## MOON PERSONA

Duality is strong in this archetype, especially when it comes to inspired public expression versus quiet introvertedness and creation. You move in phases, you can be in full moon, living in between both realms of light and dark, or opt for a new approach altogether and completely reinvent yourself and hide away in dark and transformative reflection. You flip between enjoying the spotlight and at other times preferring to guide and transform from behind the conscious scenes, focusing on your inspired creativity.

At times the idea of retreat sings to you. Sacred solitude. You are a holistic her-mit of sorts. You rejoice in channeling your artistic side, and to some you are seen as quite eccentric and woo-woo. (These are personally my favorite types of people.) At other times you like to stand up and shout your expressions. You only choose to fully be of influence and power when you are at your best, on full beam, and feel it is the right time. You are constantly in motion with new ideas, creative action, and reflection.

Ever improving and fine-tuning your evolutionary creative cycle, your energy has a huge affect on others, and you are conscious of this, hence you often opt for your own company over crowded spaces. And although this lonely safe spot is what you crave, you are never truly alone as you have such a wide reach, sis-stars surround you regularly, wanting to be in your energy and company. These polar opposite sides of you are at constant push and pull on your evolutionary journey.

## MOON CHAKRA

### Throat and Third Eye Chakras

The throat chakra is located at the center of the neck, the throat. (Go figure.) It is related to our sense of expression, sound, our lungs, voice, and true purpose. The third eye chakra, located between your eyebrows, is your wisdom energy center, connected to insight, intuition, and vision. These energy centers are vital to creative visionaries. Artistic creators, Moon Archetypes are often easily inspired by their connection to their higher self.

## MOON SPIRIT ANIMAL

The white elephant is a symbol of pure, true, and authentic expression. It represents harmony and mastery, a wisdom communicated on a profound scale. Its walk is quiet, strong, and focused, when it trumpets its trunk it communicates with meaning and purpose.

## MOON EMOTIONS

Moon Archetypes can be moody and dim one minute, and bright, bold, and beautiful the next. Their changing emotions are part of their incredible spiritual connection and artistic side, which allows them to embrace the vulnerability that comes with creative expression. These fears can easily consume a Moon Archetype, causing her to retreat. It is important that a Moon Archetype respects these phases of her emotions and knows that the dark side of the moon will always shift into brightness again. You will feel most challenged when you lose your sense of direction, you will feel helpless, disconnected, stuck. It is in living alongside these emotional shifts that the Moon Archetype will learn great insights and growth. It can be challenging, but with each evolutionary experience the cycle will become easier.

## MOON MANTRA

I accept the beautiful cycles that make up my evolutionary lessons. I use these phases to go inward, and express outward my inner dreams, visions, and conscious wishes for change with clarity. I stay true to my purpose and express my truth.

## MOON ZODIAC

The Moon Archetype has parallels to the traits seen in the star signs of Cancer and Pisces. Both of these star signs understand emotion, are sensitive, intuitive, and often seek an escape from the world; they have a tendency to be shy and introverted, which are unique to the Moon Archetype. Pisces, represented by two fish swimming in opposite directions, is a great summary for moon energy. These polarizing dualities are the core of the Moon Archetype—the black and white phases of growth in your self-development journey. The moon temperament can be wildly different depending on what day it is and the phase of the evolution cycle you are in. I like to call them the masked mystics. However, don't be fooled; they are incredibly perceptive, often able to see both sides of a story very instinctively.

## MOON SEASON

Winter, reflection, hibernation, and renewal.

## MOON CRYSTALS

Moonstone, also known as the Goddess stone, is a powerful aid to those looking to harness their intuition and tap into their true higher voice. It is essential when you feel disconnected from your intuition or blocked. Amethyst supports your spirituality and third eye, helping to heighten and stimulate spiritual insights, dreams, and can help keep you in balance. Essential for a Moon Archetype with such strong dualities.

## MOON AROMATHERAPY

Goddesses have a sacred practice using herbs and oils in moon rituals for centuries. They purify, carry prayer, and heal. Essential oils that help to open your imagination, grant you clarity of mind, and stimulate expression are peppermint, frankincense, cedarwood, sandalwood, rosemary, patchouli, and basil. These are most effective worn on your neckline and temple points to help keep your throat and third eye chakra in their natural elements and help you connect with your higher Goddess self.

## MOON FOODS

The general rule of thumb for feeding your Moon Archetype is purple. Think purple and red grapes, blueberries, and chocolate! Yes, chocolate increases your intuition and helps to focus and clear the mind. Should you be feeling out of sorts some dark chocolate and meditation may help you feel more settled and connected. Moon Archetypes also need all the juices to keep their creativity flowing: grape juice, fruit juices, teas, even coffee will help with your expression. Hydration is key for clear intuitive downloads and expressions of the higher self.

## MOON FLOWERS

Angelica is an edible flower that supports both intuitive and imaginative expression. It can be candied and placed on top of chocolate cake, yum! Or added to a raw cacao hot chocolate when your creative and spiritual communication channels need some sweet stimulation. This flower is also believed to help support communication with your guides and angels.

## MOON PHASE

Every phase of the moon is definitely important to the Moon Archetype, as every phase offers a unique lesson. However, the phase where this archetype will be at its most powerful and at its highest Goddess potential is actually when it is sitting 50 percent illuminated and 50 percent in darkness, in the first or third quarter of the moon phases. This is when you will be most in balance and able to harness conscious and inspired expressive action.

## MOON MASCULINE BALANCE

The key to balancing the Moon Archetype when you are too masculine is elimination. Evolving with moon in balance and harmony will require you to shed your skin from time to time as you grow. Letting go. The need to control is a good indication you need to balance out your masculine mindset to receive the new, which is your feminine mindset. To do this, surrender things that no longer serve you, such as relationships, thoughts, bad habits, expectations, and destructive patterns. This will mean you step out of your lunatic moon side (we've all been there), aka control freak, and shift into a space of peace, surrender, and acceptance.

If you are out of alignment with too much feminine then you are giving too much of your love and time away to others and feel tired, emotional, and energetically empty. This is an alarm bell to get your Goddess affairs in order and focus the next moon cycle on yourself, first and foremost. If you have too much masculine happening you will feel like you need to win, like you are battling, at war with others or yourself. Eclipse what isn't serving you to grow and expand. Especially if you are feeling over the moon in an over it kind of way!

**MOON RETROGRADE**

When moon is out of sync, or evolutionarily taking you backward, you can find yourself eclipsing, foggy, intensely passionate, and often feeling twisted as you struggle to shed the old and step into new beginnings. To others you may even seem stubborn, narrow-minded, or regimented. Like the Roman Goddess Diana, you are known to be pure and virginal; however, you have a vengeful streak when crossed. As with all Moon Goddesses, you have a changeable and unpredictable nature. The key is to not let past guilt or unforgiven lessons consume your soul. Past lovers, regrets, mistakes . . . they all show up when the moon element is regressing in retrograde. While it is important to digest and dissolve these thoughts and rising disappointments, it is essential to apologize and release. (Aka, don't text your ex!) Don't start a war. If Karen from accounts stole your favorite coffee mug, let it go. If you become like the Greek Goddess Hecate, the Goddess of darkness, it is a pretty good sign you are in retrograde and need to get back into alignment.

Instead, forgive yourself. Take the lessons and drop the baggage preventing you from stepping forward. This can be a strong negative pull for many Goddesses, creating setbacks when the pull of the moon is repressed. Remember, your power is in your phases, acknowledge a phase of your life, take the lessons, let go, and look forward to the new moon. Even if it means sitting in a void until you have digested what is stirring in you.

Ask yourself this: "What is anchoring me, preventing me from rocketing to the moon?" It might be time to drop anything energetically dragging you down or casting a shadow on your light. Don't be afraid to confront your darkness—it won't infect you, it won't destroy you. More so, if you don't, it might just consume you. Or worse, make you stuck and unchanged.

The most beautiful thing comes from these moments. You will change your opinion on something. And that, that is an evolutionary breakthrough when you forgive, empathize, understand, and move forward with new insight. That is when you know you kicked your retrograde moment to the conscious curb.

## Moon Life Phases

Understanding that your archetype, like you, can change and evolve, let's take a look at what a moon-dominant archetype might experience in different phases of life. A Moon Goddess will experience heightened intuition, a call to nurture and heal, and be gifted opportunities to surrender, release, and constantly reinvent herself. Throughout her Maiden, Mother, and Crone phases moon energy can play a pivotal role in a Goddesses' evolutionary experience.

### MOON MAIDEN

Like the Goddess Rhiannon, you are passionate, inspired, free! With your white horse in tow you enter a phase of great changes, a journey of self-development, and enter the arena to face huge life shifts and transitions.

Fittingly symbolized by the waxing moon, a Moon Maiden is youthful, self-aware, and focused on developing her strengths. Ever curious and optimistic, a Moon Maiden always seeks out the spiritual lessons in life, she feels deeply, down to the root of her core, and with every experience, turmoil, lesson, blessing, and challenge gains strength in her ability to read instinctively and intuitively. She begins hopeful, learns to heal, and grows toward becoming whole. Moving forward, she understands life's light and dark phases and the evolutionary lessons in both.

### MOON MOTHER

You've got more of an Aphrodite Goddess energy going on when Mother phase enters your life journey. The theme: love, self-love, and sexuality. What it means to be a woman, a mother, a lover.

## GODDESS (R)EVOLUTIONARY: TARYN BRUMFITT

We have learned from the evolution of life, both as a species and in our personal journey, that out of chaos comes liberation. It is just surviving the chaos that can be the challenge! Amen.

Today, in the hustle and bustle of an on-demand, live-streaming, 24/7 society, we often look for ways to turn off. To numb ourselves. To quiet our intuition. To fill our void.

This is a tale of a modern-day transformation. Of a Goddess facing her demons and releasing beliefs and habits that no longer served her. The void Taryn Brumfitt faced, which many of us can relate to, was negative body imaging and stereotyping. Fearlessly confronting her dark side of the moon, she founded the Body Image Movement along with creating the documentary film *Embrace*: "We're on a quest to end the global body-hating epidemic."[1]

At one point, Taryn considered plastic surgery to "fix" herself after being crippled by body image issues. The shift was her choosing to not change her beautiful Goddess curves, but instead to change her attitude toward her body. As she admitted in a *HuffPost* blog: "It's taken a lot of effort, time and energy but I can tell you there is nothing better then a) loving your body wholeheartedly, lumps and bumps and all and b) telling society where they can shove their ideals of beauty."[2] Result, a new phase in life empowered in loving the body she lives in as well as a spark of a global call for woman to step out of their body fears. To empower and liberate women to love their bodies in all of its phases, shapes, and sizes. Learn more about her courageous Goddess journey and movement at www.bodyimagemovement.com.

Entering Moon Mother, the Goddess will find herself showing up for service with a sense of purpose and action in her step. She will offer her time, love, energy, and support, and can often become so much of a giver she forgets to receive. It is not uncommon for a Moon Mother to grieve her sanctuary and solace in this time of mothering those around her. Yet she has evolved to understand her responsibilities, loves to feel needed, called upon, and is at the peak of her power in her ability to manifest moon energies for herself and those around her. This is often why those she cares for see her as strong and magical. Easily releasing old habits, beginning new chapters, and seeing evolutionary lessons come to fruition with every moon that passes. This is a time of great expansion and development, something Moon Archetypes thrive in.

### MOON CRONE

Entering your final lessons in life you will embrace your inner Goddess Morrigan. You have gained great wisdom, become intuitive, almost psychic in your ability to feel out life and those around you. You illuminate the truth and the lessons in front of you. Teaching and guiding those who surround you from your stories of transformation, tales of growth. When the moon is waning you are at your height of prophecy, a calming influence to those around you, teaching modern magic and the art of being agile, almost shape-shifting through any evolutionary experience.

Gone are the days when you could be shaken off balance, or off center. You are one with the earth, the world, and the experiences that greet you, nothing deters you as you enter completion; understanding and accepting all that you have been through; forgiving, releasing, and rebirthing from many moons of evolutionary experiences.

# MOON MODALITIES

> "THE HEART IS CAPABLE OF SACRIFICE. SO IS THE VAGINA. THE HEART IS ABLE TO FORGIVE AND REPAIR. IT CAN CHANGE ITS SHAPE TO LET US IN. IT CAN EXPAND TO LET US OUT. SO CAN THE VAGINA. IT CAN ACHE FOR US AND STRETCH FOR US, DIE FOR US AND BLEED AND BLEED US INTO THIS DIFFICULT, WONDROUS WORLD. SO CAN THE VAGINA. I WAS THERE IN THE ROOM. I REMEMBER."
> —EVE ENSLER

## Moon Cycles

Keep track of your menstrual cycle—there are loads of great apps for this. I personally use Clue. Mark your cycle dates, and mark the dates of the new and full moon. Or just keep a diary, note down the date, the moon phase, any health comments, like extra cramping or bloating, your mood, and your dreams!

Miranda Gray, author of *Red Moon*, joins me in believing that many of our ancestral teachings still exist in mythology and nursery rhymes. Although I don't recall a "Mary had a little period" lullaby before bed![1]

Gray argues there are two traditional menstruation patterns: "White Moon" bleeding, or menstruating with the new moon and ovulating with the full moon, and "Red Moon" menstruation, which is bleeding with the full moon and becoming fertile with the new moon.[2] Your period will attune to both cycles over the course of your life, but it's fascinating to note what's going on in your life energetically as your body cycles.

I personally track my cycle using femme tech. There are some great apps out there that help you keep track of your cycle and what moon phase you are synching with. I use My Moon Time. So, what is your body trying to tell you?

### WHITE MOON

If your body follows a White Moon cycle, you'll tend to bleed during the new or waning moon. Since biodynamics have shown that the earth is most fertile during full moons (when you ovulate), this cycle is most traditionally linked to fertility and motherhood. If you are a "White Moon" woman, you'll likely feel a surge in your intuition during your period, and will feel the urge to withdraw for nourishment and self-renewal. In other words, you're tapped out energetically and have given the month your all—it's "you" time.

### RED MOON

This cycle follows the full moon, meaning that your body bleeds during the waxing or full moon and is most fertile during the new or waning moon. Because full and waxing moon phase energies are outgoing, vibrant, and creative, some feel this is counterintuitive to menstruation. Not so. In ancient times, the Red Moon cycle was associated with shamanism, high priestesses, and healers. Women who tend to menstruate with the full moon are said to focus their darker and more creative menstrual energies outward, rather than inward, to nourish and teach others or themselves from their own experience. Many times, women with this cycle will be more focused on self-growth, development, mentorship, and creativity.

## Moon Cycle Dream Journal

Keep a dream journal close to your bed while you have your menstrual cycle and take note of any visionary dreams you may have. It is also worth exploring the meanings behind your dreams, so invest in a dream dictionary or Google the meaning of your dream when you wake up. The idea is to take key elements and jot them down as soon as you open your eyes—colors you see, how you felt, key people, places, actions, and objects.

## Moon Sign

We are all probably familiar with our star sign, or sun sign. But exploring our moon signs can bring big insights into our potential. Think of your moon sign as what hides underneath your passions and emotions, while your star sign reflects your principles and personality. Some astrologers define our moon sign as our unconscious. These traits can be your primal nature, your innate way of being. To discover your moon sign you need to have an idea of the time, date, and place you were born, as the moon sign changes every two to two and a half days. There are lots of fun online moon sign calculators worthy of a Google search.

# Moon Phases and Meanings

If you are ruled by the moon element, it makes sense for you to look to the moon for guidance. So, look up, what phase is the moon in? Below are the phases of the moon and their associated evolutionary energy.

Take note of what moon you were born in. You can use a site called Astrocal to find out where the moon was on your birthday. Then plot big moon shifts into your calendar; also note the zodiac energy that the moon will bring into your life, to align yourself and understand why you may be feeling in retrograde (aka, backward), full moon lunatic mode, like retreating from the world, creative, or reflective! Sync your energy with the phases and evolve your understanding of what energy the moon can bring to your day.

## NEW MOON: CRONE PHASE, WISDOM

Intention time—this is a time for new moon, new you. And to think less about me, me, me manifestations. Think, how can your intention, habit, goal transform the world around you, evolve you as a person, and help you contribute to the world. I always like to ask myself this—if my greatest wish was granted would it just benefit my life, or would it benefit the world? Honestly. Ask yourself this question.

The new moon is a fresh start. With it comes the energy of new beginnings, the start of a new lunar cycle. If you were born in a new moon you will be charged with this fresh blast of energy that will no doubt leave you with a creative streak through your Goddess soul. Why? Because the new moon brings new passions, seeds of the new, and cultivation. This also means it is a great time to shed those things that no longer serve you, to ditch bad habits, or reflect on your behavior. This makes it a powerful time to reflect, evolve, and commit to a new phase, and a new approach to living well, and living fully. New wisdom is taken on board with new insights. Awareness. Make this a ritual, a time to routinely check in on your conscious actions.

## WAXING CRESCENT MOON

The energy of the waxing moon brings with it momentum and manifestation. Those seeds that your thoughts created and planted in your consciousness are beginning to sprout. It is a time to echo these wishes for the world. The key to this energy is to remain focused on your intentions. Of channeling your energy into your mission, your passions, your heart. If you are born in the energy of the waxing moon you will often be accused of being a dreamer. In fact, you are a visionary. You can see a better tomorrow, and harness your energy to create just that. Fruition is on the horizon and you are the sort of gal who rolls up her sleeves to ensure everything is in order, to see those changes sprout.

### FIRST QUARTER MOON: MAIDEN PHASE, INSPIRATION

The first quarter signals a space of hopefulness. It is an ideal time to be optimistic and positive about your dreams and passions. It is a time where you can step into your place in the world. Embrace your playful and optimistic side.

### WAXING GIBBOUS

This moon is, get this, one of the most powerful phases in which to experience a spiritual evolution. Put this moon child on your calendar. For those born in this waxing gibbous moon energy, you will be driven to deeply and profoundly question the meaning of life. The key to your success is continual growth and development on all levels, seeking eternal learning from love, emotions, experiences—life! This is a powerful time for development, when the bud is preparing to bloom. You are in balance, half illuminated, half in darkness. Digesting lessons and growing. An equal time for analysis and for expression.

### FULL MOON: MOTHER PHASE, NURTURE

Full moon, full beam, full bloom—the full moon brings with it the energy of fertility, transformation, completion, and abundance. Think of this time as an emotional victory lap. This energy can seem overwhelming to many as it is a heightened time of magic, emotion, guidance, and healing. It is a time to recharge, regroup, realign, and come back together. Many people will dream at this time, feel psychic and deeply connected. This often brings with it sensitivities. Those born on a full moon are ruled by their emotions,

## GODDESS GEM

*Kundalini* is a Sanskrit term from ancient India that identifies with the feminine, creative, and evolutionary (yes!) energy of eternal wisdom that lives inside every human being—male and female. This energy is commonly represented as a snake coiled three and a half times around, sitting at the base of our spine, and is the focus of the teachings in Kundalini yoga practice, which rises this energy through the chakra/energy centers. This definition differs in many spiritual teachings, but the essence of its energy is quite similar in being a dormant energy that when awakened, risen, and harnessed can be powerfully creative and enlightening.

and are often passionate, deeply caring, honest people. Full moon Goddesses are intuitive people who trust in their gut. This is the ideal time for some to feel chaotic, others inspired. Find a ritual that speaks to your truth. A gathering, or solitude—feed your emotional state and trust in your inner guidance. Some full moons you may feel you need the medicine of the company of your sisters, others you will seek seclusion. Become conscious of what ceremony speaks to you. Follow whatever will leave you feeling full and fully charged.

## WANING GIBBOUS

The energy of the full moon begins receding from the expansive and emotional full moon, becoming smaller, and will call upon you to release and let go, to squeeze out anything you are energetically needing to surrender. It is a time to consider what serves your higher purpose, what feeds your soul, what leaves you feeling awakened and alive. It is a summons to clean out and cleanse yourself in the lead-up to a new cycle.

Those born in the energy of a waning gibbous—e.g. me—are considered the caregivers of the universe, usually the humanitarians, and those of service. They can be as equally calm and caring as they can be compulsive, strong-willed in character, intuitive, and idealistic. They have an eagerness and sometimes urgency to make the world a better place. This energy can be harnessed in the waning gibbous to help make yourself and your world a better place, by focusing on the positive and removing the negative in preparation for your next evolutionary growth phase, approaching in the next cycle.

## LAST QUARTER MOON: ENCHANTRESS, SOVEREIGNTY

This phase is when we weave our lessons, insights, emotions, and learnings into how we act and behave. Our core values become reflected in how we show up. It is, in a sense, a phase of coming into an awakened adult, with the child learning and experiencing or "growing up" from the full moon cycle.

## WANING CRESCENT

This is the dark side of the moon, literally. Waning is the energy of revelation from reflection. When we are in darkness, we reflect, we go within. In this energy, we can be gifted those aha moments that spark transformation. Not only is this healing, it is also profound in your development. Too often we attempt to quickly claw our way out of dark spots in life. This is a powerful phase that has just as important a weight as when we are in full bloom. It represents completion, graduating from the lessons. This is the time to withdraw from the world, rest, and reflect. Think of it as a womb, the safe and sacred space where new life is given, where you are rebirthed. A powerful time to contemplate, and complete your thought process, on those lessons learned from the cycle that is coming to completion. The energy of the moon decreases and so will you, so it is important that you go easy on yourself.

Those born in the waning energy are often connected to other worlds and can be accused of being dreamy or ungrounded. They are in fact very spirituality gifted.

## SOLAR ECLIPSE

This is when the sun's brightness is blocked from humanity, allowing darkness to watch over us—and with it can come darker energies. This is a powerfully recognized time in many cultures, religions, and global landmarks, as it is a time of protection, meditation, and spiritual ceremony. In this energy, it is best to seek to be well grounded and earthed. Those born now are, for this reason, very anchored and centered people, who have a grounded walk to life. They are very passionate, objective, and independent. They are often looking within for answers, rather than seeking them externally.

## LUNAR ECLIPSE

With the energy eclipse we see the shift to put us on the right path. This time can often see abrupt change and severe shifts. Often relationships can end suddenly, or we are forced to make decisions and move in a new direction. While it can feel like upheaval, it is a powerful time of change. The trick? To go with the flow and be conscious in shifts and changes. Those born on a lunar eclipse are super-charged on Goddess energy, intuitive, creative, compassionate, and empathetic. They have a strong sense of purpose, are devoted to service, and strive for balance in all things, from society to their own lifestyle.

# Native American Moons

Native Americans lived by the seasons and moon instinctively. Many tribes would record time with the seasons and moons. Full moon names and records varied from tribe to tribe. Today, almanac records note the moons by month with reference to the Native American moon insights. Add these to your conscious calendar to help your Moon Archetype stay aligned with the energy at hand.

Each is an observation of an animal, or shift in nature that happens with the moon as witness. Be it animals howling, the seasons changing, animals appearing, or harvesttime. For Goddesses, this is important as it shows you when to harvest your ideas, plant, retreat, and pursue in life. Use these different moon energies to align with your evolutionary journey to help guide you. Explore the different meaning of each moon and learn about the unique energy each moon can bring to your life.

**January:** Northern Hemisphere: Wolf Moon. Also known as Old Moon.

Southern Hemisphere: Hay Moon. Also known as Thunder Moon.

**February:** Northern Hemisphere: Snow Moon. Also known as Hunger Moon.

Southern Hemisphere: Red Moon. Also known as Corn Moon.

**March:** Northern Hemisphere: Magpie Moon. Also known as Worm Moon.

Southern Hemisphere: Harvest Moon. Also known as Corn Moon.

**April:** Northern Hemisphere: Egg Moon. Also known as Pink Moon.

Southern Hemisphere: Hunters' Moon. Also known as Harvest Moon.

**May:** Northern Hemisphere: Flower Moon. Also known as Corn Moon.

Southern Hemisphere: Beaver Moon. Also known as Frost Moon.

**June:** Northern Hemisphere: Strawberry Moon. Also known as Honey Moon.

Southern Hemisphere: Cold Moon. Also known as Long Night Moon.

**July:** Northern Hemisphere: Hay Moon. Also known as Thunder Moon.

Southern Hemisphere: Wolf Moon. Also known as Old Moon.

**August:** Northern Hemisphere: Red Moon. Also known as Corn Moon.

Southern Hemisphere: Snow Moon. Also known as Hunger Moon.

**September:** Northern Hemisphere: Harvest Moon. Also known as Corn Moon.

Southern Hemisphere: Magpie Moon. Also known as Worm Moon.

**October:** Northern Hemisphere: Hunters' Moon. Also known as Harvest Moon.

Southern Hemisphere: Egg Moon. Also known as Pink Moon.

**November:** Northern Hemisphere: Beaver Moon. Also known as Frost Moon.

Southern Hemisphere: Flower Moon. Also known as Corn Moon.

**December:** Northern Hemisphere: Cold Moon. Also known as Long Night Moon.

Southern Hemisphere: Strawberry Moon. Also known as Honey Moon.

## Moon Centers

In Kundalini, Yogi Bhajan teaches that every woman has eleven moon centers. These are sensitive physical areas that are connected to the lunar energies and affect how we handle life. Yogi Bhajan's teachings share that women are sixteen times more intuitive than men and are more emotional, because we are more affected by the moon. If women can understand both the moon and our emotions, we can then be sixteen times the intuitive leader of a man—fueled by knowledge and emotion. #Supermoonpowers

Your moon centers each hold different qualities and you will move through each center in about two and a half days. You can begin to connect with what moon center you are in by becoming more aware of the feelings and behavior you experience from the list of centers and their corresponding energy points and traits listed below. (Moon Centers Mediation follows.)

**Hairline**—clarity, stability, focus, and connected at this time.

**Cheeks**—emotional, sensitive, and a time when you can seem out of control or alienating to those around you. Seek balance, yoga, meditation, and breathe through the illusion of emotion at this time.

**Lips**—communication, expressive, and our verbal words can express if we are in balance or not at this time.

**Earlobes**—intelligence, ethics, righteous, and likely to participate in activism at this time. Be careful not to be judgmental.

**Back of the neck**—romance, optimistic, and flirtatious. Again, not a good time to be making big decisions.

**Breasts**—compassion, giving, and usually the time we find it hard to say no. Be conscious of your boundaries.

**Belly button/navel**—insecurity and vulnerability. This is a time to empower yourself and go inward with meditation and reflection. Avoid chocolate.

**Thighs**—affirming, productive, and structured so you will be organized. This is usually a time to tick things off to-do lists.

**Eyebrows**—imaginative, unpredictability, creative, and playful. Don't make big decisions now. This is a good time to imagine new possibilities, create business ideas, etc.

**Clitoris**—talkative, sociable, and charming. You are vibrant and it's a good time to focus on new relationships rather than homing in on existing ones.

Vagina—depth, sharing, very social at this time; however, you want intimate gatherings with like-minded people or to spend time in your own company.

**MOON CENTERS MEDITATION**

Aligning your moon centers (believed to help balance your menstrual cycle) in meditation is as simple as tummy time! It is believed if a woman does this meditation for forty days or more, she can break the cycle of any habit.

Lie on your tummy with your arms by your side, palms facing upward, with your chin point resting on the floor, head straight; focus your eyes on your brow point. Stay here for three to thirty-one minutes and chant silently, repeating *sa ta na ma* over and over like you would with a mantra . . .

**SA: infinity, cosmos, beginning**
**TA: life, existence**
**NA: death, totality**
**MA: rebirth, resurrection**[3]

> ## GODDESS MUSING . . .
>
> Still curious about all the beautiful phases of your Moon Archetype? Get to know your sister archetypes. You will find complimentary powers and lessons in the water and sun chapters. Be sure to dabble in between the pages and phases of these elements to see what revolutionary insights ring true and what you might shine light on. That's the beautiful thing about the moon, it is ever moving, and so too should you.

## Harness the Moon Goddess Energies

To channel your Moon Goddess energy create a bedtime ritual. Light white or silver candles. Look up at the stars, sky, and moon. Meditate and imagine white or silver; you can imagine yourself shifting through the phases of the moon, or riding a horse or chariot across the skies like so many of your Moon Goddess companions. Focus on moving forward, learning, and acknowledging life and death in every step. Make your sanctuary a place of retreat and celebration, make it fertile with fruits, flowers, perfumes, honey, and crystals like amethyst and moonstone. Or, if you are like me, just blast "Rhiannon" and dance barefoot in your lounge with some frankincense or sandalwood incense burning. Goddess HQ. The lessons of moon energy can be dark, but they can also be a fun celebration. Enjoy the phases, beauty.

# PART III
# WATER GODDESS

# WATER MYTHOLOGY + POWERS

*"YOU CANNOT LEARN TO SWIM BY SITTING ON THE SIDE OF THE POOL WATCHING OTHERS CAVORT IN THE WATER; YOU HAVE TO TAKE THE PLUNGE AND LEARN TO FLOAT. IF YOU PERSEVERE, YOU WILL ACQUIRE AN ABILITY THAT AT FIRST SEEMED IMPOSSIBLE."*
—KAREN ARMSTRONG

As far as elements go, water is about survival, a precious element, often even sacred. Spiritually speaking it plays a huge role in many healing, cleansing, and purifying rituals, from Hinduism, Buddhism, Judaism, Islam, Taoism, Shinto, and Christianity to Wiccan covens. It has also been the home of folklore, from mermaids that lure fishermen onto the rocks, to an age where there was an enlightened underwater society, known as Atlantis, of philosophers and new-thought thinkers (like your evolutionary self).

Water relates to all things psychic, intuition, passion, emotion, and ritual. With it comes highly sensitive powers that calls on water medicine, which offers cleansing, healing, and loving abilities and powers. When confrontations or conflict arise your mantra should be "Be like water"—also a famous Bruce Lee quote! The idea is you shape-shift, you are fluid, shapeless, formless.

Water en masse can generate huge energy and movement. This energy is harnessed in springs, beaches, rivers, pools, showers, fountains, and bathtubs; being around running water will fuel you. Let the energy wash over you and flow through you. From your dreams to your thoughts. From your friendships to your emotions. From your self-reflection to your power.

THE WATER ARCHETYPE HAS THE POWER OF HINDSIGHT. IT GIVES YOU THE OPTION TO CONFRONT AND LEARN FROM EMOTIONAL EXPERIENCES.

The Water Archetype has the power of hindsight. It gives you the option to confront and learn from emotional experiences even if you are no longer in that moment. Water's power isn't just in how you respond, it is also in how you reflect. Acting when it is a wise reaction. Mostly at peace in the ebb and flow of tides and Mother Nature's weather.

Water energy is partly ruled by moon energy—her power pulls and pushes the tides. You speak to the air and moon, nourishing and quenching earth. This water and air energy surrounds you in your day-to-day. This energy comes from the west like a sunset over the ocean; it signifies an end of a cycle, a digested lesson that will no longer repeat in your life. This energy in a Goddess can be seen as a ceremony of change. An awakened acknowledgment that a fresh cycle is on the horizon. You are in the stages of cleansing away the old, in preparation for new wisdom to wash up on your shores.

You are highly adaptive. You mold to your circumstances, making you able to cope and evolve in almost any situation. Because of your conscious flexibility, it means you are also quick on your feet, often operating in a very instinctive and intuitive fashion. This is commonly a trait exhibited by older souls, those with life experience or many life lessons under their belt. It could be due to you having to mature early in life because of family circumstances: The loss of a parent or the splitting up of a family teaches you to remain agile in your home setting, and re-silient emotionally.

The ability to so openly welcome change and easily adapt will make your evo-lutionary journey easier than most. You are highly receptive. Your intuition allows you to have one foot ahead of everyone else in your evolutionary mission.

## Water Mythology

WATER GODDESSES AROUND THE WORLD SHARE THE SAME STREAM OF STORY LINE: *PASSION*. THEY ARE GODDESSES WHO WERE RULED BY THEIR HEART.

I am sure some of the best stories you like to tell your girlfriends are the emotion-ally charged tales of heartbreak, loss, disaster, and triumph. Emotion is the key to a story, and it is what touches others. So it is not surprising to see stories of Water

Goddesses around the world share the same stream of story line: *passion*. They are Goddesses who were ruled by their heart. These patterns of love, passion, desire, hurt, anguish, and jealousy are archetypal because of how universal they are to every Goddess.

From the time of Atlantis to Nordic regions to the Ganges, we can see that our Water Goddess mythology connects to cleansing, purity, and healing. She is expressive. I personally find it interesting that many of the Goddesses of the sea had diva-sized tantrums, what could only be considered as tsunami-sized mood swings! I guess when we think of the varied states of the ocean, from big waves to eerily flat and calm, we can see that these deities were not without their flaws, much like us. Rolling waves of emotion, cycles of life, evolving to immortality. Water brings life, but it can be equally destructive. When we think of the balance of our inner warrior and Goddess energy, this swing to operate from one or another energy can also be the difference between cool-calm-collected and deadly waters!

We can observe these emotional tales of love, intrigue, and heartache and relate them to our stories. The motifs in the mythology of Water Goddesses can be exchanged for people and experiences in our own personal, evolutionary history. The persistent lover, the one we love so dearly we fear losing, the one mistake we made that gave us metaphorical monsters even! Water mythologies are stories of truth that tell the depth of our emotional transformation.

## ANUKET (EGYPTIAN GODDESS)

The first ancient Egyptian Goddess of the river Nile, she is associated with fast-moving things like water, arrows, and gazelles. Since the time of the first Nile floods, it has been common for people to throw coins, gold, and jewelry into the river to thank Anuket for life-giving water. Sobek, another Nile deity, was the god of the Nile, the army, the military, fertility, and power, and was represented by the Nile crocodile, symbolizing protection.

## ATABEY (CARIBBEAN GODDESS)

Atabey was a supreme Goddess to the Taíno religion seen in native tribes throughout the Caribbean Islands, Puerto Rico, Haiti, and Cuba. She is worshipped for her influence over fresh water and fertility—with water being all things life. She is believed to be the spirit of lakes, streams, and oceans.

### BENTEN (JAPANESE GODDESS)

The symbol of beauty, love, wisdom, arts, good fortune, water, and sea, Benten tamed her husband, who was a dragon, and is often depicted as riding dragons. As a Goddess, she originates in India, being seen in Hindu and Buddhist myths, often depicted with eight arms carrying a sword, a jewel, a bow, an arrow, a wheel, and a key. Her remaining two hands are joined in prayer. See, even Goddesses are great at multitasking!

### BOANN (CELTIC/IRISH GODDESS)

This knowledge-thirsty lass was punished for being a rebel. Legend has it that there was a sacred well that contained the source of knowledge that was off limits to all but the god Nechtan (her husband) and his servants. Boann ignored the warnings and as a result the well was violated, making it flood and rage into a river that dragged Boann away, making Boann the River Goddess.

### CALYPSO (GREEK GODDESS)

Calypso (aka Kalypso) wanted to capture herself a hubby. The Greek sea nymph lured Odysseus in with her singing and then held him prisoner for seven years in an attempt to make him her immortal husband. Think about how most guys tend to get an eye twitch at the idea of marriage for just one lifetime; imagine an immortal marriage. He ended up leaving the island on which she held him hostage on a raft, like Tom Hanks in *Cast Away*. There is no mention in any ancient scripts of whether he had a volleyball for company or not.

### CETO (GREEK GODDESS)

Ceto (aka Keto) is a Sea Monster Goddess who is the mother of other sea monsters. She is pretty much the Goddess in charge of anything badass in the sea: monsters, sharks, you name it! Like any mother might joke that her children are "fearful creatures," Ceto's actually were! From a giant ship-crushing crab to a hundred-headed serpent.

### GAṄGĀ (INDIAN GODDESS)

This Hindu Goddess is the personification of the river Ganga. Hindus believe that bathing in her river cleanses sins and promotes *moksha*—the release and liberation of life and death. The river is the symbol for the cycle of life, with families immersing their dead relatives' ashes in the river to help bring their spirits closer to moksha. Millions of Hindus make the pilgrimage to plunge themselves in Ganga every year. In Hinduism, touching water is accepted as spiritual; it is believed that water has positive vibrations and the ability to pass on energy.

### HINA (PACIFIC GODDESS)

While there are contradictory tales all over the Pacific about this Goddess known as Hina, Sina, or Ina, one thing is consistent— her Pacific popularity. She represents feminine energy, and in many stories is associated with the moon, the ocean, and female activities like tapa making, as well as healing. She is believed in some cultures to be the face in the moon, pulling the water.

> ## GODDESS GEM
>
> Many Water Goddesses of our time are writers, singers, artists, and poets—they express their emotion through their art. One of the ultimate Goddesses of our time with her emotions as her weapon is Rupi Kaur. She writes about our world, femininity, love, and life in her healing, cleansing, and powerful poems. Connect with a Goddess who is in the flow of her expression by following her on Instagram, buying her books, or seeing one of her live readings. Your story will crash into hers, as her words and emotion flood you with healing—I promise.

### MAZU (CHINESE GODDESS)

Mazu, also spelled Matsu, is a popular Chinese and Taoist Goddess. Patroness of the sea, she watches over those traveling on the ocean, protecting seafarers, fishermen, and sailors on their travels. Mazu is widely worshipped in China and Taiwan, especially in coastal regions. It is believed she had a talent for predicting the weather and warning when not to venture out to sea.

### RAN (NORDIC GODDESS)

This Goddess of the sea is rumored to have had a net with which she tried to catch men out at sea. It is believed she is responsible for orchestrating storms and waves (said to be her nine daughters) that kill. She spent most of her life collecting lost valuables at the bottom of the ocean and then casting them into her giant net, which she wore as a skirt. This is one sassy stormtress who liked bling!

### SALACIA (ROMAN GODDESS)

Ever have a guy hit on you and try to tell you he is a dolphin trainer? Well, for the Roman Goddess of salt water, Salacia, when her man, Neptune, proposed to her with a dolphin, she accepted, becoming the Salt Water Goddess. She represents calmness, serenity, and purity. Originally hiding from Neptune in the depths of the Atlantic Ocean, treasuring her virginity until his dolphin-clam-chariot thing convinced her he was her beau.

### SEDNA (INUIT GODDESS)

Known as the mother of the sea, Sedna's story is linked to creation. There are several versions, but they all tend to end with her being thrown out of a boat. When she tries to climb back in her fingers are cut off, leaving her to sink into her new oceanic home. Her fingers become the seals, walruses, and whales hunted by the Inuit. Hunters pray to her to promote hunting, but the vengeful vibe she gives out means the prayers are less of worship and more of diplomacy. Happy wife, happy life. Happy Sedna, happy sea!

## EVOLUTION EXERCISE: EMOTIONAL SURGE

Confession, my favorite place to cry is the shower. Your exercise for being a Water Archetype is to express yourself unapologetically, without feeling the need to brush your tears aside, to be hidden behind closed doors, or to keep your meltdowns to the safe sanctuary of your car when driving home from a rough day while listening to Céline Dion.

Your exercise is to allow the next surge of emotion, no matter what it is, flow through you. No matter where you are, no matter what you feel. Use your words to explain the story of why you feel like you do, the challenges that you are faced with, and how you would like to evolve from the lesson at hand. Let your emotion be the reason you need to express yourself, and let your wisdom and insight be your expression.

### SEMIRAMIS (ASSYRIAN/MIDDLE EASTERN GODDESS)

Daughter of the Fish Goddess Derketo, she was known as the great warrior who conquered Ethiopia, Libya, and Egypt. Semiramis was also believed to be a sexually voracious woman who slept with her soldiers and then had them executed, refusing to marry and give up her power. She is said to have restored ancient Babylon, invented the chastity belt, and invited Goddess worship. This is one Goddess who is often referred to in myths and historical scripts, keeping all things Goddess-boss sacred since way back when.

### TIAMAT (MIDDLE EASTERN GODDESS)

This Ocean Goddess, revered by the Sumerians, Assyrians, Akkadians, and Babylonians, was so badass she got it on with the god of fresh water and as a result gave birth to sea serpents and merpeople (can you imagine the doctor's face—"it's a mer-boy!").

**YEMOJA (AFRICAN GODDESS)**
A Goddess from the Yoruba religion, she is motherly, protective, and comforting. She can cure infertility in women and represents all things female: conception, childbirth, parenting, love, and healing. Like many women, she doesn't anger easily, but if you push her too far she can become destructive, and as violent as the sea in a storm. She is often depicted as a mermaid, connected with the moon, ocean, and creation.

## The Keys to Activating the Water Archetype's Power

**Flow, receptive to change**

**Healing, releasing or purifying**

**Sip from the cup of wisdom, swallow new insight**

**Cleansing**

**Detoxifying**

**Surge in awareness**

**Stream of consciousness**

**Loving**

**Agile**

**Peaceful**

# WATER EVOLUTION ESSENTIALS

SHE IS A MERMAID, BUT APPROACH HER WITH CAUTION.
HER MIND SWIMS AT A DEPTH MOST WOULD DROWN IN.
—J. IRON WORD

personally really resonate with Oshun, not only because she is a woman who knows how to love with her whole heart, with kindness, and with a turbulent temper (while it takes a lot to get her angry, when she snaps, god help you), but also because she is known as the "mother of all orphans" (something the abandoned, orphaned child in me adores). Not only that, Oshun was the maternal African Goddess of sweet and fresh waters. She is also known as Laketi, the Goddess who responds, she is in essence the Goddess who shows up, who protects those less fortunate, who makes sure those who need love are fed and watered.

Oshun is love, sensuality, compassion. And like her deity love sisters seen from Greece to Egypt, Oshun was the Nigerian version of Diana, Venus, Aphrodite, Ishtar, or Astarte—all Goddesses who heal the sick and bring fertility and prosperity to others. Oshun's protection over water is life to many Nigerians where millions live without access to fresh and safe water, and thousands die.

In Yoruba mystical teachings she is a witch who dances, flirts, and then cries to her followers because no one can love to the depth of what she craves, she aches for the world, believing this earth is not as beautiful as she knows it has the potential to be. And I think her tears are valid! This world needs some serious work.

I know you'll relate to her story. It's too good. At the beginning of the world all the deities got talking about how it should all be. Earth. Beings. Life. All the plans of creation were underway. Oshun, who, like most women, wasn't a fan of personal insults, overheard a male deity pass a comment that she wasn't important and couldn't really contribute to this "man's work." (I mean, really!)

Oshun thought, "Well, you'll see, I'm the Goddess of love, and I'm outta here!" Leaving the other deities to it, taking her love with her, she took refuge on the moon to observe the others at work. With her, she also took the sweet waters she governs, and as you know, without water there is no life. So now, the men have no love, and no life. They can't create anything. The earth is dry, barren, empty.

When this is recognized and all the gods have consulted with each other and realized they can't do it without her, Oshun is summoned to return. Oshun expresses the pain they caused her by their insult and belittlement. Ashamed, the gods apologize. Learning that if Oshun was to ever leave again, it would put the world in a very powerless and dangerous position. My favorite part of the tale is when Oshun accepts the apology but says, clearly and in her full embodied Goddess manner, "Don't let it happen again." Pointing out to the gods their evolutionary lesson at hand.

This tale is very relevant to today's modern Goddesses. The cracks in our society, where love has gone, are beginning to show. Be it no water on the earth. Be it children without food. The abuse of power. Resources. Rape. Pillage. Trafficking. Greed. These are where we need to call on Oshun to return. Call to the divine feminine to show up. Oshun and you are similar. You both have been insulted by your society. But you both are powerful and can contribute to healing this world. And like Oshun, it can't be done without you. This story teaches us to call out to your inner Goddess Oshun to respond. To return to your place in the world. To bring back love and tell the world to not let it happen again.

## Water Archetype Personality

YOU ARE AGILE IN YOUR APPROACH TO AWAKENING, WHICH MAKES YOU RESILIENT AND PERSISTENT. A GODDESS ENERGY THAT IS INDEED A TRULY TRANSFORMATIONAL FORCE TO BE RECKONED WITH.

You are interesting because you flow, but you also have highs and lows. You can be an easy adopter of change and transformation. Fluid with the current of change, you lay open-armed, fully submerged in everything this lifetime has to teach you. You flow with the transitioning tides. Your tendency to dive right in really does mean your journey in self-development can be sink or swim. You are agile in your approach to awakening, which makes you resilient and persistent. A Goddess energy that is indeed a truly transformational force to be reckoned with. Dang!

Your rapid reactions and quick responses means your life is most definitely never dull. You seek out movement, free-flowing shifts in life, and are easily frustrated when you are plugged up, pushed to conform, or squeezed into spaces far too small for someone of your beautiful energetic size. This makes you hard to catch, meaning lovers and those close to you in your lifetime may be challenged to keep up with the raging rapids of your revolutionary roller-coaster approach to living. And the highs and lows of your emotions. However, you are refreshing to those who cross your path, because of your fast-paced honesty, and straight-shooting forward approach to living and showing your emotions, which makes you pure yet powerful.

## ASSOCIATED ELEMENTS

Water element is highly connected to the energies of the moon, air, and sun elements. These three elemental chapters are worth exploring for the Water Archetype as each can push, pull, swirl, or even heat water. Water Archetypes are fluid and easily influenced by the push, and pull, of these associated elements; it is not uncommon to see an air or sun god at war with a Water Goddess. The stuff evolutionary storms at sea are made of. Take the Yoruba Goddess Oya from Africa and the Amazon, who is a dark Mother Goddess of all things storms; with her comes lightning, death, and rebirth. She embodies rain, air, and fury—weaving together many elements to become a force! Be it the tidal pulls of the moon, or the onshore or offshore gales of the wind. Or how it rises into the clouds with the heat of the sun.

When water is influenced, a fierce revolution of healing or destruction can result. Change can be sudden when a storm is brewing. Therefore moon, air, and sun are essential in helping the water element move forward, change shape, shift, and reflect on the raw and untamed emotion and experience that comes with any evolutionary journey.

## WATER PERSONA

You approach change with a fluid attitude. You, like water, can easily be altered and transformed. Your emotions can quickly boil, you can steam with anger, you can be hit with a tsunami of feelings, and quite easily overflow with insights from your evolutionary experiences. One of your karmic lessons is learning to contain yourself. It is common for Water Archetypes to struggle for and against security. You crave structure while at the same time crash against it. Your evolutionary experience will ebb and flow, like the tides. It is vital for you to seek and constantly soak up new wisdom and insights to ensure that your evolutionary motivations don't dry up. You are incredibly expansive when you focus your energy on transformation. You can freeze, reflecting deeply and learning quickly from your lessons, just as quick as you can melt away old beliefs and limiting thoughts.

## WATER CHAKRA

### The Sacral and Crown Chakras

Commonly associated with the lotus flower, the crown chakra represents purity, renewal, and enlightenment. Located at the crown of the head, it is connected to our brain, our thinking, and universal and spiritual wisdom. It is even said to be affected by what type of water we consume—fluoride blocks your crown chakra. The sacral chakra is located at your navel and is connected to creation, strength, and resilience.

## WATER SPIRIT ANIMALS

Fish, crocodile, and most aquatic sea life are considered to be the most ancient in the animal kingdom. These animals are wise in decision-making, often with a clear focus and vision. They also have a soft underbelly, meaning that while wise and focused, they are also sensitive and vulnerable.

## WATER EMOTIONS

You are quick to react. Easily influenced emotionally by your environment and those around you. While you are passionate and dive straight into everything you do, you can also stir things up quickly, making waves or withdrawing from those around you.

## WATER MANTRA

I listen to my higher self, and feel insight as a vital force within me. I am strong and solid in my lessons, and fluid and transformational with change, understanding I am easily influenced, and within that lay my lessons.

## WATER ZODIAC

Water Archetypes have similar traits to that exhibited in water zodiac signs, like Cancer, Pisces, and Scorpio. These star signs all share a deeper understanding for the psychic and spiritual dominions. Some being sternly against their existence, others diving deep into their mysterious realms. Each of these water zodiacs are instinctive, intuitive, insightful, and emotionally intelligent. Water Goddesses seen across many cultures, from Goddess Ganga in India to Goddess Ran in Norse mythology to the Greek Goddess Ceto, house traits similar to these water signs in that they are sensitive, compassionate, emotional, intuitive, and feel deeply. So deeply that mood swings are common to nearly all Goddesses with water influences, as they see and experience things with such meaning and clarity that they can even empathetically cleanse and digest others' evolutionary experiences for them. For this reason, it is common for both water signs and Water Goddesses to enjoy helping, guiding, healing, or protecting others.

## WATER SEASON

Autumn, shedding the old, release.

## WATER CRYSTALS

Crystals of purity, cleansing (similar in nature to water), and those that help to support water staying whole and together; crystals that offer a frequency like clear quartz, blue kyanite, and azurite. These crystals help to clear away negative energies and keep your energy in alignment as you explore your transformation and changes. Blue aventurine is also connected with the water element; the crystal brings reasoning, love, and communication to a water type's road to awakening.

## WATER AROMATHERAPY

Essential oils that are best diluted in water for Water Archetypes include lavender, eucalyptus, chamomile, and sandalwood, to name a few. These oils support quieting mental chatter, as you change old habits that no longer serve you, and help to awaken your higher consciousness to guide you in your evolution. They help calm a water energy, which is prone to sensitivity and heightened emotions. The water element promotes love, peace, forgiveness, de-stressing, purification, and healing so it is common for Water Goddesses to both enjoy and benefit from these essential oils when diffused or steamed in their Goddess sanctuary.

## WATER FOODS

Foods that purify and also help to detoxify the body are ideally suited. Try to stay away from processed foods and focus on foods that balance and nourish you during your transformation. Highly detoxifying foods include sprouts, wheat-grass, cucumber, leafy greens, and infusing water with cucumber and mint to help flush your system.

## WATER FLOWERS

Flowers like violet and campanula will help you to keep your Water Archetype in check and double as edible energy-balancing foods! If your waters are feeling murky or unsettled add them to the space where you rest or meditate to help clear your sacral and crown chakra energies—making for some smooth sailing ahead.

## WATER MOON

The full moon. Like the duality of water being high and low, the pull of the moon can mean Water Archetypes may experience extreme highs and lows at the time of the full moon. Use this time as a space to focus on being in a calm and positive state of mind in order to experience the transformational and recharging energy of the full moon. If you let your karmic lessons take over, you may find yourself behaving like a raving lunatic during a full moon.

## WATER MASCULINE BALANCE

Water element in balance means emotional balance. You are neither high nor low, you just are. When your balance is off, when you have too much masculine, you can seem angry, aggressive, or action-driven in your emotions—be it vengeful or jealous. The flip side is too much feminine, you can seem the victim, in denial, or unwilling to confront hard emotions. With a risk of being turbulent in your reactions, your emotional sensitivity, and your response to your experiences, it is key to keep your waters cool and in check. Become in tune with when you may feel a storm of feelings, a wave of emotion, and know when to take time away for yourself to work through those so you are not at risk of crashing upon others. Are they masculine or feminine emotional drivers? Take note.

With feminine energy in this element there is also a risk of becoming stag-nant in water, allowing yourself to become putrid in unpurged emotions, al-lowing them to sit still in you and fester. Let these flow through you. Expressing

# GODDESS (R)EVOLUTIONARY: INSPIRING LEADERS

Women who are not afraid to be vulnerable are warriors in my book. Courageous in the face of conformity. Women who let tears stream down their face and don't hurry to dry their flood of emotions. *Harvard Business Review* has concluded, in an article about management, that good leaders get emotional.[1] The author, Doug Sundheim, shares, "Emotions are critical to everything a leader must do: build trust, strengthen relationships, set a vision, focus energy, get people moving, make trade-offs, make tough decisions, and learn from failure. Without genuine emotion these things always fall flat and stall. You need emotion on the front end to inform prioritization. You need it on the back end to motivate and inspire."

So, this isn't a tribute to one Goddess doer who let her emotions rule her vision and inspired many, this is a tribute to the many emotionally powerful women leaders out there, with a summary of Goddesses who I find personally inspiring that I think might inspire you on your journey as well.

- Frida Kahlo, the ultimate expressionist, an artist who prided herself on ever evolving in the face of challenges both in health and love. She was her own inspiration, her own muse, who was ever trying to better her being. Her emotion was expression and individualism.
- Cleopatra, a pharaoh from BC Egypt whose wisdom and foresight rejuvenated the country's economy. The way she lead and loved has been imprinted on history, most famously for her love affairs with Julius Caesar and Marc Antony. Her emotion was service and love.
- The Rani of Jhansi, known as the Indian Joan of Arc, was the queen of Jhansi State and became the lead warrior in the first direct confrontations in the war for India's independence from Britain. Her emotion was courage and protection.
- Joan of Arc, the village girl who transformed herself into the French heroine and saint whose faith and courage in rebellion lead troops to defeat the English. She was later burned at the stake, but has been immortalized in our hearts. Her emotion was faith and liberation.
- Virginia Woolf, an English writer who evolved how we consume literature. Birthing the use of stream of consciousness, which saw a new dimension to narrative and storytelling. Her essays and novels touched on some of the world's most pressing issues at the time, from politics to discrimination against woman. Her emotion was honesty and education.
- Marie Curie, the physicist and chemist who pioneered research in radioactivity that now heals millions of cancer patients worldwide. She was the first woman to win a Nobel Prize, and the only woman to win twice. Her emotion is curiosity and selflessness.

And of course, the list could go on to consume all of this book if I was allowed to! Mother Teresa, Princess Diana, Jane Goodall, Oprah Winfrey, Arianna Huffington, Sheryl Sandberg, Mirabai, Jane Austen, Florence Nightingale, Helen Keller, Coco Chanel, Katharine Hepburn, Rosa Parks, Indira Gandhi, Billie Holiday, Malala Yousafzai, Maya Angelou, Anne Frank, J. K. Rowing, and so many more. All of these woman tell the arc of Goddess in their evolution: transformation, self-discovery, selflessness, service. They overcome challenges; they stand to voice injustices, be it in health, environment, business, culture, or society. Be it with a pen, a sword, support, or speech—they all showed up. Women who helped shape and change our world with their emotions in the charge are worth taking note of. Why? Because they weren't afraid to care.

and releasing these emotions in an appropriate and conscious manner is essential to keeping in balance through your evolutionary experiences. Easier sometimes said than done, so go easy on yourself. Sometimes your feelings will just flood out. So is life!

## WATER RETROGRADE

When water is in retrograde, you will feel like you are swimming against the current. Like you are being sucked out from shore into the ocean. You may feel out of your depth, a drowning or helpless sensation. You may feel stuck, like you are caught in a downward spiral like that of Goddess Ix Chel, the Mayan deity who has a destructive nature. All Water Goddesses have a healing and destructive element to their power; it is important to ensure these energies are in balance so the negative attributes of water don't consume you.

Evolutionary-wise, you may be stuck, anchored in water and prevented from flowing forward. Ask yourself, "What can I learn here? How can I grow?" The emotional waves of water can make you feel fine one minute, a victim, seasick, and out of balance the next. This is a sign that you are being dragged under by things that you need to resolve, digest, or graduate from. In order to float, you need to free yourself from what is holding you down, and let it all go. The key is to not allow yourself to freeze over in your evolutionary progression. Melt away limiting thoughts and beliefs, dry off your soul, and start over.

# Water Life Phases

Understanding that changes and shifts can happen suddenly for Water Archetypes, it is not uncommon for them to feel sudden self-development growth spurts and evolutionary progress. They can jump between life phases depending on their mood and emotions, at times having the wisdom and insight of a Crone, at other times having the fierceness and rebellious tantrums of a Maiden with an ego-driven inner child. They are fluid, never truly true to any one phase.

### WATER MAIDEN

Like the Maiden Goddess Persephone, Water Maiden symbolizes vulnerability, the child in all of us. A Water Maiden is young in her ability to release her emotion, often letting her feelings get the better of her. She is insightful and intuitive beyond her years, which makes it hard for her to rationalize why she feels things or sees things not yet experienced. Like Persephone, a Water Maiden is eager to explore and experience, not afraid to venture to the darker realms and explore the depths of her subconscious.

A Water Maiden's journey is of deep healing. On the surface a Water Maiden may seem barren and even forsaken, beneath her surface unfolds self-knowledge and shifting emotion. Just like the Goddess Persephone, a Water Maiden is not afraid to face her inner monsters. Thus making a Water Maiden phase as turbulent as it is transformational, a powerful phase of breaking bad habits and destructive cycles.

### WATER MOTHER

A Water Mother encompasses all things creation, destruction, fertility, and nature. She is life. Within this phase comes the responsibility of protection, vision, and knowledge. Everything from the feminine form; the feelings a Water Mother experiences become fertile, ripe, and harvested. Like the Goddess Yemoja, you become creative. Be it in life, children, art, or gardening. You inherit a call to the primeval womb to birth new projects and opportunities, gifts from your visions and ever-evolving intuition. You will nurture anything you touch. Sharing Goddess Yemoja's power to make anything you touch fertile, to soothe and heal those who suffer, to love and grow the world around you. You treat all experiences and all emotions that rise like motherhood. A chance to cradle the life and lessons around you.

**WATER CRONE**

Unapologetically the Water Crone owns her feelings. Addressing them as they rise and fall within her. She can forecast the storms within her from her emotional experiences and intelligence. Like the Water Goddess Kuan Yin, you have evolved a deep understanding of mercy, compassion, and empathy. You are strong in your ability to forgive those less evolved in their experience and emotions. You understand with everything and everyone comes great opportunity for healing. Your heart has expanded as wide as your insight, like the ocean wide and vast. People see your ability to heal others as similar to the magic of Kuan Yin—insightful, intuitive, and instinctive—which comes with age and experience.

# 11

# WATER MODALITIES

*"EVERYBODY SAYS WOMEN ARE LIKE WATER. I THINK IT'S BECAUSE WATER IS THE SOURCE OF LIFE, AND IT ADAPTS ITSELF TO ITS ENVIRONMENT. LIKE WOMEN, WATER ALSO GIVES OF ITSELF WHEREVER IT GOES TO NURTURE LIFE."*
—XINRAN

## Water Rituals

**BATHING:** Soaking your soul and body in water, particularly salt water, is essential to feeling balanced and immersed in water energy. Incorporating Goddess essentials like petals, rose water, Epsom salts, and essential oils will soothe and calm your inner waters. Explore oils that serve your energy. (Refer to the essential oil list in the Air Element section.) This ritual is cleansing, purging, and detoxifying.

**ROSE WATER:** Adding some rose water to a facial mister will help to refresh your skin throughout the day. Plus, it seems dang divine! Rose is cooling, and supports soft, supple skin. Using alkalized or filtered water, add your rose water then add in a rose quartz and an amethyst crystal, and you have yourself a Goddess

DIY facial for on the go! These crystals support self-love, reduce inflammation, regenerate skin cells, and heal the skin.

**OIL PULLING:** Yep, ditch the mouthwash and replace it with sesame or coconut oil. Twenty minutes swishing it around the mouth and then spitting it into a rubbish bin, not down the drain, otherwise you'll have a Goddess blockage on your hands. It is believed that bacteria cling to the fat in the oil, removing bad bacteria that cause bad breath, and it also supports healthy gums. A healthy mouth boosts overall wellness.

**RAW MILK:** Swab your skin with a cotton pad soaked in raw or full fat milk, or go one better—get your Cleopatra on and bathe in it. Raw milk

# GODDESS GEM

I need you to channel you inner Erin Brockovich and do some H2O CSI work, soul sister. Look into what might be added into your local water supply; this can usually be found by simply googling your local water treatment facility. While buying bottled water is tempting, from a plastic bottle perspective you might as well become a cheerleader for let's burn the world, high five for global warming, I never liked those cute green sea turtles anyway.

Don't worry, I am not about to hand you a shovel and campaign for you to start your own village well! Thankfully new innovations and our evolving minds are seeing more alkalized water solutions pop up, meaning there is a long list of options to suit every Goddess lifestyle. In the end, bottled mineral waters tend to be alkaline. Non-mineral bottled waters are unlikely to be alkaline. And adding mineral powders to regular tap water can make it more alkaline.

Instead of buying bottled water or supplementing with minerals, you can also buy a water ionizer, which creates alkaline water via a process called ionization. There are also some great filter systems that you can use. I like to keep a GoPurePod in my drink bottle for honey-booboo-holistic-spin filtered water on the go-go juice! The pod just sits in my drink bottle and has both positive and genitive charges helping to replenish the minerals taken out of the water, and take out any nasties that may be added! I also like to add naturally concentrated mineral drops to water that I might not be able to filter, just to make sure my body is getting the aqua alkalized high five it deserves. Balanced water—check! Balanced me—check!

Side note, I totally vibe with sparkling water, it tickles my throat chakra and seems like a treat—turns out in my quest to research all things hydration I unearthed a sobering discovery—making your water sparkle makes it more acidic and changes the pH balance of the water. Still better for you than the dark side, aka cola, but all things in balance right! Cheers to that.

is said to be good for inflamed skin, helping to cool and soothe. If you are vegan, coconut milk has the same properties.

## Alkaline Your Vessel

One of the quickest, easiest, and most straightforward ways of staying in tune with your soul is to drink lots of water—around six to eight glasses every day is the widely accepted amount—to help cleanse and flush your system of toxins. Throughout nearly every spiritual script, water is referenced as the pure essence of cleanliness, purification, and consciousness, not just through consumption, or rituals such as baptism, but also as a way to journey through adversity and onto calmer shores through the imagery of oceans and storms.

## Clarity Meditation

Think of your consciousness like a sponge soaking up water. Now, let's pretend the water is contaminated, dirty, or stagnant—would you want to soak it up? Think of the world around you like an ocean; aim to keep it clean, pure, flowing, and sparkling. Your "ocean" is made up of your friends, your work, your lifestyle, your attitude, and what you eat, say, and do. Do you need to wring out your sponge, clean up the energetic environment around you, and begin soaking up cleaner waters? Meditate on your waters, sensing the cleanse and purge of the waters, the ebbs and flows of the tides.

## Purge and Cleanse

This is a cleaning and releasing tool you can use to help you wash those non-serving bad vibes away! Taken from the Hawaiian culture practiced by the *kahuna*, here is a deep-healing and transformational exercise called *ho'oponopono*. The theory behind ho'oponopono is that when we forgive others, we are releasing any attachments, guilt, or regret. It is believed that inside our unconscious minds we carry all the significant people from other relationships. In essence, this exercise will help you cleanse your mind, like a detox for your unconscious self.

Find a quiet space and say out loud this cleansing tool that works to bring your state of being back to its original state—zero. In a sense flushing out and purging memories from this lifetime, or past lifetimes, that may be dictating to your subconscious and in effect limiting your evolution of both body and mind. It is crucial to understand that our

## GODDESS MUSING . . .

Did this chapter leave you with your Water Archetype glass half full? Fully submerge your soul in the pages of your element supplement chapters. Remember these elements have a great influence on your evolutionary journey: air, sun, and moon. You'll find conscious clues within these elements, which seem intent to push and pull you to change and grow in this lifetime.

body and our environment are not the problem with physical or mental illness, but the effect and the consequence of memories repeating in the subconscious that need to be released and cleansed.

Read out loud: "I'm sorry. Forgive me. I love you. Divine creator, father, mother, child as one. If I [your name] have offended against myself, my family, relatives, and ancestors in thoughts, words, deeds, and actions from the beginning of my creation to the present, I ask for forgiveness. Let this process cleanse, purify, and release all the negative memories, emotions, blocks, and energies, and transmute the unwanted vibrations into pure light. And it is done. Thank you. Thank you. Thank you."[1]

## Harness the Water Goddess Energies

Allow yourself to spend time in the company of water. Now, for time-poor, modern-day people this can seem like torture, but trust me on this. Allow yourself an hour to sit with water. You can meditate by it, or simply observe it. Become hypnotized by its flow. Notice how it is never in a rush, but it still moves and reaches its destination. Notice its agility, how it shifts, floats, and changes form. Embody water. Be like water. This can be making time to sit on a beach, or watch a river or stream, or simply watch the flowing tap as you fill a bathtub or have your morning shower.

# PART IV
# EARTH GODDESS

# 12

# EARTH MYTHOLOGY + POWERS

*"WOMAN AND EARTH ARE INSEPARABLE. THE FATE OF ONE IS THE FATE OF THE OTHER."*
—MYSTIC MAMMA

Honoring the earth and considering the natural world as your primary teacher have been connected to many forms of Goddess lifestyles. From the pagans to Native Americans, Vikings, Hindus, and witches, many religions' beliefs centered around the natural world. The earth Archetype carries power in wisdom and knowledge, strength from growth, and fruitful prosperity as you harvest your lessons and learnings.

The earth element and energy bring stability, fertility, foundation, and awareness to your body or vessel. The earth is a source of energy at the heart of all things and encompasses all the elements. Like you, earth is the womb, the energy from which all things sprout and bloom. Honor your fertility, your ability to be mother to all.

Respect that this energy is quiet, and sometimes heavy. This is a time to ground, center, grow strong, root, and rejuvenate. This is a valuable time to learn, expand, and reflect. Earth energy breathes life with the full moon, spawning a hive of activity. This is a powerful time for the Earth Archetype to meditate deeply on her lessons and understand her growth from the last cycle. Allow yourself to be at peace in the darkness, in the mystery of learning. Find your true north in this time, and gravitate toward sowing seeds to reap in the new cycle. Bury those things that no longer serve you with their transformational learnings, so they can grow into new beginnings.

This element and its Goddess energy is in all things from caves to woodlands, gardens, farms, kitchens, nurseries, and forests. Use these earth spaces to help harness your power. Smell the sweet flowers. See new life amidst the rotting old cycles. Walk through nature with the drum of your root chakra, rooting your Goddess energy with your truth. Receive your knowledge in your learnings. It will come in your ability to reflect and recharge in this time. Think of how the earthworm burrows deep into the soil, the cow grazes in the lush green pastures, or the ant gets to work underground. This is your time to dig your toes into Mother Nature, and feel safe burying your head in her earthy lessons and consoling energy, in a time that some could feel as darkness, but you know as all-encompassing mothering growth and the soil from which springs new life, and a new phase of energy.

You are deeply perceptive. You have the ability to read energies, observe elements of people unseen by many, which can make you far more observant and cautious of other beings, more than most. Trust this. You are incredibly logical in a lot of your approaches to self-development and will spend a lot of time digesting every element of your life lesson. This attention to detail will serve you greatly, just be sure not to get too stuck in the mud of it all. Your stomach speaks to you. You feel evolutionary shifts in your gut. Butterflies in your stomach will guide you to exciting opportunity. An ache or stab to your stomach will warn against a wrong step for an Earth Archetype. You'll literally feel sick to your stomach. You are extremely sensitive and in tune with the steps you take while on earth.

## Your Deep Roots

Did you know that in Japanese folklore it is believed that kodama (spirits) inhabit trees, similar to the dryads in Greek mythology? To cut down a tree where a ko-dama lives gives you bad luck for eternity. (In my opinion, to cut down any tree is probably worthy of some seriously bad juju.) In ancient times, kodama were be-lieved to be *kami*, nature deities, that dwelled in the forest. Like Earth Goddesses!

When I was writing this chapter, my partner decided to roll up his sleeves and do some gardening. When I decided to take a break from writing I went out to see he had cut down a huge yucca tree. I was as furious as a fairy in *FernGully*! I felt such a wave of emotions, mourning the tree's death. My partner grew up on a farm, so while being very in tune with nature, he is also comfortable with chop-

## GODDESS (R)EVOLUTIONARY: JANE GOODALL

When it comes to Earth Goddesses of our time Dr. Jane Goodall really is the queen of the environment and animal kingdom. Her work as a primatologist, ethologist, anthropologist, and UN Messenger of Peace has helped guide thousands globally in how they contribute to all things in nature. She has famously taught, "Only if we understand, will we care. Only if we care, will we help. Only if we help shall all be saved." Her work has always been about those who cannot speak for themselves. Something that us Goddesses can pay tribute to.

Goodall has been a leader in conversations about conservation. Educating the world not just on environmental and natural world issues, but also on the art of dialogue around change. My favorite quote from her relates to you and your evolutionary journey: "You may not believe in evolution, and that's all right. How we humans came to be the way we are is far less important than how we should act now to get out of the mess we have made for ourselves." Proving to be an Earth Goddess, to evolve, you must contribute, every little action counts.[1]

ping, cutting, and killing to sustain a property. While I wouldn't consider myself a total I'm-going-to-chain-myself-to-this-tree-or-so-help-me-Gaia kinda gal, that day I grieved a loss. It sparked me to look into spirits and trees, and I found the tale of kodama resonated.

So, if you have ever felt a presence in trees, a whisper in the forests, or a cry from a fallen tree, you may relate. My poor farmer boyfriend was shocked to see it had rattled my chakras so badly, and said in an ever down-to-earth blokey manner, "She'll be all right. Next time I'll replant it somewhere else. I won't give it the chop, babe." To which I replied with a cutting blow of sass, "How would you like it if I just chopped your leg off!"

This whole tree surgery situation made me realize I was more of an Earth Goddess than I originally thought I was. I always feel at peace when I have nature surrounding me, be it under a tall oak, lying in the grass, or even with a bunch of fresh flowers to sweeten the air of my sanctuary. Ralph Waldo Emerson wrote, "The earth laughs in flowers." And I would have to agree!

You, Earth Goddess, are deeply rooted to Grandmother. You feel and ache when both earth and your nature are not respected. This is an energy of deep grounding. Your power comes from Mother Nature, her flowers, herbs, animals, and beings.

## Earth Mythology

# AS WOMEN, WE ALL HAVE A SPECIAL MATERNAL UNION WITH MOTHER EARTH BECAUSE WE SHARE HER ABILITY TO CONCEIVE, CREATE, AND BIRTH NEW LIFE. YOU COULD SAY WE ARE SIMPLY BRANCHES OF HER FAMILY TREE.

From the cycles of the seasons to the celebration of harvests, Mother Earth to many is the source of creation, the source of life. As women, we all have a special maternal union with Mother Earth because we share her ability to conceive, create, and birth new life. You could say we are simply branches of her family tree, so it is no surprise that stories about Earth Goddesses are essentially just feminine fables.

Regardless of what culture or time in history, motifs in mythology and symbols in our stories all weave together earth's elements. Earth always has reference to being the maternal mother, the hub of creation, source of knowledge, and nourishment of life—from the Tree of Life to the fruits of Mother Nature. For her animals, who represent human qualities and behaviors as we evolve and grow as people. The shades of green are symbolic of growth, fertility, death, and rebirth. The circle of life, seasons, and duality is told in the tales of transformation between gods and Goddesses.

We human beings have endless questions about earth: How did it begin? Why do things exist? Why are we here on earth? Mythology has been a source for our exploration, ideas, and understanding of our Great Home, and to find meaning in our journey on it.

### ANU (CELTIC/IRISH GODDESS)

This is one mystic mama! Goddess of all things manifestation, magic, moon, air, fertility, and abundance, she shares corresponding connections to Danu, and was believed to rest in the Paps of Anu, two breast-shaped hills that were a reminder that the earth was her motherly body. (Side note: Whenever I see a mountain I think, Anu's other booby!)

### ASASE YAA (AFRICAN GODDESS)

Worshipped by the Akan tribe of West Africa as their Mother Earth, she is the deity of fertility, planting the seeds of truth. When her people want to prove their trustworthiness, they kiss the soil with their lips so that Earth Mother can help them speak their truth.

## AUTUMNUS (ROMAN GODDESS)

An easy one to remember, she is the Goddess of autumn and represents all things fruitful in nature, like crops, harvests, and reaping fruitful soils. A good Goddess to call on when you plant the seeds of business.

## BHŪMI (HINDU GODDESS)

Known by many names she is regarded as Mother Earth. She shares many traits with the Indo-European Goddess Gaia. She is often depicted to have four arms to show the four directions, and no shortage of jewels and jewelry to show her status as a queen in the heavens. Her many names—Bhūmi, Bhudevi, or Bhuma Devi—as well as the epithets Dhra, Dharti, and Dhrithri, which mean "that which holds everything."

## CERES (ROMAN GODDESS)

Known as the Goddess of corn, she represents agriculture, fertility, harvest, crops, and motherly relationships, and is connected to all things earth and food. She is often connected to secret rituals performed by women who plan to store and prepare plants for eating, to keep the plants healthy for feeding family and loved ones.

## CHICOMECOATL (AZTEC GODDESS)

Known as the Goddess of nourishment, she is also represented by all things corn. She is represented with red paint, and like many Aztec deities was worshipped with human sacrifice. Yeah, think of that every time you get a corn kernel stuck in your throat or teeth! Every September a maiden was dressed up as the Goddess, sacrificed, and the blood used to anoint the statue of Chicomecoatl to give her life.

## COATLICUE (AZTEC GODDESS)

The Aztec Earth Goddess and mother of the gods, she was the composer of Aztec life, a creator and a destroyer; she even gave birth to the moon and the stars. She goes by many names, Teteoinnan (mother), Toci (grandmother), and Snake Woman. Snakes are a symbol of fertility and birth.

## CORN MOTHER (NATIVE AMERICAN GODDESS)

This Goddess is also on the corn buzz like Ceres. However, she brings abundance and healing to the earth. In some stories Corn Mother was accused of witchcraft for producing corn kernels by rubbing her body. Before she was killed she offered advice on how to move and plant her body to grow crops, with her burial site sprouting maize. She is also known as Selu or Santa Clara.

### CYBELE (TURKISH/GREEK GODDESS)

Cybele, the Anatolian mother Goddess, was also a symbol of prosperity. The Greeks believed she rocked up on a lion-drawn cart with a raging, disorderly, and party-like entourage cranking some sick beats and drinking wine, and she quickly earned a polarizing reputation as a foreign, exotic, mystery Goddess. In Greek mythology, she was equated to Earth Goddess Gaia and Harvest Goddess Demeter, and was associated with mountains, wild animals, and fertility. I can make the connection to the "wild animal" part through her inner party animal side!

### DANU (IRISH/CELTIC GODDESS)

In Irish mythology Danu is worshipped for being mother of all things earth, the gods, fertility, wisdom, and wind. Her offspring are believed to be the fairy people who are skilled in magic.

### DEMETER (GREEK GODDESS)

We can all pay tribute to she who is essentially the Goddess of all things cakes and donuts, and all the yums! Demeter was the Harvest Goddess of grain and was known as the baker's Goddess. Her festival is about all things from fasting to feast. The saying that "a cupcake is just a muffin that believed in magic" can be attributed to Demeter if you ask me.

### DURGA (HINDU GODDESS)

Girl, imagine what you could achieve if you had eight arms to juggle all those daily tasks of yours. Let's put it this way, Durga, the ultimate Mother Earth Goddess, rides a lion, defeats demons that even the gods cower from, and generally gets shit done. She is worshipped primarily in eastern India during harvest season. Personally, she is one of my favorite Goddesses to call upon when I need backup.

### FJORGYN (NORDIC GODDESS)

This Nordic giant pair is both female (Fjorgyn) and male (Fjorgynn). Fjorgyn was believed to be the wife of Odin (the king of the gods), mother of Thor, and mother of the Goddess Frigg. Fjorgyn means "earth"—she was known as an Earth

Goddess. It is argued that Jord may have been Thor's mother, but interestingly the translation for Jord is also "earth." So, either way, we can confidently say that Thor was a product of a feminine Earth Goddess.

## GAIA (GREEK GODDESS)

Pretty much the spiritual boss of earth. Gaia is the ancestral mother of all life: the essential Mother Earth Goddess. She parents the sky and the sea, and was born at the dawn of creation—mother of all. And we must all admit, this Goddess has one glowing global reputation. Captain Planet, she's our hero. . . .

## HUICHI (JAPANESE GODDESS)

This Goddess is a fireball of energy. Farmers worship her, offering her fire to spark their energy to get through the harvest, fueling their labor and energy in exchange.

## LAKA (HAWAIIAN GODDESS)

This Goddess is more commonly connected to all things fertility and reproduction, aka life. She is believed to have invented the hula dance—movements well known to pay tribute to the natural elements and Mother Nature. Any Goddess with moves like that deserves to be mentioned in the evolution of dance.

## NU GUA (CHINESE GODDESS)

In Chinese mythology she was believed to be the first human on earth. With a human head and a snake-like or fish-like body, she was the handywoman of earth, refurbishing the heavens, establishing marriage, matchmaking, and even building a palace for spirits. If you ask me, she doubled as an architect and cupid and moonlighted as a Goddess.

## POMONA (ROMAN GODDESS)

The Goddess of all things fruitful, she guarded orchards and harvests. She was believed to be a wood nymph residing in all things nature from the rivers to the trees.

## RENENUTET (EGYPTIAN GODDESS)

Recognized largely throughout ancient Egypt as the cobra, Renenutet was a Goddess of all things nourishment and harvest. She had a cobra's head with a woman's body and was the beneficiary of many offerings during harvest season.

**SELU (NATIVE AMERICAN GODDESS)**

Selu, in Cherokee, means "corn." She was widely worshipped by nearly all Native American tribes to bring abundance in harvest, weather, and growth. It is believed that she planted her own heart so that corn could sprout from it so people wouldn't go hungry. Today, she is also referred to as Santa Clara.

## The Keys to Activating the Earth Archetype's Powers

**Grounding and centering**

**Planting new thoughts**

**Burying old habits and behaviors**

**Rooting in truth**

**Giving space to reflect**

**Digesting new lessons**

**Retreat and rejuvenation**

**Reconnection**

**Solitude**

**Rooting and stabilization**

**Strong, steady steps—like a drum**

**Underworld or underground**

**Still, like a rock**

## EVOLUTION EXERCISE: GRADUATION CEREMONY

Harnessing your earth element, what can you destroy to then transform in your life?

What might need to die in order to create rebirth and a new cycle?

Honor both phases as part of your growth, experience the grief in an ending, as well as the joy of graduating, progressing, and changing in a new way. You can do this by placing sticks, flowers, or leaves into water and letting the earth element be carried away and purified by the water element. You can also burn things that symbolize what no longer serves you, with sun or fire element. Or you can celebrate new birth in your life by planting new seeds or plants, or picking fresh flowers and acknowledging the start of a new phase in your life. Kind of like an Earth Goddess graduation ceremony!

# 13

# EARTH EVOLUTION ESSENTIALS

TREAT THE EARTH WELL.
IT WAS NOT GIVEN TO YOU BY YOUR PARENTS,
IT WAS LOANED TO YOU BY YOUR CHILDREN.
WE DO NOT INHERIT THE EARTH FROM OUR ANCESTORS,
WE BORROW IT FROM OUR CHILDREN.
—ANCIENT INDIAN PROVERB

Sometimes I swear us woman should have evolved an extra set of arms by now. We simply have become the masters of multitasking. Truth is, your ability to develop, to handle more, to be more doesn't just personally evolve you. It evolves the world. And since so much about Earth Goddess is actually about creation, time, devotion, and learning, what better Goddess is there than Kali, who has the benefit of four arms! And it is no wonder, because she has a lot of transformational work at her hands.

While many wouldn't consider her an Earth Goddess exactly, this Hindu Goddess of destruction and transformation symbolizes earth's energy. Birth, life, death, and rebirth. With her sword of knowledge, Kali cuts away anything that no longer serves us, slicing away ego and illusion. This powerful Goddess is feared by those who don't understand the natural cycles of life. I hate to break it to you, if you haven't already worked it out, but there will be destruction and transformation—whether you opt for it or not.

Kali is the embodiment of Mother Nature, she washes away the old with natural storms and burning fires to make the ground fertile for new crops and new life. She also represents time, the eternal spiral of change, seen in the creation, destruction, and rejuvenation of all things. Kali reminds us that, in the aftermath of life's storms, good can and will come. She points out to us that in life sometimes things must break in order to be rebuilt to be stronger and wiser. With destruction comes transformation—they are twin sisters. She, like earth, is a symbol of the power of eternal transformation and life. With the bad, comes the good.

## Earth Archetype Personality

# YOU CARE DEEPLY ABOUT THE EARTH'S JOURNEY, AND THE BEINGS THAT INHABIT IT. YOU ARE INCREDIBLY EMPATHETIC.

You are an earth angel in every sense of the word. You are the salt of the earth. A total Gaia Goddess. You care deeply about the earth's journey, and the beings that inhabit it. You are incredibly empathetic, to the point that you can be too influenced by the energy of others. For this reason, you can most likely be found recharging in your home, your sacred sanctuary. An earthy homebody! Your mission is humanitarian work, to improve the lives of those around you, be it simply the stable rock of a family, the center point of a business, or the strong and steady growth of a conscious idea or business.

People like to listen to you, you may not speak often, but your words are profound when you do. And while you are often pulled in many directions by other souls, environments, and experiences, it is just as vital that you have alone time to rest and recharge. You are at home in your alone time or with those you love deeply. You bask in the simple pleasures of life. You value family. Close friendships. And seek meaningful, deep-rooted connections with others. You seek things deeper than surface bullshit. Girl, you are about those genuine relationships. The stuff soul mates are made of. In fact, you crave these connections for stability and meaning.

People are drawn to you. You have a way with them. You are a social butterfly in some sense, connecting to all walks of life. But you find true reward in service, creating space, products, and services that improve the lives of others. In this, you are incredibly self-sacrificing of your time and energy. You give beyond what many believe possible. You are a true Goddess, helping others transform themselves alongside you.

### ASSOCIATED ELEMENTS

Earth element is highly connected to water, sun, and air elements. While the Earth Goddess gives life, these other elements are essential to sustaining life. Earth needs all of these elements not just to survive, but to thrive. These three elemental chapters are worth exploring for the Earth Archetype as they weave together the complex tapestry of the Earth Goddess. A series of threads reliant on the next to ensure growth, life, and expansion. Earth Archetypes are grounded, stable, slow, steady, loyal, and respect other stable beings. This is why air and water, two very fluid elements are important in helping the earth element move forward and are essential to an Earth Archetype's evolutionary journey.

## EARTH PERSONA

You are incredibly hardworking, down-to-earth, a creator in both nurturing life and creativity; you are emotional, sensitive, intuitive, and empathic. What a beautiful conscious combo! You are ruled by your gut, and intuition is very important to your evolutionary experience. A lot of elements are in play to ensure you are in balance, all stemming from how you fuel your evolution with food, your environment, and how you digest insights. You can easily become somber and melancholy, deep in reflection. It is important your energy does not become too dark and moody.

## EARTH CHAKRA

### Sacral and Root Chakras

Located at your navel point, the sacral chakra is connected to digestion and genitals (aka, your appetite will be off, or you will be emotionally eating, and you will either demand sex or be repulsed by it). The sacral is the hub of creation, both emotionally and reproductively. The sacral on a Goddess level relates to the Mother, the Maiden, and the Crone. Bringing fertility, sexuality, birth, nurture, and wisdom in the cycle of her lifetime. It is the ever-turning energy of our creation and feminine power that is essential to your evolutionary survival. The root chakra is located at the base of your spine and is concerned with your foundation, survival, and basic needs.

## EARTH SPIRIT ANIMALS

Elephant, wolf, horse, dolphin, whales—animals that move as a pack or a pod. These animals reflect a deeper understanding and the presence of compassion and patience. Something dear to you.

## EARTH EMOTIONS

You are extremely expressive through creativity, sex, and your relationships. You speak and think deeply, and reflect on your feelings more than most, which can make you quite sensitive. You deeply value your relationships and what others think of you.

## EARTH MANTRA

I walk forward trusting in my intuition, safe in the environment and experiences I create. Deeply rooted in my truth and purpose. I digest my experiences and use these lessons to express my fully evolved self. I am here not just to survive; I am here to thrive.

## EARTH ZODIAC

Your earth nature resembles much of that exhibited in the zodiacs Virgo, Taurus, and Capricorn. Earth signs are genuine and authentic souls, and much like all Earth Goddesses they are reliable, determined, practical, and responsible. They are grounded, real people. Like Goddesses Durga, Gaia, Isis, Artemis, and Frigg, you can rely on them to show up, like the earth, ever rejuvenating the world around them. They are most comfortable when they feel rooted, with solid foundations. Often having a slow and steady approach to the evolutionary race. Digesting one lesson at a time before moving forward. They are the peacekeepers, the meditators, those who see beauty in the world no matter the circumstance. There is no issue too difficult for earth energy to solve.

## EARTH SEASON

Winter, hibernation, reflection, and renewal.

## EARTH CRYSTALS

Crystal colors associated with your element link to all things sacral chakra and earth. Earthy yellows, oranges, reds, and browns will all serve your earth energy. Crystals like amber, tiger's eye, red jasper, and citrine offer creation, grounding, romance, and support your sensitivity. These will serve as very balancing for you and grant you stability in times of trial and transformation. Hematite is also connected to the earth, providing a strong structure and grounding support.

## EARTH AROMATHERAPY

Rooting herbs and oils that are healing and grounding are important for the Earth Goddess and can be rubbed into the skin, so the scent can walk with you in your day. Oils for Earth Goddesses include cypress, patchouli, and ylang-ylang, which are sweet, tropical, calming, and sensual, helping to settle and soothe the earth energy. Citrus oils like orange and bergamot are superb at supporting Earth Archetype's creativity, which stirs the earth element energy of peace, fertility, stability, growth, and abundance. These scents also support an Earth Goddess's root chakra, helping her to feel grounded and centered.

## EARTH FOODS

Sweet. Fruits of the earth. Oranges and citrus will support your digestion and help awaken your creative outlets and open you up to new ideas (very important when you are under evolution). Sweet teas, juices, or smoothies like mango, strawberry, lemongrass, lemon, ginger, and honey will soothe and recharge you during times of change. Foods that fuel your strength (earth) and flow (supportive elements of air and water) that have both proteins and oils are salmon, nuts, and seeds. For orange-colored foods think carrots, oranges, salmon, and sweet potato.[1]

## EARTH FLOWERS

Again, earthy orange comes into play when your evolutionary experience is in full bloom. Flowers like calendula and gardenia that double as earth elements inspire decor and edible garnishes. Both support creativity and expression, and are connected to your element, zodiac, and sacral chakra.

## EARTH MOON

Crescent moon. The Latin word for "crescent" is *crescere*, which means "to grow," or "to bring forth and create." The waxing crescent moon symbolizes growth, change, and creativity. This moon phase is when you will be inspired to seek out the new in life, seed change, and be at your most inspired. Note it down in your calendar, Goddess, so you can take some time out to really harness this time to fuel your evolutionary journey.

## EARTH MASCULINE BALANCE

When earth element is out of masculine balance, you can energetically feel destructive, turbulent, like your life force is running on empty. You may feel dry of hopes or ideas, barren of fuel and substance, and find yourself stuck feeling like the victim. Asking yourself "Why?" Questioning your values. Seeking purpose. Looking

## GODDESS (R)EVOLUTIONARY: RACHEL CARSON

Today's Earth Goddesses are those who are protectors in everything from the soil, the foods we harvest, and the humanity who eat them. These Goddesses are those who fight pesticides, finding solutions to grow healthy food for a growing population who indeed are faced with the reality of food shortages as our global population rises. But progress shouldn't come at the price of our health and well-being. Pesticides have been connected to female fertility issues, cancers, and birth defects widely reported through multiple environmental and science studies. The first warning, not of banning pesticides but of reducing their use to ensure the health and well-being of those who farm and consume products produced with pesticides, came in 1962 from biologist, ecologist, and author Dr. Rachel Carson. Her work promoted the misuse of pesticides and in turn became a major focus of JFK's presidential research.

Today, the education and protection of both farmers and the general public from the health effects from pesticides is still a real problem globally with woman continuing to step up and continue the conversation around pesticide concerns. From America's Rachel Carson, Britain's Georgina Downs, India's Vandana Shiva, to Malaysia's Sarojeni Rengam—today there is now a movement in an international Pesticide Action Network for a pesticide-free future. All seeded by the warnings of woman.

for meaning in life. You can feel like you're on the brink of catastrophe. Warning signs are a huffing and puffing sense of frustration, worry, anxiety; a stubbornness, and feeling like you could combust and have a meltdown all at the same time. Your own personal climate change moment! The key? Nature. And gratitude.

First, get outside. Not just outside in the outdoors, but also outside of your head. Allow yourself to settle. Rest. And calm down in the company of plants, trees, flowers, and animals, even a patch of grass will do. If a flower can grow through concrete, you can grow through this. Second, be thankful for all that is surrounding you, flowing through you, and ahead of you.

Alternatively, if you are feeling like you are too much in your feminine earth element, you may have Goddess symptoms of being so connected with nature that you want to opt out of society and human engagement altogether. While this can be tempting, and I can't blame you for feeling like that, you are here to help guide others in how to learn growth, balance, and to take care of the earth. You need to be her voice. What is the saying? "If a tree falls in a forest and no one is there to hear it does it make a sound?" Your voice is needed, and if you aren't there, no one will hear it.

**EARTH RETROGRADE**

A step further than being out of balance in earth energy is moving backward in earth energy, regressing in retrograde. To not bloom or grow, but to die, rot, or decay. When your earth element is evolving you can manifest and grow anything you choose to focus your attention and energy on. Like Goddess Cybele, you are fruitful and harvest the seeds you sow. Be it new learnings, experiences, understanding, opportunities. When Earth Archetype is in retrograde, you can find you bring worries and anxieties into existence. You become consumed by the weeds of worry, and the thorns of "what if." It is essential to keep in mind what you love, the vision of where you are going, and what you are grateful for. Like any Goddess, there is an element of magic in you. What you lend your thoughts toward is what you begin to grow. When you find yourself in need of planting some positivity, simply be maternal with yourself, nourish, nurture, and cradle yourself through it. Reassurance, love, and warming positivity can be healing, so surround yourself with things that help you look forward with gratitude.

# Earth Life Phases

The Earth Goddess is ever reinventing herself. Rejuvenation is the key to her ability to adapt and grow no matter the environment or circumstance. In every Goddess phase she blossoms, ascending to a new level of deep-rooted growth and understanding. This growth is strong and steady as she shifts through each phase, evolving with age and experience.

**EARTH MAIDEN**

With Earth Goddess comes consciousness. With a woman's consciousness comes earth consciousness—they walk hand in hand. The Earth Maiden is the earth; she encompasses the womb of all woodland creatures. The home of all growth, expansion, abundance, and fruition. Like Artemis, Earth Maiden is independent, a huntress; she is strong, agile, and focused on developing skills and observing her surroundings; she grows alongside her environment. She sees lessons where most would step on or over opportunity. She studies growth. She is sharp, poised, a warrior in her quest to evolve. Leaving no rock unturned in her curiosity and determination to expand in every way, shape, and form.

## EARTH MOTHER

The epitome of love and support, the Earth Mother is unrelenting in her quest to nurture and protect. Like the Goddess Demeter, the Earth Mother phase is about nurturing those around you. A time of perseverance, determination, and commitment to matters of the heart. Like Demeter's love for her daughter Persephone, you will follow any path—even ones of destruction—if it means putting the things you love front and center. She embodies trust, loyalty, and the cycle of birth, life, death, and rebirth—helping relationships end and new ones bloom. Earth Mother knows her place, while also knowing when her assistance is needed. Like a mother with an empty nest, she has evolved to understand you can love from near and far as a mother's love can never be lost; it is present in everything: a seed sprouting, a flower blooming, a bird singing.

## EARTH CRONE

As with all things in life, Earth Crone has evolved to understand with love comes war, beauty, life, and death. She is balanced, understanding, insightful, and a wealth of knowledge and magic. The Earth Crone is grandmother, elder, keeper of ancient wisdom; like Grandmother Spider, she brings lessons of survival and teachings from the past, be they lessons of fire, of the art of weaving, of protection, or of life. Earth Crone is about transition and completion in this lifetime, offering guidance, tools, and insights to the generation following behind. And like Grandmother Spider taught the humans, Earth Crone offers her wisdom to the next generation of Goddesses to inherit in their quest to evolve.

# EARTH MODALITIES

*"OWNING OUR STORY CAN BE HARD BUT NOT NEARLY AS DIFFICULT
AS SPENDING OUR LIVES RUNNING FROM IT."*
—BRENÉ BROWN

### Earthing

Sometimes, you need to stop. Stand. And connect to the cause, your purpose, your why. This simple earthing exercise only takes a few minutes and will help to ground you back to your roots with Mother Earth. Find a patch of grass or soil and take off your shoes. Stand tall on the patch of earth, close your eyes, and breathe in deeply and calmly. Imagine your feet growing roots deep into the earth, anchoring you. Imagine your spine growing tall like a tree. You, shedding worries like life-lesson leaves. Stay still and feel the breeze swirl around you. When you are ready, slowly open your eyes, wiggling your toes happily on the earth before you finish.

### Earth Sanctuary

Inject some Mother Earth into your Goddess sanctuary! My home is riddled with crystals. You can find gemstones, rocks, and geodes under pillows, on my coffee table, in my undie drawer—I even have a clear quartz hanging in the east window of my living room and in my bedroom, and a crystal dream catcher that radiates rainbow prisms and positivity throughout my sanctuary every sunrise and sunset.

I have given hanging crystals to friends for everything from baby shower gifts to bachelorette party baubles, and I even sneak them into tiny terrarium gardens so even my plants have crystals for company. After all, plants and crystals are both products of Mother Earth, so, in my opinion, it's no less weird having a crystal on your countertop or a couple hanging from your bedroom curtain rod than it is having a potted plant in your house. Both potent treasures to bring indoors from Mother Earth, in my Goddess opinion.

Here is a list of earth gemstones and attributes you can include in your sacred sanctuary.[1]

### ROSE QUARTZ

Rose quartz helps heal the heart with peace, comfort, and love. Use it when you need a little extra support as you heal from a breakup or recent loss.

### MOONSTONE

Moonstone supports intuition and spiritual growth. (One of my personal faves!) Use it when you're in the middle of a transition, as it will help you stay connected to your soul and higher self.

### AMBER

Amber helps drown out negativity and support romance. Use it when you're experiencing challenging times in a relationship and need an extra dose of positivity.

### OPAL

Opal helps you find inspiration and channel your imagination. Use it when you need to overcome a creative block and tap into your more artistic side.

### CITRINE

Citrine helps you focus on abundance and success. Use it when you're studying and need to retain information.

### AMETHYST

Amethyst is a spiritual-growth stone that supports sobriety and stability. Use it when you're exploring your higher spirituality but want to keep one foot firmly planted on the ground.

### LABRADORITE

Labradorite supports magic, intuition, and your psychic abilities. Use it when you're tapping into your inner mystic and looking to harness your intuitive superpowers.

## CLEAR QUARTZ

Clear quartz provides power, clears energy, and offers clarity. Use it when you want to rid your home or office of stagnant negative energy.

## ANGELITE

Angelite is a calming stone that offers serenity and helps to connect you with your guides. Use it when you're learning to tap into the knowledge of your Goddess guides and ancestors.

## OBSIDIAN

Obsidian helps in protection and grounding. Use it when you're traveling and want to hold on to a piece of home.

# Earth Goddess Totems

It's not uncommon for a Goddess to feel an affinity to an animal—a connection, something that draws them in. It may have been your favorite animal from childhood (no, a chicken nugget can't be your spirit animal), a favorite pet, or perhaps an animal you have had repeated sightings or dreams of. Our spiritual guides present themselves to us in the format we are willing to see them, and it is natural for many Goddesses to connect with their guides through an animal.

Pay close attention to the animals in your life, as this may well be the way your guide is trying to connect with, protect, and lead you through trouble. You can keep the energy of your Goddess totem in the forefront of your mind by wearing jewelry with the animal on it, adding figurines to your altar or workspace. I personally find I like to use Animal Medicine Tarot Cards when I need an Earth Goddess totem to guide me. Each card has a different animal, which has its own unique nature. These traits can be linked to what I might be doing, or need more of in my Goddess behavior.

Below is a list of some common animal spirit guides and what they symbolize. The key to finding your totem is to follow your Goddess intuition. You may already have a sixth sense of what it may be. It may be an animal you have an affinity with, you've had an experience with, that constantly keeps popping up for you . . . whatever the clue, here is the meaning behind famous Goddess animal totems and what they may be calling you for.

## SNAKE GODDESS

From the Goddess serpent and snake seen, from Greece to India, as the symbol of life, energy, healing, and movement between the spirit worlds, and renowned for its ability to transform or change its skin—you are adaptive, intuitive, and empathic. You are a healer, your connection to all things energy makes you more in tune with those around you than most.

## BIRD GODDESS

The Goddess bird, seen from Egypt to Old Europe, represents water, movement, emotion, and healing. Bird totems are some of the oldest totems associated with Goddesses, with birds like the owl representing the Crone, or wisdom. Birds take flight and are messengers to the world, fueled by passion and harnessing emotion for change and healing. You are expressive, and have a message for the world. Let no one label you or clip your wings. Soar, and know your soulful song will fall on the ears of those who need awakening.

## COW GODDESS

The Cow Goddess, seen from the Minoans to the Baganda tribes of Uganda, represents all things life from the production of milk. Female cows were rarely killed for meat or leather, being used to sustain life. The cow symbolizes life, from the resemblance cow and bull horns have to the shape of female reproductive organs and horns to the crescent moon. You're a nurturer, nourishing those around you with energy, love, compassion, and wisdom.

## BEE GODDESS

The Bee Goddess, seen from Greek to Hindu mythology, is symbolic of the priestess and female workers, healers, honey as medicine, and the responsibility of pollination, spreading wisdom and insight. You, dear one, have shamanic energy to lead, to put in the work, and to report for service with the goal of healing as your intention. You work hard. You consciously collaborate. You are a creature of divine duty. Austeja, the Bee Goddess's name, comes from the verb "to weave." Her Goddess nature was to guard over her hive, family, and community, and ensure fertility and the multiplication or growth of her home.

## CAT GODDESS

The Cat Goddess is seen from Egypt to Old Europe and represents wisdom, independence, strength, and success. She is often connected to being the Goddess of warfare, bringing with her the energy of balance and protection. You seek justice and equality in the world. Graceful, independent, playful, and intuitive you are a watchful eye for the world. Observing wisely, and ensuring balanced results, keeping the world in balance. You value your freedom, and seek to ensure there is freedom for all.

## SPIDER GODDESS

The Spider Goddess is a master weaver; she is patient and symbolizes the feminine energy of creation in her masterful web. She is seen in Egypt as the totem for divine mother, Neith, creator of all. In some Native American tribes, the Spider Goddess is seen as an extension of Mother Earth energy. She represents the feminine, in her darkness, as well as in her beautiful talent to weave, unify, and create. Her many eyes see many perspectives. You have a wise outlook on life, are insightful, and have a visionary approach to building your world around you. You connect people and projects. Bringing people and ideas to fruition. The Spider Goddess is one that used to scare me, then frustrate me, as it watched over me while I wove together the words of this book, and while I am still not a huge fan of spiders (shudder), I appreciate their Goddess magic now!

# Mother Earth–Inspired Altar

Pick a shelf, windowsill, or even just your bedside table to create a sacred space to keep your earth element treasures together. This could include your crystals, flowers and herbs, a figurine of your animal totem or Animal Medicine Cards, rocks, shells, feathers. This can become your own grounding altar where you can anchor your earth roots through meditation or earthing exercises to help focus your attention on what earth lessons may have been given to you, and balance you in your earth energy.

## Sync with Earth Seasons

The following is a chart of the seasons and what we should be focusing our attention on to stay in sync with Mother Earth.[2]

| | |
|---|---|
| **Spring**<br>**Spring Equinox** | Meaning: breakthrough, new growth, new projects, seed blessings<br>Energy: birthing, sprouting, greening<br>Affirmation: I plant new goals, ideas, and habits that will flourish with nourishing love, energy, and focus. |
| **Summer**<br>**Summer Solstice** | Meaning: community, career, relationships, Nature Spirit communion, planetary wellness<br>Energy: togetherness, celebration<br>Affirmation: I surround myself with like-minded souls who lift me up, inspire, support, and challenge me. I celebrate these relationships. |
| **Autumn**<br>**Fall Equinox** | Meaning: thanksgiving, harvest, introspection<br>Energy: appreciation, harvest<br>Affirmation: I am thankful for all my abundances in life, be they experiences, relationships, lessons, or learnings. I reap the seeds that I sow. |
| **Winter**<br>**Winter Solstice** | Meaning: personal renewal, world peace, honoring family and friends<br>Energy: regeneration, renewal<br>Affirmation: I give myself space and time to recharge, reflect, and reinvent myself. I focus my time on regeneration and will emerge renewed. |

## Mother Nature Remedies

Every Goddess has a flower and herb that resonate with her, and there is also a flower and herb for each zodiac sign and every chakra. Each of the twelve signs and seven chakras can benefit from the properties of certain plants, which help to heal, grow, balance, and inspire. Look up your sign and add these evolutionary organic tools by filling your garden, refrigerator, and home with these brilliant gifts from Mother Nature. As you learn about each flower's and herb's healing properties, you will begin to become more aware of which one you crave, and why you may be craving them. These natural remedies and offerings from Mother Nature are essential, not only to heal illness but to help prevent illness by keeping us in balance.[3]

| Zodiac Sign and Dates | Flowers, Herbs, Fruits, and Vegetables |
|---|---|
| **Aries, March 21–April 19**<br>**Ruling Planet: Mars**<br>**Fire Element** | Calendula, Geranium, Poppy, Red Rose, Tulip, Daffodil, Tiger Lily, Nettles, Cayenne, Red Clover, St. John's Wort, Milk Thistle, Ginger, Coriander, Marjoram, Mustard, Onion, Garlic, Leek, Chive, Radish, Horseradish |
| **Taurus, April 20–May 20**<br>**Ruling Planet: Venus**<br>**Earth Element** | Daisy, Lilac, Lily, Violet, Geranium, Foxglove, Licorice, Slippery Elm, Anise Hyssop, Sage, Thyme, Dandelion, Spinach, Peas, Potato, Sweet Potato, Apple, Fig, Apricot, Strawberry, Olives, Grapes |
| **Gemini, May 21–June 20**<br>**Ruling Planet: Mercury**<br>**Air Element** | Parsley, Dill, Anise, Lavender, Marjoram, Lilac, Peppermint, Lemongrass, Caraway, Basil, Maidenhair Fern, Orchid, Chrysanthemum, Plum, Orange, Grapefruit, Grape Juice, Raisins, Apple, Lettuce, Cauliflower, Spinach, Carrot, Celery, Green Beans, Tomato, Cayenne, Garlic, Ginger |
| **Cancer, June 21–July 22**<br>**Ruling Planet: Moon**<br>**Water Element** | Daisy, Jasmine, Morning Glory, Lotus, White Rose, Lily, Water Lily, Peppermint, Spearmint, Lemon Balm, Parsley, Mushroom, Brussels Sprout, Broccoli, Cabbage, Cauliflower, Sweet Potato, Pumpkin, Banana, Apple, Pear, Watermelon |
| **Leo, July 23–August 22**<br>**Ruling Planet: Sun**<br>**Fire Element** | Marigold, Sunflower, Dahlia, Peony, Anise Hyssop, Calendula, Motherwort, Rosemary, Mint, Ginger, Anise, Saffron, Chamomile, Dill, Fennel, Parsley, Coconut, Corn, Mustard, Pineapple, Orange, Grapefruit, Olives |
| **Virgo, August 23–September 22**<br>**Ruling Planet: Mercury**<br>**Earth Element** | Violet, Aster, Chrysanthemum, Narcissus, Dill, Fennel, St. John's Wort, Lavender, Marjoram, Licorice, Carrot, Parsnip, Barley, Oats, Rye, Wheat, Millet |
| **Libra, September 23–October 22**<br>**Ruling Planet: Venus**<br>**Air Element** | Orchid, Freesia, Daisy, Rose, Violet, Primrose, Pansy, Columbine, Parsley, Juniper, Mint, Thyme, Yarrow, Angelica, Broccoli, Eggplant, Spinach, Peas, Sweet Potato, Artichoke, Watercress, Pomegranate, Apricot, Fig, Plum, Grape, Olives |
| **Scorpio, October 23–November 21**<br>**Ruling Planets: Mars and Pluto**<br>**Water Element** | Calendula, Geranium, Peony, Honeysuckle, Hibiscus, Gardenia, Aloe Vera, Ginseng, Ginger, Coriander, Basil, Wormwood, Mushroom, Peppers, Rhubarb, Leek, Onion, Garlic, Horseradish, Mustard, Radish |
| **Sagittarius, November 22–December 21**<br>**Ruling Planet: Jupiter**<br>**Fire Element** | Red Rose, Carnation, Peony, Jasmine, Calendula, Dandelion, Sage, Anise, Nutmeg, Mint, Beet, Tomato, Turnip, Watercress, Olives, Asparagus, Endive |
| **Capricorn, December 21–January 19**<br>**Ruling Planet: Saturn**<br>**Earth Element** | Thyme, Magnolia, Pansy, Hemp, Ivy, Knapweed, Baby's Breath, Camellia, Trillium, Heartsease, Rosemary, Tarragon, Chamomile, Marjoram, Banana, Olives, Mushroom, Tomato, Onion, Lettuce, Cauliflower, Cucumber, Spinach, Radish, Broccoli, Beans, Lentils, Pumpkin, Fig, Garlic, Mustard |

| Aquarius, January 20– February 18 Ruling Planet: Uranus Air Element | Bird-of-Paradise, Orchid, Gladiolus, Trillium, Chamomile, Catnip, Passion Flower, Myrrh, Frankincense, Cinnamon, Clove, Kava, Comfrey, Spinach, Beet, Rye, Barley, Parsnip |
|---|---|
| Pisces, February 19– March 20 Ruling Planets: Jupiter and Neptune Water Element | Jasmine, Lilac, Water Lily, Poppy, Orchid, Calendula, Wisteria, Clematis, Echinacea, Eyebright, Mugwort, Kava, Nutmeg, Anise, Oat Straw, Asparagus, Mushroom, Beet, Tomato, Seaweed, Watercress, Olives |

| Chakras | Flower and Herbs |
|---|---|
| Root Chakra | Bee Balm, Dandelion, Red Rose, Ginger, Thyme, Oregano, Sage, Elderflower, Wild Lettuce Leaf |
| Sacral Chakra | Calendula, Squash Blossom, Gardenia, Cilantro, Saffron, Damiana, Maca, Pine |
| Solar Plexus Chakra | Dill Flower, Fennel, Melissa (also known as Lemon Balm), Lemongrass, Chamomile, Rosemary, Fenugreek |
| Heart Chakra | Cherry Blossom, Jasmine, Lavender, Cilantro, Parsley, Mint, Green Tea, Yerba Santa, Hawthorn Berry |
| Throat Chakra | Borage, Nigella, Basil, Peppermint, Clove, Echinacea, Licorice, Comfrey |
| Third Eye Chakra | Angelica, Astello Indigo, Star Anise, Mugwort, Lavender, Juniper, Rosemary, Eyebright, Gingko, Feverfew |
| Crown Chakra | Campanula, Camass, Phlox, Violet, Lotus, Anise, Lavender, Tulsi, Comfrey, Mugwort, Frankincense |

# Harness the Earth Goddess Energies

Make space for yourself to be in the company of earth's creations, be it an animal or familiar (a type of animal guide that we usually find becomes our pet or an animal we share a deep connection with), be it with flowers and their essences, fruits, trees, soil, or a garden. The key to connecting to Earth Goddess energy is to listen. Listen to her birds, the sounds of the trees, the hum of insects. What does

## EVOLUTION EXERCISE: GIVE A LITTLE

Ever just feel like grabbing the world by the shoulders and shaking everyone within it? You know, like getting your mama boss Goddess on and wagging your finger at everyone and saying, "Play nice."

See, I believe we all have a bit of Mama Earth in us. That caring, take-no-shit, giving-mothering face all Goddesses wear from time to time. So, mama, this exercise is about you honing that side of yourself. Stop focusing on what you can earn, win, or take in this lifetime and ask yourself, "What can I give?" Make a promise to yourself that you will give something to the world and the souls on it every day. It can be offering guidance, support, positive energy, encouragement, justice, love! Let your kindness be as constant as the changes in your life.

earth energy tell you? If you sit with her, actively listening, she will tell you things to help spark your expression and creativity. Just as her flowers bloom, and tree trunks grow tall and tower, so too will your inspiration and energy. Notice how nature is ever still—the trees, flowers, plants all seem to just be. However, within, deeply rooted, they are sprouting change, ever growing, expanding, and evolving. Doing in the simplicity of being.

## GODDESS MUSING . . .

Insights not enough to fill your hungry earth element void? This does not surprise me. I mean, growth and transformation are what an Earth Goddess does best. Skip straight to your supplemental chapters on water, air, and sun. After all, Earth Archetypes evolve best when breaking their conscious comfort zones and pushing beyond the surface of their beliefs. You understand that the best leaps forward often come hand in hand with discomfort and setbacks. Spread your roots and venture out to the other chapters.

# PART V
# AIR GODDESS

# AIR MYTHOLOGY + POWERS

*"I WOULD LIKE TO BE THE AIR THAT INHABITS YOU FOR A MOMENT ONLY.
I WOULD LIKE TO BE THAT UNNOTICED AND THAT NECESSARY."
—MARGARET ATWOOD*

Wind knows no boundaries; it connects us all and touches everyone and everything. The air and wind have long been associated with all things magic and spirit from the ancient Greek priestesses of wind to the Native American ceremonies and chants of the four winds. Air calls to all cultures, from all corners of the globe. It touches all of us. Flows through all of us. We all breathe the same air.

Wind. Air. Oxygen. It breathes life into us. Heals us. Helps us to fly. Carries with it everything from sounds to smells to seeds. I want to share a story with you, something that always taps on the windows of my soul when there is a gust of spirituality in the air. Whenever I am feeling low. Whenever I am cursing the skies or generally just pissed off with life, I am always gifted a dandelion seed. It sounds strange, but many people close to me would agree that dandelions seem to follow me everywhere.

One time, when I was little, my mother and I were in the backyard resting on the lawn, pulling dandelions, and blowing the seeds in one big puff to make a wish. "Where do the seeds go?" I curiously asked, watching the seeds drift away, floating in the spring breeze.

"They will find a new home and grow up," replied my mother, who had moved on to placing a buttercup under my chin. (There is an old wives' tale that if a buttercup lights your chin yellow then you like butter. I, being the ripe age of four, loved butter, on everything!)

"Like me?" I asked my mother, who leaned in, interested to understand how I had jumped to this conclusion.

"Like you?" she asked, picking up a nearby dandelion, ready to hear my explanation.

"Yep! See, when I was adopted I was blown out of my home and went on an adventure to find a new one, that is how I landed with you, and now I am growing up." I blew out the dandelion, successfully spitting all over my mother's hand before laughing.

"You were the answer to me wishing on a dandelion," she replied, before giving me a cuddle.

Dandelions have shown up in all sorts of life situations—the death of my mother; they filled my windowsills when I suffered a broken heart; they will float past me in the car, or even when I am out on the water—a reminder that we can always move freely, grow, and wish!

Also, a very good reminder to me that as much as I love Mother Nature I am also totally allergic to her; hay fever takes over my face, I sniffle and snort like some crazed seasonal bull, and scratch at my watering eyes like some kind of snuffling Pollen Goddess. Again, a gift from old mate wind, who carries airborne particles like dust, pollens, pollutants into the nasal passages, and makes my sinuses explode! Cheers, air.

————————

With air, comes thought. Air, and the wind it is carried by, brings with it a powerful and fresh message of light, wisdom, and beginnings. Its energy lies in the east, where the new day starts with the sun rising. Air energy signals change, a new day, a new opportunity, and a new cycle.

Air totems are weavers and messengers. The spider that weaves its web and catches the fly. The bird that sings its songs from the trees and soars through the sky. With it is offered a high perspective, an observant and wise view of the world. Knowledge in watching. Listening. The Air Archetype's season is spring, the birthing of new life. With it comes the opportunity to gain new insights.

Your concentration at this time will be deep, and your connection to all things magic and the divine will be strong. Using the wind magic to surround yourself with the smoke of sage or sandalwood incense will give you clarity. You may find feathers. Surround your sanctuary with the fresh scent of flowers and scented candles. Fill your senses with the energy of this element.

Just as the rooster crows at dawn, and the birds chirp and stir, so too will your soul with the new messages of change and ideas that will birth at this time. Your space for this energy is in morning—walk out and feel the brisk air on your face, listen to Mother Nature, and let the energy of the wind carry into your ears and

## GODDESS GEM

The air can carry with it scents. Be they the nostalgic aromas of baking for Christmas, or healing and spiritual scents—smells identical to that which our ancient ancestors and elders would use in their rituals and in their healing remedies. I am 100 percent positive you have practiced aromatherapy at some point in your life. Whether choosing a perfume that resonates, or sniffing a candle, or choosing a beautiful smelling soap, aromatherapy is an ancient air art form that you can easily plug into your modern daily life. When we connect with the scents we enjoy, we can instantly get picked up, calmed down, or transported—kind of like Mother Earth's version of drugs without the nasty side effects.

People have used natural herbs, flowers, incense, oils, and perfumes throughout time to connect body, mind, and spirit in a sweet-smelling cloud of spiritual wellness. The ancient Chinese, Hindus, Israelites, Carthaginians, Arabs, Greeks, and Romans all practiced forms of aromatherapy as well. While the earliest use of perfume bottles in Egypt dates to around 1000 BC, it is believed that the art of aromatherapy itself originated from both the Greeks and the Chinese.[1] Greek mythology maintains that the knowledge of fragrance and perfume was something only the gods and Goddesses were gifted with, and that knowledge of aromatherapy and its ability to influence health and moods was a sign of status.

heart. Air energy for Goddesses is about imagination and inspiration. Your brain will be ignited with creative ideas.

Air is masculine; it is action. Air passes through all things, all elements, and is a time for you to take note of new ideas being carried on the winds of change. Let the movement of air around you help your energy stir and bind your imagination and actions together. Air is a light and active energy. Know that with this energy you can truly make your dreams take flight.

### ONE THING VITAL TO THE AIR ARCHETYPE IS NOT TO UNDERESTIMATE HOW POWERFUL YOUR INFLUENCE CAN BE. WHEN A STRONG GUST HITS YOU, YOU CAN'T HELP BUT MOVE.

One thing vital to the Air Archetype is not to underestimate how powerful your influence can be. When a strong gust hits you, you can't help but move. A chilling breeze can be hard to ignore, and a warming breeze can be a comforting embrace. Your energy can easily surround others, and although gentle, it can be equally powerful. Your intellect is also a source of strength.

You are deeply reflective, ensuring your analysis and assessment of your situations and surroundings, ever learning. However, this does result in you not being present at times, when you are lost in your head. This is part of why you love big social gatherings, because they offer an opportunity to engage in a conscious classroom to observe and grow from. To truly harness your power and to aid your evolution, ensure you are taking away the real lessons from your observations, not the fear-driven ones. Learn with your heart, not only your head. Be present in your surroundings, show up, and show yourself.

# Air Mythology

## IT IS NO SURPRISE THAT THE STORIES OF AIR GODDESSES HAVE SHIFTS, PLOT TWISTS, AND OFTEN RUTHLESS CHANGE AT THE HEART OF THEIR STORY LINE.

Across many cultures, air has been associated with the divine from the Chinese, Greeks, and Romans to the many indigenous cultures. Generally speaking, it is said winds from the south and east bring good omens, a sudden shift in the change of direction of air can mean transformation. So it is no surprise that the stories of Air Goddesses have shifts, plot twists, and often ruthless change at the heart of their story line. Remember, with great change comes great transformation. That is air's signature and evolutionary calling card.

### ARCE (GREEK GODDESS), ALSO KNOWN AS ARKE

Messenger for the Titans, Arce had wings to carry messages through the winds. She was the sister of the Rainbow Goddess Iris, and is believed to be the faint second rainbow next to her Goddess sister in the skies, where she hid after Zeus stripped her of her wings. For the record, Zeus seems kinda ruthless with all his damning, transforming, and stripping.

### BRIGID (CELTIC/IRISH GODDESS)

Girl was the Goddess of all things weather, poetry, and crafts. Her story has evolved through time, from pagan to Christian influences. She has been associated with all things spring—fertility, feasting—and is similarly equated to Athena and Hestia. She is also connected to the fire element.

### EOS (GREEK/ROMAN GODDESS), ALSO KNOWN AS AURORA

One of my favorites, this is the winged Goddess of the dawn. Also a Titaness, this soul sister rose with the sun each morning after nightfall. Her brother and sister were god and Goddess of the Sun and Moon.

### HATHOR (EGYPTIAN GODDESS)

This Goddess had taste; she takes care of all things sky, beauty, love, and music. Now that is a great gig! She rocks all things feminine, love, and good vibes. She is believed to be the "mistress of the west," welcoming and guiding the dead to their next life. (In many cultures, the dead are buried with their heads facing west to help them cross over. This is also why many people, me included, believe you will have a more awakening and energizing sleep if you point your head east when you rest. Those with their head west will find it harder to rise with the sun in the morning.)

## EVOLUTION EXERCISE: LISTENING TO THE WINDS

This exercise will help you ease into shifts and changes that the air element brings with the support of your sister Goddesses. Venture outside, and if there is a breeze face it, if there is no wind, lay back and watch the clouds.

Now close your eyes and listen to the wind. (I know, a Pocahontas moment.) Allow yourself to settle, rest, and ground as you listen to the whispers in the wind.

Think of your favorite Air Goddess if it resonates. Allow your feelings, your energy to swirl and spiral, moving within you. If you ever feel stuck, or in a rut, use this exercise to help ease you into your changes ahead. I like to journal my challenge, and then after the meditation, write what I saw, felt, or heard. It is interesting what you may see when your eyes are closed and the wind has your ears for its audience.

### ILMATAR (FINNISH GODDESS)

The virgin spirit of air. She was bored of the sky, sick of counting rainbows, and having messy hair from the wind (may I recommend a topknot, sister). The east wind felt sorry for the Goddess, and gifted her what she had been longing for—a son, who became the child of wind.

### KHAOS (GREEK/ROMAN GODDESS), ALSO KNOWN AS CHAOS

She was the first thing to exist in the world; born from darkness and night, she swirled into existence before Gaia was created. See, chaos can be beautiful! In

Greek, chaos means "yawning" or "gap," and she was believed to be between the earth and the sky, the air that beings breathe.

### SARANYA (INDIAN/HINDU GODDESS)

She was Goddess of the clouds and the dawn. She was the wife of the sun; however, it wasn't a blissful union. It is believed Saranya couldn't handle her husband's raging heat and was believed to have hidden from the sun in the wilderness, also becoming Goddess of all animals.

## The Keys to Activating the Air Archetype's Power

**Shifts and movement**

**New thought and insight**

**Witty**

**Flexible and agile in change**

**Positivity**

**Knowledge or study**

**Travel and freedom**

**Visualization**

**Higher perspective**

**A sense of magic and synchronicity**

**A new perspective**

**Rediscovery**

**Independent**

**Selfish**

# 16

# AIR EVOLUTION ESSENTIALS

*"AERODYNAMICALLY, THE BUMBLE BEE SHOULDN'T BE ABLE TO FLY, BUT THE
BUMBLE BEE DOESN'T KNOW IT SO IT GOES ON FLYING ANYWAY."*
—MARY KAY ASH

This is a story of the Goddess who didn't need the wind to blow up her skirt to put on a show, who throws caution to the wind. . . . Sheela-na-Gigs, aka "the old hag of the breasts" (has a delightful ring to it doesn't it), was carved into history in the form of stone figurines riddled throughout old Ireland and Britain. The figurines were quite unique in the sense that they showed the pagan Goddess Sheela exposed and flashing an insanely exaggerated vulva. (Apparently, she was most recognizable for her huge vagina, oh my.)

It is said that the lustfully liberated pagan Goddess would bait men with her "lady bits." Fishing in the air, with her skirt over her head, playfully enticing men to bury their woes, worries, and hardships in her body. Most men rejected her, probably walking by thinking she was crazed and confused, though when they oc-

casionally accepted her unique invitation, Sheela would swirl and transform herself into a beautiful woman gifting the man kingship. Much to his surprise! Seems he went from clit to crown!

Scholars and historians also believe that carvings of Sheela served as a protector against the "evil eye." These carvings are seen in France, Spain, Britain, Ireland, even Norway, with figurines showing a woman's legs spread and the triangle of the sanctuary of a woman's womb, believed to bring health, a fertile harvest, and to ward against evil.

Sheela-na-Gigs also managed to carve out a reputation for herself in history as a Fertility Goddess. Her figurines were often brought to weddings, homes, and birthing circles. But my favorite story about her of all: Her go-to move was to lift her skirt up to warn off evil spirits. A pagan practice called *anasyrma*. Leaving us to wonder: *Is this superpower to warn off the evils of the world a potentially lost art form?* I'll leave that to your discretion. No judgments here!

Truth is, a Goddess never judges or belittles another sister let alone name-calls her. Our sexuality is a spiraling and empowering force that grants new life. Now that is a superpower if ever I heard one.

## PLAYFUL, SWIRLING, LIGHT, BREEZY, AND FREE-SPIRITED GODDESS SHEELA TEACHES US THAT OUR FEMININITY CAN BE AS ALIENATING AS IT IS ENCHANTING.

Playful, swirling, light, breezy, and free-spirited Goddess Sheela teaches us that our femininity can be as alienating as it is enchanting. Regardless of what others may view in or speak of you, own your full beautiful bodies and confidence to raise your chick heads high. Live unapologetically. You don't hear the wind whispering "excuse me, pardon me," as it rushes through the hair of thousands of women marching the streets. No. Instead it has the back wind of liberation. It inflates our souls, and helps us rise; it flies out of the doors and windows of change pushing out discouragement and belittlement to welcome in the brave, Marilyn Monroe–skirt-blowing, sexy, intelligent, and determined vixens.

Sheela is a total heroine, and I raise my skirt to the evils of the world in Goddess salute. Sheela and her stance on flashing bids us to swirl and shift the ideas that would once embarrass us, instead they empower us. Skirts blowing, knickers out (or no knickers depending on the evil company you may be keeping), and all.

## Air Archetype Personality

## CHANTS AND CALLS CARRY THROUGH YOU, YOU AS A SACRED CARRIER, PROTECTOR, A SOUL THAT CAN BE EASILY TRUSTED BECAUSE OF YOUR UNWAVERING PURITY.

The winds of change whisper to you and with great reason, Goddess. You are the call of change, something you approach with true Goddess grace. Chants and calls carry through you, you as a sacred carrier, protector, a soul that can be easily trusted because of your unwavering purity. You are gentle. Real. Your ethical approach to evolving is one of the most authentic of all archetypes. You are not driven by ego or self-promotion. You operate simply from love. Pure. True.

When confronted by challenges and conscious blocks, which fight against your purity, seeing darkness in others you can gust, whirl, and blow off course. Easily hurt and frustrated by the carelessness and selfish intentions of others. You often find yourself swept into social settings, surrounded by a range of souls each with various lessons to share with you. You find this exhilarating, exciting, because you are on the edge of your comfort zone. You love this variety of energy around you; however, it equally leaves you consciously guarded. Something that can truly stop you from ever deeply connecting with others, never truly letting people close enough to touch you. Very few people ever truly see the wind, they only feel that this is a key in your evolutionary experience.

## ASSOCIATED ELEMENTS

Air is highly connected and supplements sun, water, and earth elements. The Air Goddess travels between worlds, kissing the sky and carrying whispers to the earth and seas, she shape-shifts and transcends. These three elemental chapters are worth exploring for the Air Archetype, because Air Goddess is connected to and sister of these elements. Air Goddesses are loving, gentle souls, who are social in nature, liked by all, but also often experiencing wide groups of acquaintances and no real deep connections. Floaters, as I like to call them. They can move almost too freely. This is why sun, water, and earth—three very strong, healing, and grounding elements—are important in helping the air element catch up to her purpose, and are essential to an Air Archetype's evolutionary experience with learning true connection.

## AIR PERSONA

The Air Archetype can be seen as flighty or a pushover as their personality is so passive and pure. This genuine gentleness is indeed a power of this archetype if harnessed correctly. Their ability to bounce, shift, and sway with the changing winds make them dynamic and fast in their approach to change and transformation. Something they take in their stride and do with exquisite grace. An Air Archetype is most certainly not aggressive in her approach to evolution, and will often shy away from big, disruptive, and confronting challenges, opting for a more subtle attitude to self-development. Their personality is personal, often keeping matters dear to their heart close to their chest, what many may not realize, as they often are seen in groups and happy socializing. However, in truth, the Air Archetype is indeed a very introverted and guarded energy to evolve with, polarized by this craving for a collective consciousness in which they can feel safe and at home.

## AIR CHAKRA

**Heart Chakra and Solar Plexus**

Your heart chakra is located in your heart's center and is connected to all things anger, fear, love, and trust—signs that the majority of this evolutionary experience are about the lessons served in emotion. Allowing yourself to experience life with all of your heart. The solar plexus is located at your abdomen or upper stomach region and is connected to your confidence, self-worth, and self-esteem. These two emotional and self-love experiences lay at the heart of the Air Archetype's journey.

## AIR SPIRIT ANIMALS

The deer or antelope represent the Air Archetype. They symbolize the heart—yep, think Bambi. They are gentle creatures that are sharp and quick to respond to threats easily heard in the whispers of the wind. The action they take is always graceful and innocent, moving lightly and nimble with change.

## AIR EMOTIONS

Air Archetypes, viewed from the outside, look to be very calm and collected. However, from an inward perspective their emotions can be a whirlwind of judgments, anxiety, and swirling doubt. They are often trying to make sense of what they think and what they feel. They can be warm one minute, and cold the next depending on how they have perceived someone's comments. Often allowing themselves to get upset by jumping to conclusions too soon. One of the main emotions Air Archetypes will need to master is trust. They are generally quite delicate and soft in their emotions. This is often the root of a lot of their inability to deeply connect and experience profound change, as they opt for surface relationships believing they are safer because of the energetic distance between them and others. The air is after all hard to catch! When they shift from the belief that surface relationships can't hurt them to surface relationships don't serve them, true transformation can begin. In fact, it is within this deep experience of love, connection, and sometimes hurt that the real lessons await the Air Archetype.

## AIR MANTRA

I walk with conviction, trusting in my action and knowing that running or dodging my lessons prevents my development. I allow people to see and experience all elements of me. In all my forms and in all my beauty. May the winds divide and organize to aid my progress forward.

## AIR ZODIAC

Air types share the traits of that seen in air star signs, including Libra and Aquarius, which represent the winds of change. Like Air Goddesses they are flirtatious, playful, and expressive. They carry ideas and action in their evolutionary mission. Similar to air star signs, Air Goddesses are rather liberated! This power of air signs to deliver a breath of fresh air can be very supportive to others stuck in their evolutionary experience. That is why you may find a lot of like-minded souls being blown into your company. You are actually quite deep and intelligent, with many air signs exhibiting a wide intellect due to their observant nature and gentle approach to reason. Like Air Goddesses Hathor, Eos, Khaos, and Brigid, you are alert, awakened, and curious, your approach to evolution often helps lead a path for others similar to you to follow. You are truly an individual, making for a fun and unique evolutionary road ahead of you.

## AIR SEASON

Spring, new beginnings and rebirth.

## AIR CRYSTALS

Crystals like emerald, topaz, labradorite, and fluorite are ideal for the Air Archetype. They support balanced thoughts, quieting mental chatter, and helping to calm and harmonize emotions. These crystals also vibrate with the frequency of the heart, helping to support self-love and inner peace. These stones are grounding, stabilizing, and protective, ideal for supporting the air type to love and trust fully. Blue calcite is also connected to the air element, carrying visions and spiritual messages.

## AIR AROMATHERAPY

Best diffused or smoked into the air surrounding you, Air Goddess essential oils help aid your circulation and free-flowing energy. Goddess oils like neroli, geranium, or lemongrass help to uplift your mood and shift your focus to a more positive perspective and keep your energy circulating. Frankincense will calm your anxieties and provide peace of mind when you are opening yourself up to trust and are finding the shifts and feeling of ever being light, bright, and breezy a bit stressful. Letting the air carry the scent or smoke swirl around you is a sacred Goddess ritual that will aid air types to feel truly settled and at peace in times of big change or challenges.

## AIR FOODS

Leafy greens are your go-to, Goddess. They support love and compassion and also give your hearty nutrients. Lettuce, kale, spinach, and arugula are all rich in vitamin K, which will help the air type to feel grounded, strong, and release any blockages easily. Meals made with love are essential to the air type, so foods that bring up loving memories are also very supportive to Air Archetypes in their journey. Meals can reconnect them to a loving home, partner, or experience in their life. These meals are the way to an air type's heart.

## AIR FLOWERS

Cherry blossoms are soothing, kind, and compassionate, radiating love. They are great decor in the home or garden of an air type, but can also be found as a decorative garnish. Delicate and soft like the air type.

## AIR MOON

Supermoons are the Air Archetype's most confronting and transformative tool. Supermoons occur when a full moon or new moon happen when the center of the moon is closest to the earth, and happen on rare occasions. The moon appears bigger, and its pull is even more powerful. These supermoons are powerful pathways for the winds of change. With each supermoon offering a change in meaning.

## AIR MASCULINE BALANCE

When air is out of masculine-feminine alignment and you are in a more masculine form of energy, you may find yourself trying to make logical sense of the world around you. Rationalizing experiences and your emotions. Air can symbolize *prana*, the breathe of life, and also faith or the flow of your spiritual energy. When air gets out of balance you may feel like it is hard or impossible to believe what you can't see. Love and spirituality are not seen, but, like air, are felt. It is important for you during this time to try to focus your energy on what you feel versus what you think.

Air tends to be a more masculine element because of its movement and logical natures. The feminine side of air comes into play when you want to connect with all things spirit, fairies, angels, ghosts—whatever you believe in. The spiritual and magical association with air and the wind and whispers that are carried within is a powerful element to empower your mystical side if you can believe in things that you can't always see. You can't see the air, but it is there. You can't see love, but you know when it is present.

**AIR RETROGRADE**

Wind is not static, it is made to bend and weave. When air is in retrograde your life feels like it has no movement. Breathless. As though your spirit to move forward has no air in its lungs. You may feel like you are stuck, or in retrograde, being pushed backward by the winds of unchanging times. The element of air is best thought of like the number eight. It is ever flowing, in and out, like the infinity sign. Much like the triple Goddess, ever rebirthing, dying, and rebirthing. A cycle, a spiral of movement. Both air and the eight creates change, usually in personal power such as your career or finances. It is about abundance, prosperity, progress. As an Air Goddess you are programmed to change, to move, to evolve. So naturally, when an Air Goddess becomes stuck, you may not be listening to the change of wind, or be willing to adapt to the change it brings, which, as a result, may stop the organic flow that comes with air. Like walking into a room that has been closed up for too long, it will seem stuffy for you energetically. The key is a balance of control and spontaneity. Go where the wind takes you rather than waiting for the doors to fly open.

# Air Life Phases

It is no surprise that the free-floating Air Goddess floats between different Goddess phases similar to that of water. Behaviorally you can be near impossible to predict,

## GODDESS (R)EVOLUTIONARY: WRISE

We used to seek shelter from the wind. Raise our hands to shield our eyes so we could keep walking and evolving, often walking into a headwind, every step took effort, took energy. Today, we see wind as a symbol of shifts and change, we see wind as something that connects us and carries us, it puts the air into our sails to push us forward, we even gather it as renewable energy! The wind is a doer in itself.

So, this isn't about a woman who works with wind, this is about Women of the Wind. Women of Renewable Industries and Sustainable Energy (WRISE) is a strong foundation and force across the renewable energy economy; it has an empowering purpose: to change our energy future through the actions of women.[1] By building community, promoting education, and cultivating leadership, WRISE advances women and inspires its members and the public to unite in raising their voices for others. The winds of change you could say.

From wind turbines, energy planning, and meteorologists to new resource systems and solutions, more and more women are stepping up to manage and harness wind to help heal and sustain the earth. The foundation works to get more women into tech roles, advance them, and help raise their voice in the sustainable resources space. These women give a whole new meaning to the term "girl power"! To learn more, check out wrisenergy.org.

which means you can easily encompass the triple Goddess in one day! You can be playful and innocent like a Maiden one second, bold and direct the next, and then gentle and still—like shifting winds.

### AIR MAIDEN

The Air Maiden is all about mind. Air Goddess will feel inspired, motivated, and almost weightless in her ability to explore philosophies, theories, and knowledge many would find abstract. Like an eagle, you soar to new heights in your quest to observe. Looking upon life like an eye from the sky. Like Air Goddesses Hera, Aura, and Ilmatar, you are restless and have a tendency to be bored easily. When conflict or arguments arise, an Air Goddess needs to learn to stay and focus on communicating with clarity. This sense of fight or flight is a key for an Air Maiden to master in this Goddess phase. Instead, she must learn to evolve in her ability to be still in times of confrontation so as not to skip out on any potential transformational lessons from life.

## AIR MOTHER

Air Goddess in Mother phase encompasses Goddess Danu, an Irish protectress. Weaving together wisdom with wind—the divine magic in flow—her name means "flowing one," and is perfectly fitting for an Air Mother as her wings of wisdom carry her through this phase. Her children, called the people of Goddess Danu, are believed to be the fairy folk, pixies. Her wings symbolize inspiration and wisdom, bringing comfort, fertility, and abundance to her water and lands. Showing us the long-standing friendship that the Air Goddess has shared with the water and earth elements. Air Mother is about community, and the bounds of friendship and family. An Air Goddess will go to great lengths to shelter her tribe and ensure their safety. The energy of Air Mother encompasses new beginnings, creation, transformation, creativity, and enlightenment. She realigns the truth and empowers others.

## AIR CRONE

An Air Crone is worldly, universal. She sees all things as one, connected. The dark void and all-consuming truth of Air Crone energy is best harnessed by the Goddess Khaos (Chaos). Khaos was the first Goddess, born from vast darkness and splitting into the universe, a symbol for the triple Goddess: Sky as Maiden. Earth as Mother. And the dark existence beyond as Crone. She birthed our beginning, and with Crone energy raises our attention toward endings. Air Crone is about our darker energies, respecting the circle that cradles life as seen in all things human journey in nature. Air Crone is about acceptance, forgiveness, protection, and communication with spiritual realms and our guides. Air Crone guides the Goddess for her final flight, allowing her wisdom and strength in experience to be the wind lifting her wings.

# 17

# AIR MODALITIES

*"WHEN YOU OWN YOUR BREATH, NOBODY CAN STEAL YOUR PEACE."*
*—ANONYMOUS*

## Breathe Life

Something both science and spirituality agree on is that when we breathe deep, for long periods of time, we not only relax but we can transcend and dream. The art of deep sleep and the mystery of dreams has interested us beings of all backgrounds throughout history, with records of dream analysis dating back to approximately 3500 BC, and records of it being studied in ancient Egypt, Greece, Babylonia, Phoenicia, Japan, and the Americas, to name just a few.[1]

When we breathe deep into our energy centers, and allow our body to rest, letting oxygen rejuvenate and restore our body for the coming day ahead, we are also often gifted dreams and messages from our ancestors and guides. This is our way of digesting events and emotions that have hit our subconscious.

While breathing is a native instinct for you, when was the last time you practiced mindful breathing? You know, focusing your attention on every inhale and every exhale. Let's get our Air Goddess on and take five to bring our attention to our breath and give thanks to something we take for granted daily. Breathe life into your chakras, feel the air swirling through your Goddess energy centers, shifting and blowing energy around your mind, body, and soul. Refreshing and rejuvenating like a light summer's breeze.

Try these different breathing exercises; they can help relax you when you are stressed or dealing with lots of change, or support you before you rest to help aid a deep sleep.

### BELLY BREATHING

Place one hand on your stomach, relaxing your belly, and slowly inhale through your nose, bring-

## GODDESS GEM: WIND PIPES

Listen to the wind. Be it the wind blowing outside your window, flutes, or peace pipe melodies.

I have the utmost respect for Native American culture and traditions. They have always respected a connection to the elements, and have a connection with the wind themselves. Native Americans believe the wind is a divine messenger, with air carrying spirits. They believe that the air and wind encompass all that we cannot see but can feel—like our soul, spirituality, and love. Just because we can't see something doesn't mean it is not there or doesn't exist.

You can still feel the wind on your face although you cannot see it. Pipes feature strongly in Native American culture, from peace pipes to medicine, war, and wind pipes. Peace pipes are believed to be a sacred link between the earth and the sky—fire and tobacco in a pipe resembles the sun and source of life; during a ceremony, prayers are made to the four directions of the wind. The flute was used by shamans and healers and medicine men for everything from meditation and courtship to healing. The healing nature of the Native American flute is still widely used today.

ing air into the bottom of your lungs. Your belly should rise as your lungs expand full of air. When your lungs, belly, and rib cage are full, pause for a moment, before you gently release the air out again from the top of your lungs to the bottom. Taking a few deep breaths like this can help reset your nervous system, and even affect your vagus nerve, which slows down your heart rate and calms the body and mind.

**ALTERNATE NOSTRIL BREATHING**

This breathing technique is from Deepak Chopra and is known as *nadi shodhana*, or "alternate nostril breathing." It will help transform anxiety and the feeling of being unsettled or ungrounded into a quiet and calm mind.[2]

❀ Sit in a comfortable seat with your spine straight, shoulders relaxed, and chest open. Close your eyes and take a few deep breaths through your nose to bring your attention to your breath.

❀ Simply place your right thumb over your right nostril and inhale deeply through your left nostril filling up your lungs.

❀ When full, close off your left nostril with your fourth or ring finger (from the same right hand).

❀ Lift your right thumb, and then exhale smoothly out of your right nostril.

## GODDESS DOER: MICHELLE OBAMA

A modern Air Goddess who masters the slow-mo, fan hair flip, as much as she does the winds of change and insight is Michelle Obama. Her work to educate and school millions of girls around the world through her Let Girls Learn initiative shows that the air energy knows no barriers. This Goddess used her time and platform while First Lady of the United States to help air out global issues about education for girls. Joining her in this mission and sharing their wisdom for the next generation of Goddesses is Erna Solberg, Malala Yousafzai, Oprah Winfrey, Hillary Clinton, Ellen Johnson Sirleaf, Emma Watson, Her Highness Sheikha Mozah, and Tererai Trent, to name just a few. Woman who know the value of education in the evolution of any Goddess, ensuring that as many woman worldwide get access to the wisdom and opportunities they are entitled to have.

❀ Close your right nostril with your right thumb. Breathe in again, and when your lungs are full, close off your left nostril with your fourth finger, lift your right thumb, and then exhale smoothly through your right nostril.

❀ When your lungs are empty, inhale through the right nostril, closing it off with your right thumb at the peak of your inhalation, lift your fourth finger and exhale smoothly through your left nostril. Repeat this for about three to five minutes or until you feel your breath has become effortless and your mind is calm.

### UJJAYI BREATHING

This technique is also known as "victorious breath," and chances are if you ventured into a yoga class you have heard someone doing this. It is the practice of breathing a deep, slow, and long inhalation through your nostrils, and then exhaling through your mouth, relaxing the jaw, almost expressing a *ha* sound as you take a long, slow, and gentle breath out. We sometimes do this intuitively when we are stressed. The deep sigh calms the nervous center and helps to relax our bodies and mind. Essential for evolving Goddesses stuck in traffic.

## Dream Journaling

In many cultures dreams are respected as visions and insights carried to you by the air element. As a Goddess, you should take note of your dreams and pay attention to any hidden meanings a deep rest may bring you. Pay attention to symbols in your dreams, colors, how you are feeling, what you are experiencing. When you wake up try to note down everything you remember. For example, I may have dreamed I was sailing on a ship and ended up diving deep into the water, and then it turns black and I sit quietly on the bottom of the ocean. (A real dream I had recently.) I would write down ocean, sailing, dive or jump in, swimming, black, sitting, and then reflect on these words, or look them up in my library of dream dictionaries. There are lots of great dream dictionaries and websites available to explore the meaning of these Goddess gems that come to you in your dreams. So go out and be your own dream detective, and learn what clues your dreams are telling you.

## Aromatherapy

Here are a few natural oil blends that stimulate and transform different moods to get you started. These oils can be burned into the air, placed in your temple or shrine, if you have one, applied to your pulse points, put onto a cotton ball and slipped into your pillowcase, or added to water and sprayed as a mist through your hair and over your clothes. The trick to working with aromatherapy is to go with your gut and use scents you enjoy. This step on your search is almost all about pleasure, so relish it![3]

| Blends | Mood |
|---|---|
| Orange, Jasmine, Grapefruit, Rosemary, Sandalwood, Peppermint, Lemon, Ginger, Basil, Frankincense | Fatigue, low energy, unmotivated, unfocused, confused, lost |
| Vanilla, Ylang-Ylang, Lemon, Orange, Chamomile, Bergamot | Stress, overworked, run-down |
| Jasmine, Orange, Rosemary, Cypress, Bergamot | Self-esteem, nurturing, love, self-care |
| Frankincense, Rose, Orange, Lavender, Jasmine, Clary Sage, Sandalwood, Ylang-Ylang, Bergamot | Sadness, grief, loss, change |
| Chamomile, Lavender, Mandarin, Sandalwood | Anger, agitation, hate, forgiveness |

## Wind Chant Meditation

My dear soul sister Anita Sanchez shares her connection to people, earth, and spirit, ending her talks with a wind chant to the four directions to teach and connect us all. Using the learning from her Native American heritage, Anita's storytelling beseeches us to adopt a new view of our planet and to do away with the illusion that we are somehow separate from the earth. She challenges us to seek out and honor the interconnectedness between people, earth, and spirit. I personally find her chant so moving it makes me tear up. Anita is the author of *The Four Sacred Gifts: Indigenous Wisdom for Modern Times*. Change is in the air my fellow Goddesses![4]

This meditation and chant is a song of gratitude to Mother Earth, or what Anita's indigenous people call the Great Mystery. You chant the song each time as you turn to face the four directions—east, south, west, and north. The song is: "It is said, it is said: Thank you, Thank you Great Mystery. Thank you. Thank you Great Mystery."[5]

## Harness the Air Goddess Energies

Stand with your face to the wind. Like the Air Goddess let your hair be tossed in the breaths of air as you smell and listen to the wind as it swirls around you. Breathe it into you. Make yourself one with the air as you let it fill your lungs. Let the wind carry sweet scents to your nose, and whisper stories in your ears. Let it embrace and encompass you. Acknowledge the chaos and destruction in the wind as it whips past you, and equally bow to its ability to breathe life into what it brushes past, carrying seeds of rebirth in its winds. You can do this outside with the wind in your hair, or visualize it by listening to wind instruments and smelling your favorite aromatherapy scents.

## GODDESS MUSING . . .

The Air Archetype has an emotional evolutionary road awaiting them. If they can harness their power to be present and shift through their barriers to trust those around them, their lessons lay before them. If the eager winds of the Air Archetype have swept you away, you can continue exploring the wide and wonderful new world of all things wind and wisdom by studying up on Air Goddess mythology and folklore. And don't forget that the sun and earth elements also come into play in your evolutionary conscious winds of change.

# PART VI
# SUN GODDESS

# SUN MYTHOLOGY + POWERS

*"TURN YOUR FACE TO THE SUN AND THE SHADOWS WILL FALL BEHIND YOU."*
*—UNKNOWN*

We are all made of stardust. We all have fire in our hearts. Now this isn't just woo-woo mumbo-jumbo; scientists would agree with me on this one! You see, nearly every element on earth was formed in the heart of a star. You are a little piece of star, a little piece of sunlight—literally! And just like our beautiful sun is a star, it had to evolve, expand, and evolve some more to master the art of all things light.

Fire is the essence and elemental energy of the Sun Archetype: intense, creative, destructive, and passionate. It creates warmth, light, motion, and action. And like the sun leads us through our day, Sun Archetypes are leaders, trailblazers, fire warriors who share their torch of transformation with the world.

So, Sun Goddess, let's ignite your glowing, bold, shining, beautiful side, and dip into all things

sun-soul. Position that pretty head of yours so the sun crowns you with a halo of light; we can coronate you into the realm of all things daring, dazzling, and sun-drenched. This chapter is all about sun-kissed skin and sun-shining good vibes. So, grab your natural SPF, some coconut oil lip balm, and your bikini, because we are going to sun our souls with some seriously enlightening soul food.

Unlike the other elements, sun/fire is transformative, born out of a spark of change. It has been used to warm our sanctuaries, to cook for our loved ones, shine light in darkness, guide us, and unify us around the fireplace. Sun is symbolic of motivation and movement, born in you when a passion is ignited. You will feel a fire in your belly, a call, urgency, or frustration, sometimes even anger. Some of my dearest teachers have called this emotion the "raging unicorn."[1] I have described it as trying to talk to a Goddess while she is in labor. You are pregnant with creativity. Birthing new ideas. And as with all things birth, this can be a beautifully transformative and equally challenging yet rewarding energy to be in. So, full permission to huff and puff in the throes of this energy, but take responsibility for your firecracker energy, indeed, sparks may fly!

Harnessing energy is the number one Goddess power of the Sun Archetype. What they focus their time on. For this reason, this makes sun types incredibly perceptive of energy vampires, and they have no issue with expressing their conscious concerns with people who just feed on their energy or hard work. Their truth is white hot. Pure. Honest. At times hurtful to those more gentle air types, their intention is never malicious. If anything can be said for sure, Sun Archetypes are heartfelt, energetic, and have a lust for life.

## Sun Mythology

# SUN MYTHOLOGY IS ESSENTIAL FOR WOMEN TO UNDERSTAND AS IT REPRESENTS LIGHT AND CONSCIOUSNESS. PROGRESS. ACTION. ENERGY ESSENTIAL TO ANY MODERN GODDESS EVOLVING TODAY.

Sun mythology is essential for women to understand as it represents light and consciousness. Progress. Action. Energy essential to any modern Goddess evolving today. Our evolution has been largely tracked alongside the sun from calendar to celebrations.

Today, we are more likely to think moon when we think of feminine and Goddess, but the Sun Goddess represents the power and force of the sun and its warming energy, something that historically was feminine but somewhere along the evolutionary mythology lines switched to masculine. No biggie!

Mythically speaking, Sun Goddess stories depict a shift away from a matriarchal society where the eldest female was usually the boss. Profound, this gender shift in Goddess mythology, and especially sun mythology, was a portrayal of female divinity changing with the rise of the gods and the shift to a single masculine god.

With our matriarchal hats on, it is easy to see when the warrior woman might have felt forced to throw in her Goddess towel and opt for a mystical reputation under the radar of the night sky.

Take the solar Goddess of Alaska, Akycha, she escaped to the skies after her own brother raped her. Not cool. In pre-Islamic Arabia, the Sun Goddess was known as Torch of the Gods, Attar or Al-lat. She was honored daily by pouring libations at roof-top altars. Her name was subsequently rumored to be masculinized to Allah. Her other name, Shams, along with her attributes, became associated with a male sun god, Shams-On. The Babylonian sun god was Shamash, clearly related.[2] Starting to connect the conscious dots? Seems even our Goddess ancestors were all about shifting, changing, and evolving—seeing our stories, myths, and legends change throughout time.

We can't be sad or pissed about the evolution of and changes to our myths, we must accept seeing Goddesses go from sun to moon, and from Goddess to gods to a god to gone. We must admire the change in some respects. After all, we would be big fat sun-worshipping-evolving hypocrites, would we not, for dissing them for evolving, changing, and growing—even if it is from female to male? It is insightful and illuminating to shine light on the mythical origins of the Sun Goddess and see how it shifted. It essentially could be called the great mythological sex change!

What we know for sure is that the hieroglyphics, monuments, and heritage sites show us that we have had a long fascination with the sun throughout human civilization regardless of its associated gender: from Stonehenge, to the Egyptian Sphinx, to the Aztec temple, to Machu Picchu—called the "temple of the sun." As far as landmarks go, we humans are still drawn to sun temples today, many of the top tourist landmarks around the world hold a sunny secret—they were placed to align with the summer solstice. Ever wanted to visit the Great Pyramids and Great Sphinx of Giza? In the summer solstice, the sun sets exactly in the middle of the two pyramids and crowns the sphinx with a halo of light. This represents consciousness.

The traditions of the solstices and equinoxes are always about balance, light and dark, and the earthly and celestial order of nature and life, birth and death, beginnings and endings. Human and divine representations of the sun (Apollo, Ra, even Jesus) and the moon (Artemis, Diana, the Virgin Mary), and figures representing both earthly and celestial forces and patterns, are part of how humans understand their place in the universe. They all represent our part in the greater design of existence, marking our path through the stars as we journey together. Intense, right? The Goddess was not always the sun herself, but often the force behind it. The grand controller of the cosmos, the sun, and the celestial cycles.

According to Greek mythology, Leto laid an egg that produced two offspring, the sun and the moon, Apollo and Artemis. The Egyptian Goddess Hathor hatched the "golden egg of the sun" at the dawn of creation.[3] The sun god Osiris-Ra died each night to return to the womb of the Great Mother, from whose "gate" he was reborn each morning. The same is said of the Maori sun god, who must descend into the uterine cave of the Waters of Life to be regenerated daily. Bast was originally a lioness Warrior Goddess of the sun throughout most of ancient Egyptian history, but later she was changed into the Cat Goddess, which is familiar today. Greeks occupying ancient Egypt toward the end of its civilization changed her into a Goddess of the moon.

You, like these gods and Goddesses, move like the sun and the moon, rising and falling, resting and radiating. All things in balance, like the seasons, cycles, and days and nights of life. Light and darkness are all part of your balance.

## ADITI (INDIAN GODDESS)

This Hindu Goddess is known as the keeper of light and consciousness. She is the mama of all things, having given birth to the universe. She is the mother of the gods, and in Sanskrit her name translates to "limitless" (aka, total Goddess boss).

## AINE (IRISH GODDESS)

An Irish Goddess, she represents the spark of life. She is celebrated in festivals on midsummer's eve and is considered the Goddess of summer.

## AKYCHA (NORTH AMERICAN GODDESS)

The Alaskan solar Goddess worshipped by the Inuit people, this Goddess used to live on earth and fled to the skies after her brother raped her.

## AMATERASU (JAPANESE GODDESS)

A Shinto Goddess, she symbolizes the great shining of heaven. She is the emblem of the rising sun that appears on the Japanese flag. Considered to be not just the Goddess of the sun, but of the whole universe.

### ASTRAEA (GREEK GODDESS)

Known as the star maiden (and since the sun is a star she most definitely deserves a mention) this Goddess was the symbol of purity, innocence, virginity, and justice. According to legend she will return to earth, bringing with her utopia.

### BAST (EGYPTIAN GODDESS), ALSO KNOWN AS AILUROS (GREEK GODDESS)

The Lion Goddess of sunset, she was the Goddess of many things sunset, the fertilizing rays of sun, warfare. The evolving Goddess shifted from a lioness to a cat and was, widely, a symbol of protection.

### BILA (AUSTRALIAN/ABORIGINAL GODDESS)

This Goddess was a bit of a nasty ass. Girl used to light up the world by cooking her victims on a big-ass flame. She ended up getting kicked off earth and everything was plunged into darkness. Needless to say, balance was needed. So they did what any self-respecting human would do, they caught her, tied her up, and tethered her to the earth, ensuring light for everyone. Intense, right?

### BRIGID (CELTIC GODDESS)

Imagine this lass as the chick dancing with fireballs, elegant and talented, at the next festival you go to. Brigid is a solar deity whose vibe is all things light, inspiration, and great balls of fire.

### CHUP-KAMUI (JAPANESE GODDESS)

This Goddess babe has modesty down! Word is she swapped spots with the sun god because she was embarrassed about all the sexy, saucy, and adulterous antics that took place on earth at nighttime. Personally, I think girl just wanted a view from the top.

### HATHOR (EGYPTIAN GODDESS)

I totally vibe with this Goddess of the sky—she is all about femininity, love, and motherhood. She is believed to be the mother of the sun god Ra, and is represented as a pure-white cow usually carrying food, or a beautiful woman with a solar disk in between cows' horns. She was like the Taylor Swift of Goddess pop culture back in the day; everyone knew her and dug her vibe; she was one of the most popular Goddesses in ancient Egypt. Later, her rep was challenged by the Katy Perry equivalent of ancient Egypt, Isis, who absorbed more and more of Hathor's characteristics and eventually succeeded her. Dang.

## HINA (PACIFIC GODDESS)

Stories of Hina have traveled from Taiwan in Asia, to Hawaii, Polynesia, and down to New Zealand. Across all myths she is connected to the moon, and shares a love connection to the sun god Maui. Girl had his back in almost every mission Maui ventured out on, from catching the sun to stealing fire.

## MEDUSA (GREEK GODDESS)

Now this babe is best known for rocking the ancient version of a weave: snakes. Gutsy if you ask me. The only snake I would ever get close to is YouTube sensations "I'm a snaaaaaaake"—if you haven't seen it, Google it, evolution-wise you will either raise a WTF eyebrow, or laugh. Anyway, back to Medusa, who is known as a monster who turned those who gazed on her face to stone; however, ancient clues show us she also had some hook-ups with lions, which are a widely used logo for the sun. These days we see Medusa in the height of fashion in Versace's logo, in many video games, and stories. Seems the Goddesses with the worst reps are sometimes the most memorable.

## OLWEN (WELSH GODDESS)

Imagine if your name was "golden wheel," like a car after pimp-my-ride is finished with it. Well, Olwen is the Goddess version; she is a heroine who had an overpossessive actual giant of a father who would do anything to stop her from landing a fella, since it would spell his death. Let's be honest, tough choice, right? Ryan Gosling or Dad . . .

## PATTINI (SRI LANKAN GODDESS)

Ever feel the tingle of the sun pierce your skin with its rays? That's Pattini patting you on the back. She is the Goddess of sunrays and all things heat. However, my guess is she would totally recommend tanning responsibly and getting your SPF on. Just rest assured knowing she's got your tanning back.

## PELE (HAWAIIAN/PACIFIC GODDESS), ALSO KNOWN AS PERE

This Goddess was one dangerously doomed sister. Goddess of all things fire and volcano, she was cast out to walk the earth by her father, who was fed up with her fiery attitude. She wandered the earth creating volcanoes throughout Hawaii.

## SAULE (LITHUANIAN GODDESS)

This chick knew how to cruise. She had metallic gold locks, rode across the sky on a chariot pulled by two white horses, and fought darkness like Batman fought crime in Gotham City. This girl totally needs her own Goddess superhero feature film.

## SEKHMET (EGYPTIAN GODDESS)

The ultimate reminder that sun represents balance, it's not always golden tans and chilled coconuts. This Goddess stands for all the destructive vibes the sun can produce, like drought and famine. She was represented as a lion-headed Goddess. A bright reminder that even our fave sunny little kittens can have a lioness bite to them.

> # EVOLUTION EXERCISE: EMBRACE THE DARK
>
> As with all Sun Goddesses, I admire their bright and bold side, but I also want you to get better acquainted with your darker side so you can better understand how and why your light is important. We cannot have light without darkness, and these stories from mythology remind us of that balance. When fire consumes everything, blackness is left. This exercise is about journaling one of your own personal Sun Goddess tales of transformation, when your light was extinguished. How did it feel? What pushed you out of your light? How did you reignite your sun spark? By writing out your experience and learning, you can go deeper and learn more insights. Shine light into the corners of your consciousness, and take note.

## SUNNA (NORDIC GODDESS)

This Goddess has the same ride as Saule (she also goes by the name of Sol), so I feel there are some connections to her. She also rocks the sky on a chariot pulled by two horses. She is the sister of the moon, Mani, linked to the man in the moon. These connections were even noted by scholars to show evidence of her evolution, from the Nordic Bronze Age to even Indo-European—changing names and adapting to different cultures.

## UNELANUHI (CHEROKEE GODDESS)

This sun Goddess was the boss of time, dividing the day into units. Her warmth was caught in the weave of Grandmother Spider's web.

**WURIUPRANILI (ABORIGINAL/AUSTRALIAN GODDESS)**

This Sun Goddess was said to light a bark torch across the sky, traveling from east to west every day. Using fire to guide her over the sky and under the earth.

**XATEL-EKWA (HUNGARIAN GODDESS)**

It seems like there may well have been a Goddess fleet of chicks riding chariots with pimp'n horses across the sky, because this European Goddess is also rumored to share a striking resemblance to a few other Sun Goddesses already mentioned! Obviously a popular ride for solar deities.

# The Keys to Activating the Sun Archetype's Power

Passion, checking your goals

Leadership

Creativity

Desire

Opportunist

Intensity

Imagination, visionary outlook

Power, can be destructive

Intuition

Fuel, it must feed on something (no energy is free)

Courage

Strength

Light

Illumination

Positivity

Activity, action

Obsessive

Expansion

Decisive

Daring

Prone to rage and jealousy

Focused

# SUN EVOLUTION ESSENTIALS

"THE SUN SHINES DOWN, AND ITS IMAGE REFLECTS IN A THOUSAND DIFFERENT POTS FILLED WITH WATER. THE REFLECTIONS ARE MANY, BUT THEY ARE EACH REFLECTING THE SAME SUN. SIMILARLY, WHEN WE COME TO KNOW WHO WE TRULY ARE, WE WILL SEE OURSELVES IN ALL PEOPLE."
—MATA AMRITANANDAMAYI, AFFECTIONATELY KNOWN AS AMMA ("MOTHER")

What better place to find our Sun Goddess than the land of the rising sun, Japan. Amaterasu was the Goddess of the Sun; she was warm, illuminating, gentle, and encouraging. She would glow on the faces of those around her, as she highlighted their beauty and potential. She was all things light and bright in the world.

Susanoo, the storm god, and Amaterasu had a bit of a love-hate relationship. Some scripts say they were related, other say they were lovers, but whatever they were, like many male and female relationships, they often had their differences, and often disagreed on things. Susanoo would release pent-up feelings, and his storms would shake up the world when things had become too stagnant, moving swiftly and often creating chaos—you could say he wasn't good at dealing with evolutionary lessons at the time and would often let things build up. He was all show. Brave, confident, relentless, but underneath was anxiety and insecurity.

He dreamed of visiting his dead mother in the underworld but was secretly too scared. So, in order to increase his courage, he bathed in the light and wisdom of the Sun Goddess, growing his strength and insight by observing her approach to life. When he finally felt confident enough, he excitedly flew up to the sky to visit Amaterasu. Being so focused on himself, when he flew up to see her he unconsciously cracked his light and storm winds across a thunderous sky—scaring the humans on earth beneath him. This got the Sun Goddess's attention, his new light and strong energy was surely not a good power to be in the hands of someone so ungrounded, volatile, and self-absorbed.

Forgetting they had recently quarreled (as they so often did), he was greeted by the Sun Goddess holding a bow and arrow in his direction. She was cautious of how hasty and swift Susanoo was. She was no fool to his mood swings.

Hoping to gain her trust, the storm god asked the Sun Goddess if they could create children. (Big call, I know.) So Amaterasu snapped the storm god's sword into three pieces, chewed them up, and blew a light mist birthing three Goddesses, beautiful and bright beings. Still not satisfied, Susanoo asked for five jewels from the Sun Goddess, which he crushed between his teeth and blew out a light mist birthing five masculine deities, each powerful and strong.

The storm god Susanoo again began to light up the skies with his thunder and storms in an egocentric dance and boastful celebration of his creations. (Never a good look for a deity to have a moody and unpredictable nature. #unevolvedsoul)

Hoping to share an evolutionary lesson, Amaterasu explained to the storm god that he did not make such beauty alone, it was a union, a partnership of energies that could create such beauty. Not just his masculinity alone. Needless to say, he cracked. Storming. Raging. Losing all self-control, he flipped his deity lid. Rumor had it he was so mad he even put excrement in the Sun Goddess's temple, I mean . . . *ew*.

The lesson here is that although we always hope to light up and guide others, offer warmth and see beauty in everyone, unless that person is willing to evolve and grow for themselves we cannot teach them. More importantly, it isn't our job. How you respond in moments of challenge and destruction are what define you as a being. And I'm pretty sure smearing poo in sacred spaces is right up there in terms of unevolved behavior. A great lesson in how to be, and how not to be!

## Sun Archetype Personalities

A POWERFUL LEADER, A MINDFUL MOVER AND SHAKER, A TOTAL TRANSFORMATIONAL TRAILBLAZER. YOU ARE THE ESSENTIAL GODDESS ELEMENT NEEDED TO CREATE CHANGE; YOU ARE AN ACTUAL LIGHT WORKER.

You are one beautiful firecracker! A powerful leader, a mindful mover and shaker, a total transformational trailblazer. You are the essential Goddess element needed to create change; you are an actual light worker. Why, because your energy is light! Lit up by your soul energy of fire, and a down-to-earth hard worker. You can literally light up a room with your presence; however, you are prone to the "moth to the flame" scenario, where people follow you hoping to hitch a ride on your evolutionary hard work. A big piece of your conscious challenge.

Suns are balls of energies that soar to great heights by day, and crash and burn to darkness at night. The Sun Archetype is similar to that of the Moon Archetype in that it shares extreme polar dualities. However, the Sun Archetype holds opposing energies to that of the moon. Rather than the reflection and intuition driving the moon energy, the sun is powered by intense action and fiery evolutionary growth spurts. Those with a Sun Archetype may often get burned by playing with energetic fire on their evolution journey.

Sun types may feel they need to get as much achieved in a day, as much work as possible while the sun is up. They have a fear of not achieving everything they set out to. Fearing dimness, dullness, and darkness. They actually fear the thought of never changing, never developing, never improving, and never being the brightest star. It's almost an obsession with being the best, which can be their undoing.

## ASSOCIATED ELEMENTS

The Sun Archetype is highly connected to the moon, air, and earth elements. Throughout Goddess mythology Sun Goddesses have often shifted sanctuary from sun to moon, watched over the earth, and moved through the skies, so they share an affinity with all of these elemental forces. So these three elemental chapters are worth exploring for the Sun Archetype. Sun Goddesses are passionate, driven, and dynamic. Red hot, their archetype is fueled by fire. Like Goddesses Brigid, Bast, Amaterasu, and Sol, you are like a flash of light: fast, bright, and bold. This is why moon, air, and earth, three very calming, grounding, and intuitive elements, are important in helping the Sun Goddess root to her purpose and are essential to a Sun Archetype's evolutionary experience with mastering where to put her energy, understanding energy, and supporting her energy. Like many Sun Goddess stories from mythology, if a solar deity fails to confront her darkness, to harness her light, and to confront her challenges she and the world will be consumed by darkness.

## SUN PERSONA

Sun Archetypes are busy bodies. They are most content when under fire, working, creating, and burning the candle at both ends, so to speak. They live fully, work intensely, and have a firecracker opinion on all things in life and love. This usually goes hand in hand with a firm sense of ethics toward their evolution and pedal-to-the-floor approach to speeding through self-development. People who hold them back annoy the hell out of them. (Cough, cough, earth types.) This fast-fire drive can easily see them getting lost along the way, or breaking down. Another reason why the wisdom of moon and the grounding, slow, and steady influence of earth is helpful to sun types in their evolving journey.

## SUN CHAKRA

### Root Chakra and Throat Chakra

The root chakra located at the base of the spine is our flight-or-fight energy, based on our foundations and sense of survival. This energy is an essential part of understanding the sun types' drive, feeling the need to always be creating a sense of stability of success around them. An aura of achievement is needed for them to feel content. The throat chakra is located in the neck and shoulders, and it is from here that sun types breathe their energetic fire. Expressing themselves and creating their conscious action, which makes the sun type such a powerful energy.

## SUN SPIRIT ANIMALS

Ox and bull: fiery, fast, and fueled by all things red; passion runs through your blood. You are down-to-earth, and actually have a strong connection to the earth, having a firm belief system and strong roots, which helps you to charge forward with conscious change.

## SUN EMOTIONS

Sun types are intense, and can sometimes be blinding to those around them. At times coming across as ignorant, they can be so focused and driven that they almost seem to bulldoze anything and anyone who gets in their evolutionary way. This is obviously not a very conscious action. But action is their motto. Things that halt this will quickly infuriate, annoy, and lead to a potential frustration explosion from a sun type. Compassion and patience are both virtues that you will need to master. Your energy can be warm, loving, and welcoming. Passionate about those you care about, loyal and fiercely protective. But equally scalding, and can burn those close to you if you become out of balance or unconscious.

## SUN MANTRA

I am conscious of my energy and efforts and shoot for balance, not burnout. I am conscious in my action, and give my energy to things that fuel my love for my evolved life.

## SUN ZODIAC

Sun Archetypes share similarities with that of fire signs in the zodiac: Aries, Leo, and Sagittarius. Fire signs are renowned for their loving kiss and fierce bite. Similar to many Sun Goddesses who share lioness symbolism like the Goddesses Bast and Sekhmet, and rams heads seen in the crescent and horned crowns of Goddesses, it is easy to make connections between fire zodiac signs and solar deities. As with all things, the sun's energy can keep you warm, or it can spell destruction with drought, famine, and fire. While fire burns out quickly without fuel to keep it going, it can also regenerate its power from the ashes, which is why it is vital for sun types to learn how to nurture their power to prevent burnout, but also learn how to reignite it. A flicker, a spark, can quickly rage out of control, which is why sun types need to consciously monitor their energy along their road to evolution. Like the stories of Sun Goddesses, there are consistent themes surrounding lessons of communication, strength, willpower, purification, and protection.

## SUN SEASON

Summer, fertility, and flowering.

## SUN CRYSTALS

Crystals that support a Sun Archetype's energy are those that help to keep the blazing brightness in balance, such as sunstone, which supports energy, health, and willpower. But also crystals that share the reds, yellows, and oranges of flames—like amber, carnelian, citrine, fire agate, ruby, and jasper—also help to aid positive energy, focus, and successful action in a sun type's walk to awakening.

## SUN AROMATHERAPY

Sun essential oils are best burned by candle or incense so the smoke can surround a Sun Goddess in her sanctuary, which is key to the fire element. Oils or incense that resonate with and enhance Sun Archetypes most are scents that help to sooth and settle their energy, helping to support them with their goals and manifestations. Oils including rosemary, rose, juniper, clove, peppermint, black pepper, nutmeg, and basil are all calming to fire and sun types. These are also great dabbed onto a pillow before they rest for the evening, aiding them in a calm and restful sleep. These oils connect to the solar plexus chakra, which links to our personal power and self-will—all things that will aid the Sun Goddess in her evolution.

## SUN FOODS

Root vegetables are very grounding and earthing to the Sun Archetype. Vegetables like beets, onion, potato, and sweet potato nourish the sun energies and help them to feel healthy, strong, and balanced. These vegetables are also essential in helping to regulate your immune system, something often under fire in a sun type's work-hard, play-hard lifestyle.

## SUN FLOWERS

Bee balm is a minty flower that can be brewed in a tea along with other roots, like dandelion and ginger, to help support sun energy. Bee balm has been known to support active minds and reduce hyperactivity and insomnia—often issues that plague sun types.

## SUN MOON

Red moon or lunar eclipse. The sun's connection to the red moon or lunar eclipse represents your deepest longings, basic needs, habits, unconscious mind, and ability to change your approach to life (i.e., evolve). This is an ideal time to acknowledge what you have changed about your beliefs, lifestyle, habits, and what may still need work. It is a highly intuitive time when you let your higher self help support your fiery action for the future.

## SUN MASCULINE BALANCE

Sun Archetypes can be hot to handle when they are out of alignment and have too much masculinity in their hot little hands! For all things sun, fire, and flame in life

## GODDESS (R)EVOLUTIONARY: SOLAR GODDESSES

There are lots of us taking a solar shift in how we harness the sun's energy. Many people don't realize that there are a lot of women on the front line of the energy crisis. Leading new thoughts and advances in sustainable energy to help fuel the earth with renewable energy sources. These modern-day Sun Goddesses work across the globe: Erica Mackie, PE; Laura E. Stachel, MD, MPH; Lynn Jurich; and Katherine Lucey; just to name a few.

The women leading the sun charge are also in China, where they are working to transform the world's biggest polluter into the world's leader in renewable solar energy. Seeing China adding enough solar panels in solar farms to cover half a football field every hour! Creating an energy revolution. The coolest thing: Ni Huan started it all from her backyard garden, and even hosts school groups in her garden to ensure she is empowering the next generation with not just renewable energy but also resources and insight to help fuel a sustainable future. She says, "Chinese women are very heavily involved in their children's education. Many of them want to learn about 'green lifestyles,' because they want their children to learn how to protect their future."[1]

He Yisha, a passionate self-starter and Solar Goddess, founded a solar panel manufacturing company at the age of twenty-five. Not an easy feat: "I could see that people doubted me, because I looked young and didn't have much experience, but I wasn't afraid. I just decided to treat everyone as though we're all equal, which we are." Her fearless determination has paid off in huge ways, her success means success for the earth itself—that's a win-win for all. He Yisha goes on to say, "China has a relatively high proportion of female executives, compared to other countries and I'm seeing it increase. In the professional events I attend, I'm hearing more women's voices. In China now, more and more women in the workplace are daring to express themselves bravely. Whether that's in the solar industry or any other industry."[2] Brilliant!

can easily get out of whack. You can burn so bright, you eventually burn out. Like an unruly fire, it is essential for you to create a sense of orderly chaos as you evolve, as your energy can often be too masculine and become destructive. Or if too feminine, you can be smothered by earth and water.

Too much sun energy in a Goddess can be seen as selfish, egocentric, and having unrealistic expectations for yourself. You set fire to yourself in a sense. Your challenge is to find the balance with both masculine and feminine in creating gradual change, a gentle and steady glowing burn, rather than a blazing wildfire. One can fuel you; the other could destroy you.

## SUN RETROGRADE

When the Sun Archetype is still in the sky, stuck or held down, she can become relentless in her frustrations, wicked, and can fire off at any time. With sun most commonly being depicted as a god, or male energy, it can have a streak of masculine aggression and sacrifice. In many stories in mythology the sun is a source of destruction. Like a stick of dynamite, caution is warranted.

It is important to not become erratic or angry when in retrograde. Your passion easily switches from drive and determination to dominate and destroy mode—so it is important you keep your passions in check. You are, after all, as a Sun Goddess linked to a Warrior Goddess, or Goddess of war. As with all things, balance wins any battle. The support from both earth and water elements will help stabilize, ground, and calm you when you may be feeling like you are a ticking firebomb. This is simply a sign you are beat up, burned out, and out of alignment, and it is time for you to rest and recharge. Even fires need their fuel. In fact, fires cannot burn without it. Make sure you fill your energy tanks in order to prevent a Goddess breakdown.

# Sun Life Phases

The sun is always in full unless eclipsed by the moon. For this reason, it is more common that a Sun Goddess will experience distinct Goddess phases throughout her evolution. Given that a Sun Goddess is driven and focused on progress, she will feel rewarded as she enters every phase in her Goddess lifetime. Seeing each phase as a welcomed new challenge.

## SUN MAIDEN

A Sun Goddess is a warrior in training. This is a time of finding your power, expressing your strength, and taking your place in the world. Warrior Maiden Sekhmet is a Goddess, which fits this phase perfectly. Commonly Sun Maidens are fans of war. They like a challenge, a battle, and seek to fight injustice. Sekhmet's image shows her with a lion's head, and in hieroglyphics she is called the powerful one. The lioness sums up Sun Maiden, a fierce huntress, stalking down challenges, and rising to the fight rather than retreating. A Sun Maiden focuses her attention on desire, action, spontaneity, independence, and fearlessness.

## SUN MOTHER

Sun Mother represents stability, power, fulfillment, and success. This is a time of great spirituality and self-discovery in the journey of womanhood. The act of childbirth evolves sun types in learning surrender, protection, and great responsibility. Sun Mother harnesses the energy of her body both for reproduction and for her sexuality. Sun Mothers become dedicated nurturers whether they have children or not, showing up to become committed leaders in their community and activists for change in their society. Their tribe becomes her children. She seeks to guard all. Like Goddess Brigid, her flame is a torch to shine the way for others. This is a time of leadership.

## SUN CRONE

The Sun Crone is a true matriarch. An experienced and seasoned leader, a Sun Crone, rather than withering, will find this time to be the most productive of her life. It is not uncommon for a Sun Crone to feel called to speak out, lead change, take action, and cultivate movements. She surrounds herself with a wise council. Like-minded Goddesses who like her have a fire in their bellies for positive change and progress. A Sun Crone is driven by the vision and idea of leaving an illuminating legacy. Being a trailblazer for future generations of evolving Goddesses. It is an age of mastery, spirituality, power, and consciousness.

# SUN MODALITIES

### "SUNRISE: DAY'S GREAT PROGENITOR."
### —EMILY DICKINSON

## Breath of Fire

Wake your soul up with the sunrise one morning! Set your alarm for dawn, make yourself a seat on a yoga mat, cushion, or bolster, and practice a morning meditation listening to Kirtan chants. I personally love Snatam Kaur. Google her, you will find playlists online you can listen to. If it resonates you can also try a morning Kundalini session—I like GaiamTV's online videos, in particular the "wake and bake" session with Ashley Turner. In Kundalini you practice deep breathing exercises and repeating movements that aim to awaken different energy centers and organs. It is fitting that now that we are in the sun section of the book you get introduced to Kundalini, since the key breath of Kundalini is breath of fire!

Breath of fire is a quick breathing technique in which you bring your navel in as you powerfully exhale from your nose and relax your abdomen when you inhale, breathing fast and loudly from your abdomen, out through your nose.[1]

An important instruction for breath of fire is that the inhale and exhale are balanced in strength and length. It is like panting through the nose, with the mouth closed. It is also important that women know not to practice breath of fire during their moon cycle or after the one hundred and twentieth day of pregnancy. This practice can be used with a *mudra*, or hand gesture, to do when you want to awaken your soul and body.[2]

## Sun Energy Mudra

This mudra is great for Sun Archetypes, it helps to recharge, awaken, and revitalize your energy. Clench both fists and stack your left fist on top of the right one; bring them up by your heart so your elbows point outward and your arms run in a straight line from elbow to elbow. Use this mudra while practicing your breath of fire.

## Sun Meditation

For masculine energy: From the full moon to the new moon meditate in the morning with breathing focused via your right nostril. Right nostril breathing in Kundalini yoga is believed to raise your yang and masculine energy, helping to energize and awaken.

## Sun Salutations

Essentially, we are about to do a vinyasa yoga flow, which performs a salute to the sun—a sun salutation, or *surya namaskar* in Sanskrit. As with all practices we have been exploring, there are different variations of sun salutation, so it is always best to explore the practice that resonates best with you personally. It is also important to listen to your body, so don't try to overstretch yourself. I recommend following a video demo if you are new to the realm of yoga. I personally liked *Yoga Journal*'s how-to articles and videos when I was starting out.

- ❀ Begin standing tall in mountain pose, bringing your awareness to your breath, inhaling and exhaling through the nose, focusing on your *ujjayi* breathing. (Check out the Air Modalities chapter and the ujjayi exercise.)
- ❀ Lifting your heart and circling your arms upward above your head, imagine yourself rising up like the sun, opening up to the world. You can gently arch your back to look up at your hands when you reach the top.
- ❀ Exhale and fold forward bending yourself in half—this is *uttanasana* (standing forward pose). Ground your hands on your legs or the floor and lift your spine toward the horizon into *ardha uttanasana* (half bend), imagining your back is a flat line like the sun halved by the horizon line.
- ❀ Fold back into *uttanasana* (standing forward pose), and recognize how your body is starting to warm up.
- ❀ Exhale, and step or jump your feet back, then bring yourself into downward-facing dog. Tailbone tall in the sky and your palms and feet grounded on the earth.

- Rolling through your spine, lowering your tailbone, bring yourself into a four-limbed staff pose (similar to when you are doing a push up except your arms will be tight against your body instead of wide), also known as a low plank, which is called *chaturanga dandasana* in Sanskrit.
- Inhale and roll over your toes back into your downward dog.
- Then step your feet back together, or jump your feet back together, for your standing forward fold. Back to half bend. Then raise your hands up again, bringing your hands together, and bring them over your heart center in prayer. Notice how you feel. Notice your breath. Do you feel warmer?
- Repeat the yoga sun salutations three to four times.

## Sun Scribe

Your evolution shifts like the sun and will go through phases like the moon! Make a note, scribe, or journal of your transitions, moods, and breakthrough moments in your diary, or on your smartphone calendar, to see if there is a method to your modern mystic madness. Think of it like your astrology evolution tracker. Are you more creative in a new moon, on an emotional rampage in a full moon, experience breakthroughs such as breakups, big life decisions made, or overseas holidays booked in summer solstices? And note that everything needs to be enjoyed in balance—sun can be fun, but too much and you literally get burned. When you can work with the seasons, the sun, the moon, and the stars, you will find you can understand more about yourself than you maybe realize.

## GODDESS MUSING . . .

The Sun Archetype has a lot on their evolutionary plate in this lifetime. If they can harness their power to be a strong, hot, glow of sustainable action and energy, the conscious change they can create can be huge. Their light spreads easily, making them vital to the global evolution and world shifts at hand. If you have a fire under your evolutionary butt then go back to the earth, air, and moon chapters to continue exploring all things illuminating light and fiery forward action. These elements help to fuel your fire.

## Candle Meditation

Light a candle and sit alongside it in darkness. See how the wick engulfs darkness with its light. How it gently burns. Not raging, but warmly. Allow yourself to gaze into the light and, with long and slow gentle breaths, allow your energy to encompass the candle. Notice how it isn't destructive—it simply glows. Illuminating the space around it. It has a gracious presence. It is warming. Consoling. Present, yet not consuming. Your candle can light others. You can share your sun and fire energy with those needing your warmth and spark. Take responsibility and care—your spark can, if not cared for and shared wisely, also burn and torch others. Meditate in the space of caring for your light. Taking ownership of your sun energy. Being the light keeper, giver, and caretaker.

## Harness the Sun Goddess's Energies

Whether you sit under the glow of a sunny day, by a roaring fire, or next to a flickering flame, sun energy is best harnessed in earthy, airy spaces. Dampness will dull your burn. So focus on fueling yourself with things that soar your emotion and passion. Music. People. Passion projects. Reward yourself with things you enjoy. The pleasures in life. Work with sun energy and visualize a lioness, a drum beating you on; hot, passionate colors of red, yellow, and orange encompassing you in every gracious step you take forward. The drum is your heart and purpose. The burning glow is your service. You are radiating light that the world so desperately needs.

# ACTIVATING YOUR GODDESS POWERS

*"WOMAN MAY BE THE ONE GROUP THAT GROWS MORE RADICAL WITH AGE."*
—GLORIA STEINEM

This book has been a long time consciously coming. I want it to be about change and evolution. Why? Because life has always been about how we can become brighter in every sense of the word: walking with our wisdom, being compassionate and intelligent in our reactions. Awakened in our action. Asserting a shift to balance and wholeness. A feminine future. An uprising of the Goddess within.

## GIVE YOURSELF PERMISSION TO SHOW UP FULLY. EMBODYING ALL OF YOUR GODDESS ELEMENTS IN UNISON.

Give yourself permission to show up fully. Embodying all of your Goddess elements in unison. Your water emotions, your grounded and stable roots of earth, your intuitive hunches of moon, your fiery passion from sun, and express and connect that to the voice of change from air. Becoming complete, as in completely aware of what activates your strengths and weaknesses, that your transformation triggers will be the catalyst in your change and contribution.

You respect men as much as you do women. You walk alongside them. Work with them. You love and teach them, as much as they love and teach you. We are different, yet the same and together, that is what makes our dualities strong. And within you as well! Your darkness and your light. Your ability to honor your inner masculine warrior, your awakened action, alongside your feminine nature to create the new and receive lessons will unite you in your ever-evolving ability to step forward with purpose and insight rather than feeling the need to charge ahead without meaning. You are Goddess, and you are exactly where you are meant to be: In competition with no one, in conflict with nothing. Simply on a quest for conscious change. You transform wounds to wisdom.

## Activating Your Goddess Powers

Your emotions and evolutionary elements (moon, water, earth, air, sun) can give you clues to your passions, your health, your purpose, your priorities. Before you step in any direction, ask yourself, how does this truly make me feel? Feel it out. Become aware of it. Then own what you feel. Address your emotions with the respect they deserve. Honor your energy. Take from your element and the lessons it can offer you and allow that energy, emotion, to help your growth. Allow it to be your transformational fuel. Your own personal Goddess superpower.

### GODDESS GEM: CELEBRATE

**Gather your consciousness and surround yourself with Goddesses who are, like you, stepping into their power. Eclipse the fear in feminine from your life, and put your love and lady on high beam. Fearless, topless, wild, and free. Goddesses have danced since the dawn of time—from ceremony, to sensuality, to belly dancing, to dance floors. So this gem is about the ritual of celebration. Blast your Goddess-go-to whether it is Stevie Nicks, Florence Welch, India Arie, Dolly Parton, Tina Turner, or Snatam Kaur. And simply move. Swirl your hips, bounce your booty, throw your hands up, clap your hands, and dance with your elemental energy in this moment. Why? Because you can, and because you deserve to celebrate your inner Goddess. Look how far you have come in life. I mean, girl got through some hurdles!**

We didn't see Mother Teresa sitting bummed out in Calcutta about poverty, focusing her energy on being pissed at the world. We saw her channel her emotional response as a healing love for others. Same goes for Princess Diana. Or Oprah. Or the women holding their protest signs amidst a march. Or the woman cheering another woman who helps to empower and love others. Or the woman who reads to learn how to offer her energy to a cause bigger than herself. Each equally as important as the next. Each a powerful source of emotionally charged transformational energy. These are the ones who choose to evolve from the art of being, to the powerful act of doing.

These were the ones who really won. Who were not defeated by their energy and emotions, refusing to be conquered by their dealings in life. Who chose not to be victims.

Instead, they rose to the lesson and seized the challenge. Like you, they got these cards that are dealt; these ripe pickings are, indeed, harvesttime for evolutionary development, to truly consume consciousness. Digesting it at healing depths. You feed on such experiences. They fuel you.

That is the thing about experiences that help you evolve—they are as painful as they are profound, as messy as they are miraculous. Setbacks help you step forward. And whether you want them or not, whether you are ready, regardless, they show up anyway. Life changes in the blink of a third eye. And our reactions show up, sometimes afraid, hurt, confused, impossible, untamed, and raw. Each emotion valid. And just like the experience, reactions, or the emotions, the elements show up around us whenever they damn well please too. They might be messy, but they show up anyway. You and everything you have experienced, everything you are feeling, everything that fuels you, will show up to help you move forward. To encourage you to evolve. The only thing impossible is trying to outrun it! Our ability to learn and grow is endless.

You know that turning point in all stories, where Cinderella, Snow White, Moana, the underdog, or the bullying bitch all hit transformation mode? When their journey hits a breaking point? A transformational tipping point? You know, when you have read or watched many a story cheering on the protagonist to take the chance and change her whole world as she knew it! Because girl, you are part of the solution. You never needed saving, or permission to be the true Goddess you are. And damn, I just want you to kick down any doors holding you back, and for you to own this life of yours.

## THIS IS YOUR STORY. AND THIS IS YOUR MOMENT. WHEN YOU REALIZE YOU ARE THE MAKER OF YOUR OWN DESTINY. MORE THAN THAT, THE CREATOR OF IT.

This is your story. And this is your moment. When you realize you are the maker of your own destiny. More than that, the creator of it. The mother. The life giver. The nurturer. The leader. The healer. And like all great mythical stories of Goddesses, we all arrive at the crossroads where we can choose to change, or choose to stay. So, here we are. What road will it be for you?

Your long line of Goddess DNA would lead me to assume you're leaning toward changing the world. The thread of emotions from the women before you pulse through you. You are the combination of every natural element. Of every maternal energy. You have been birthed from a line of women who have stood up, spoken up, and led with love through shifts and changes throughout history. Contributing to build the society you stand in today.

## EVOLUTION EXERCISE: NEED SOME SUPPORT?

As we begin to harness our Goddess super-power, we may focus our energies on only one area or pursuit and that naturally makes everything else go out of balance. So try to keep your Goddess energy fluid and flexible and sustainable. Here is a list of Goddesses you can call on to help support your divine feminine energy, whether you need a boost in fertility, creativity, compassion, wisdom, beauty, love, or healing.

You may connect with different Goddesses depending on your need, trust your intuition and don't be afraid to call on them. The trick, call on the one who resonates with you now—that's easy! It is also important to know that you don't always need to call on them, sometimes they will visit you: be it in dreams, visions, or in the middle of your meditation, so keep an eye out.[1]

| Aphrodite | Greek | Love, beauty, sensuality—a good one to summon when you need some self-love. |
| Artemis | Greek | Courage, independence, protection—ideal to summon when you are fearful of change or are challenged. |
| Axo-Mama | Peruvian | Fertility—call on her when you want to conceive. Best not to if you are looking for more of a contraceptive Goddess! |
| Brigid | Celtic | Creativity, inspiration, healing—she is good to call on when using your hands, be it writing, art, massage. |
| Ceres | Roman | Nourishment, healing—good to call on when you are ill or feeling under the weather. I call on her when I have chocolate cravings! |
| Diana | Roman | Hunting, purity, independence—call on her when you seek truth. |
| Freya | Norse | Love, healing, sensuality—call on her when you have relationship problems and you need some loving good vibes around you. |
| Isis | Egyptian | Nourishment, wholeness, awakening—call on her when you are studying and learning. |

| Kali | Indian | Transformation, destruction, change—summon her when you are in a transition. |
|---|---|---|
| Kuan Yin | Asian | Compassion, mercy—call on her when you are in conflict, girl will help you see both sides of the argument. |
| Lakshmi | Indian | Wealth, abundance—summon her when you need some help in the money department. |
| Sekhmet | Egyptian | War, anger, negativity—summon her in times of conflict and strife to help resolve corruption and to offer protection. She eats negativity for breakfast. |
| Sophia | Greek | Wisdom, power—call on her when you need to communicate with insight and authority. Think of her as your go-to girl boss. |
| Tiamat | Babylonian | Power, protection, magic—summon her when you need a shield of security around you. |

The women in war, in protest, in art, in business, in hospitals, in the home. The women who fed, led, taught, inspired, and told you about a better way forward. Each important. Each instrumental. You are connected to all of them, from Goddess to governess, from priestess to president, from mother to matriarch. Each of you is a vital piece of this evolutionary puzzle. There is no complete picture without every little contribution. All pieces must be present. Coming together as one. May your life be a tribute to them all. And honor their contribution as much as yours.

No woman was ever left behind or forgotten. They are alive in you. In your nature and willpower to share their stories, to tell others these tales of wisdom, of woman, of your experiences and emotional evolutionary achievements in your lifetime. Your personal stories. As educational and inspiring as any Goddess in mythology. Your journey. Your demons. Your moments of transformation.

See here's the thing. You can be anything. But it turns out your power is less in what you are and more in what you do. The old saying that "actions speak louder than words" has never been truer. Doing is where the magic happens. And magic is what you do. To do is where the mastery is. And you are a Goddess in everything you grow and become. To you, being and doing are one and the same!

———

Now, if masculine energy is what you seek—strength, leadership, logic, protection, knowledge, and courage—then you may need to yang up your energy with some of these gods.[2]

| Aengus | Irish | Youth, love—call on him when you seek playfulness and fun. I call him my young soul party god. |
|---|---|---|
| Apollo | Greek | Beauty, music, healing—summon him when you need reassurance of your beauty and to heal your self-confidence. |
| Ganesh | Indian | Strength, perseverance, overcoming obstacles—call on him when you want to give up. He is the god of pep talks and pushing on. |
| Green Man | Celtic | Fertility, abundance, sexuality—summon him when you need to up your sex drive or sexual self-confidence. |
| Horus | Egyptian | Knowledge, eternal life, protection—call on him when you are ill or seek safety. |
| Mars | Roman | Aggression, war, courage—summon him when you need to fight for something you believe in, or stand up for something. |
| Mercury | Roman | Intelligence, communication, trade—call on him when doing business or collaborating with others; he'll have your back. |
| Odin | Norse | Knowledge, prophesy—summon him when you need to tap into your intuition or seek the truth of a situation. |
| Shiva | Indian | Destruction, transformation—call on him when you have been knocked down and are in the process of learning, growing, or rebuilding. |
| Vishnu | Indian | Preservation, stability—summon him when you feel ungrounded, shaken, or unsettled. |
| Zeus | Greek | Authority, justice, abundance—call on him when you seek honesty and integrity in a situation. He is kind of like the Dr. Phil of the god realm. |

## EVOLUTION EXERCISE: COMMUNICATION ETIQUETTE

There is a certain etiquette to apply when connecting with deities. It is like walking into someone's home and not asking if it is okay to leave your shoes on. Being a conscious soul you know to show respect, but here are some extra tips to help you when communicating with your spirit squad, be it a Goddess, god, spirit guide, or spirit animal.

- **Ask for assistance:** They can usually only intervene when asked to, so don't be afraid to ask for guidance or help.
- **Surrender:** If you have asked for help, you need to let them take the reins and trust in their guidance. Don't ask for help and then screw your nose up when the answer isn't what you expected.
- **No-harm policy:** Always seek to do good. Trust me, you don't want to be summoning evil energies to do your dirty work. You should always seek help for a positive resolution or reason.
- **Don't be rude:** Say thank you, show some manners. Be grateful and you will have a kind and helpful ally. Show your Goddess etiquette off to everyone, you classy conscious cat you.

## Taking Goddess Action

### KNOWING WHAT TO BE IS THE FIRST STEP. KNOWING WHAT TO DO WITH YOURSELF IS THE SIGN OF AN EVOLVING BEING.

Knowing what to be is the first step. Knowing what to do with yourself is the sign of an evolving being. What to be, in defining your Goddess, is becoming conscious of your behaviors, your elemental energy, where you are, and what you are learning. Have a clear vision in your transformational Goddess arc, know what you want to become and where you are headed.

You don't really need to have a destination, but a direction is essential. Next comes knowing what you need to do in order to get there. Knowing what you need in order to move forward.

The transformational tools at hand to help you: your elements, your empowerment, how you can best embody your Goddess journey. Why? Because you won't get far if you never digest the lessons along the way. Or worse, if you never notice them in the first place. You. You know who you are. You know where you

## EVOLUTION EXERCISE: TAKING YOUR NEXT STEPS

Here are some practical takeaways to help you move forward beyond the pages of this book.

- **Sign up for something bigger than yourself.** It could be to support someone, to nurture something, to teach, heal, or help. It could be a neighborhood cause, a community cause, or a global cause—find out what you're passionate about and participate. You don't need to be leading a march of thousands to create change (but if that resonates, do it).
- **You can simply help a neighbor, a coworker, a stranger.** Being a good human in a world that needs good humans can be transformational in itself. Now that you are aware of opportunities for transformation and growth you will begin to notice them more, you won't ignore chances to support others.
- **Research Goddess circles,** ask around for women's groups, mentors, or gatherings that might resonate with you. Follow your intuition, trust your feelings, go where your evolutionary journey leads you. Even if it simply means handing this book on to a fellow Goddess. Every act is action.

The aim of the game of life has always been to go from here to there. Even in nature sitting still is a dangerous act, sitting can get you killed, eaten. In our case, stuck, defeated. Moving will empower you. Your emotion will move through you. This will make you feel alive! Why? Because transformation isn't about treading water, it's about riding the waves. Rest assured, it is a messy business, this change. Your awakened abilities will be tested. But know this, you were built to thrive in chaos, to create anew, to rejuvenate, to rebirth, to survive in the never-ending swirl of this world. Own that. Trust that. Be in that space. And keep doing and loving what you do.

are going. And you know that the things that happen to you from here to there are part of what makes you divine.

Everything contributes to your expansion. It isn't conspiring against you, it is challenging you to rise up, to grow, to evolve—evolving being the operative word as we never stop. It is a never-ending action. Cycles of growth. Never-ending phases of change. Eternal transformation.

Wherever you are on the transformational arc, on the evolutionary scale of things, know that your archetype, the elements, and you are forever developing. And know that you have the power to change not just yourself, but also the world around you. As you grow, the world around you grows. Like a drop of water sends ripples, the trees branch out, and the sun's rays sweep across lands, know that you can impact more than you will ever know, see, or understand, simply from your choice to do more than be.

# TAKE RESPONSIBILITY FOR YOUR LIGHT, YOUR WARMTH, YOUR GLOW. LISTEN IN ACTION. THOSE WHO HAVE THEIR MOUTHS OPEN DO NOT LEARN. LET THE WINDS OF CHANGE BE YOUR BACK WIND.

Take responsibility for your light, your warmth, your glow. Listen in action. Those who have their mouths open do not learn. Let the winds of change be your back wind. Open your arms to the potential of the world and let the elements carry you. Surround yourself with the souls of Goddess giants. Get excited about like-minded beings who do. Who like you get excited about change. From the change of the seasons to the sounds of the ocean. A sunrise. Rain. The stars. I for one am excited that you don't just claim consciousness, you act with consciousness. You move mindfully. Act consciously. Ever moving forward. Ever changing.

Make this your mantra for eternal evolution . . .

## EVOLUTIONARY EXERCISE: EVOLVE

An exercise to do every single day *to activate your Goddess magic.* Operate from your most primitive instincts: love, intuition, growth, and compassion. Never stop digesting new insights, opening yourself to new visions, and striving for all things blissful balance. Follow in the footsteps of the ancients, the elders, the Goddesses!

E—Expand: Your wisdom and beliefs systems.

V—Values: Open yourself up to all values and ways of living well.

O—Observe: Yourself, more than others, reflect and learn about yourself, both body and spirit.

L—Love: Let your organic and primitive response always be love.

V—Vision: Allow yourself to think and absorb new thoughts and dreams.

E—Equalize: Never stop growing, learning, and schooling your soul and self to find that state of balance in your life. That spiritual sweet spot.

# AFTERWORD

*"MY MISSION IN LIFE IS NOT MERELY TO SURVIVE, BUT TO THRIVE."*
*—MAYA ANGELOU*

Your Goddess story now walks. May your lineage be dusted off, no longer buried or lost. But standing, moving with you. Your ancestors' voices echo louder as you listen. You are no mystery woman, nor is how you came to be and do.

You are reborn. Like every new day, you start again. You are always different from who you were the day before. There is always an element of change in you. And that, my love, that is what makes you a Goddess truly capable of anything, because you are connected to everything.

This is your new age. It calls for a new approach. A new attitude. A new way of thinking. In this new age, anything is possible. This is your time. Be the change. Have the courage to be more. To do more.

Life isn't about small, safe steps. It's about those moments we trust, leap, and the place we go to when we didn't think we could go, or had been told we couldn't, but believed we could. Truth is we did it anyway. Live big today, and every day. Know that the old you, the old stories exist as lessons only, not limitations. The stories that have held you back don't matter as much as what you do now—that is what matters. Because the stories behind you, and the stories ahead of you, are nothing compared to what lies within you. Evolving as a spiritual being, a spiritual doer, a better human isn't a matter of "if" for you, it is a matter of "when." It is all about the "how" for you. How you choose to learn, grow, and change.

LIVE BIG TODAY, AND EVERY DAY. KNOW THAT THE OLD YOU, THE OLD STORIES EXIST AS LESSONS ONLY, NOT LIMITATIONS.

All of us can change. Not everyone chooses to evolve. But you do. Not everyone chooses to walk beyond what is tolerated, what is just acceptable. You walk amongst those who walked wild new paths to existence—that dared to say yes to walking an unknown path forward. That is what the wild woman in all of us, the Goddess, the nudge, the soul ache, the frustrating itch is; it is a roaring *yes*.

Yes, you can. Yes, you are. Yes, you will. Yes, anything is possible if you have the nerve. I look at you, and I say, yes, yes, Goddess. This was never history. My story. Her story. It was always yours. Ours. This is your day, our day, and every day, for everyone, a move forward. To gather. Together. To her.

---

There is a chant and song that whenever I hear it gives me goose bumps. Something in me is summoned. The beat of a drum rattles the earth under my feet, shaking the sleeping souls of our ancestors awake, and I feel their mission pulse through me. Reading the lyrics on the page, the words will sing to you. If you feel inclined, look online for the song by Sandy Vaughn, and let the song hit your Goddess soul.

### I Hear the Voices of the Grandmothers[1]

I hear the voice of the grandmothers calling me
I hear the voice of the grandmothers' song
She says wake up, wake up, child, wake up, wake up
Listen, listen
Listen, listen
I hear the voice of the grandmothers calling me
I hear the voice of the grandmothers' song
She says stand in your power, woman, stand in your power
Listen, listen
Listen, listen

I hear the voice of the grandmothers calling me
I hear the voice of the grandmothers' song
She says give birth, give life, mother, give birth, give life
Listen, listen
Listen, listen

I hear the voice of the grandmothers calling me
I hear the voice of the grandmothers' song
She says teach and give wisdom, crone, teach and give wisdom
Listen, listen
Listen, listen

May the rivers all run clear
May the mountains be unspoiled
May the trees grow tall
May the air be pure
May the earth be shared by all

Listen, listen
Listen, listen
Listen, listen
Listen, listen

It's time we all chanted "Wake up, wake up, listen, listen."[2] It's time to listen to our truth. Our inner callings. To hear the calling we are all being whispered, to arrive, to gather, to rise. Fact is, now you know what you are made of. Now that you know your transformational truth, there are no limits to where you can go, what you can change, and what you can become. After all, you are a Goddess.

# ACKNOWLEDGMENTS

Thank you to all the Maidens, Mothers, and Crones who made this book possible. This book was scribed by a tribe of elders, a collective of chicks, a group of guides, source, universe, God, and angels (Gabrielle and Metatron) who channeled messages through crown chakra to keyboard, and my one hopeful soul reporting for spiritual service.

To the many sages who graced me with insights and learnings to share in the pages of this book, I bow:

Zhena Muzyka, the queen who believed in this project when it was a mere seed. Thank you for your guidance, holding space for me, and helping me step into my truth in these pages.

Judith Curr, and her hardworking tribe at Simon and Schuster.

Marilyn Allen, Emily Han, and Anne Slight, who all poured love and energy into these words for the world to grow from.

To the women who led the way for me, including Marija Gimbutas, Starhawk, Caroline Myss, and Clarissa Pinkola Estés.

Women who walk along the same path as me sharing the priestess ways and support my work, thank you, sisters. Rebecca Campbell, Mel Wells, Shannon Kaiser, Amy Leigh Mercree, Rachel Hunter, Michelle Buchanan, Emma Loewe, Kayla Jacobs, Jordan Younger, Marissa Lace, Angela Leigh, Julie Parker, HeatherAsh Amara, Ruby Warrington, Taryn Brumfitt, Rebecca Van Leeuwen, Sarah Brosnahan, Jane Loewe, Kim Macky, Janelle Brunton-Rennie, Makaia Carr, Abbylee Childs, Hannah Jensen, Sarah Tanner, Erin O'Hara, and Diane Sims. And to all the women who crossed my path while this book was being birthed, thank you . . . Sandra, Kelly, Sarah, Charlotte, Leanne, Jane, Mo, Jess, Worth, Barbara, Kristen, Peggy, Cathy, Jennifer, Olivia, Roylin, Susan, Chante, Toni, Rebecca, Chris, Kathryn, Lisette, Aleisha, Lizzie, Vanessa, Jasmine, Emma, Bridget, Gaia, Rani, Mel, Jess, Julie + more.

And to the strong and loving men who supported me in this journey, especially my father, Merv, and patient partner, Brad. Who watched on while the weaving of these pages took place.

This book took a tribe, and for each of you, I give thanks.

# APPENDIX: GODDESS MANTRAS

A collection of go-to Goddess mantras to take with you along your evolutionary journey.

Everything is conspiring to evolve and grow me.

I don't strive for perfection. I know that perfection doesn't exist. Instead, I strive for progress. I celebrate what is achieved, even the smallest steps forward.

I don't see opposition. I see opportunity for change.

To change the world, I change me.

True belonging is a spiritual practice, and the ability to find sacredness in both being a part of something and having the courage to stand alone.

I need to be in balance to achieve a balanced world. I always seek to see both sides, seeking compromise, change, understanding, and peace.

I speak up and act when things no longer serve me. I leave toxic relationships. I stand up for myself at work. I show respect to myself by doing what's best for me.

I protect other women. Always knowing we are all from the same tribe. On the same team.

I will show up for other women and support my sisters. Empowered women empower women.

Make peace with the evolution process. Respect your reworked flaws weaved into who you are now as a woman.

I choose to respond. Not to react. I am conscious of the difference.

I listen always with the intent to understand, not reply.

I allow myself to be loving. I give compliments to strangers, and tell people I care about them. I love, freely.

I use my emotions as a strength, not a weakness. My emotions charge my soul. I feel out my emotions. I listen to them.

I am not wounded by my experiences; I am bettered by my experiences.

I share my emotions and story to help heal others. Vulnerable. Real. Raw.

I honor all of my emotions. Recognizing the power of both wild, angered passion and loving, driven passion.

Your emotion is your empowerment. Accept it is both a blessing and a curse to feel life so deeply.

Labels only limit. Be defined by what frees you.

I offer an insight over an insult.

I see with my heart, intuition, and soul—all three eyes. I choose to see the good.

I have healthy boundaries.

What eclipses your wisdom? Eliminate what isn't helping you evolve.

I stand up for what I believe in, while respecting others' opinions.

Respect, understanding, and taking the energy to meet someone where they are is an expression of love.

I neutralize hostile people and situations. I keep my feelings in check when handling difficult situations and don't allow anger or frustration to overcome me.

I consider everyone's point of view and use my emotional intelligence to guide me in conflict.

I give myself space in times of lessons and learnings to reflect on and receive the experience.

I nurture my community, offering support and guidance, and cheerleading those around me.

I focus on my presence over my hustle. Other women like my company.

I collaborate with others, allowing it to flow rather than force.

I am constantly renewing myself. Just as a snake sheds its skin, shed your past and start over and over again.

My feminine power is support, compassion, and unity—not to demand or conquer.

I give as much time to my darkness as to my light. Giving myself space to process all my emotions and experiences.

My sisterhood is medicine. I ask for help when I need it.

I speak my truth.

I don't let labels define me. Nor judge others.

I contribute to the world. I take awakened action. I strive for progress.

I understand that if I show up every day, even in little ways, I help to contribute overall in a big way. Less be, more do.

I give my time, and energy, to something bigger than myself.

I am not wounded. I am not a victim. I accept, learn, and move forward.

I am brave, not stuck. I step into my darkness, as proudly as I do into my light. Understanding that both teach and heal me.

I am unapologetically empowered, kind, gracious, strong.

I am a Goddess.

# NOTES

## CHAPTER 1: GODDESS WITH A THOUSAND FACES

1 "Goddess," *The Merriam-Webster Dictionary*, accessed on October 5, 2017. https://www.merriam-webster.com/dictionary/goddess.

2 Email interview by author with Tribal Trust Foundation founder, Barbara Savage, August 1, 2017.

3 Ibid.

4 Ibid.

5 Ibid.

## CHAPTER 3: OUR FEMININE ARCHETYPES + NARRATIVES

1 Joseph Campbell, *The Power of Myth* (New York: Anchor Books, 1991).

2 Ibid.

3 Dr. Clarissa Pinkola Estés, *Women Who Run with the Wolves: Myths and Stories of the Wild Woman Archetype* (New York: Ballantine, 1992).

4 Ibid.

5 Caroline Myss, *Archetypes: Who Are We?* (Carlsbad, CA: Hay House, 2013).

## CHAPTER 4: TIMELINE BY THE STARS

1 David Bokovoy, "God, Gods, and Goddesses: Making Sense of the Elohim in Genesis," *Patheos,* December 6, 2014, accessed on August 25, 2017. www.patheos.com/blogs/davidbokovoy/2014/12/god-gods-and-Goddesses-making-sense-of-the-elohim-in-genesis.

2 Ibid.

3 Ibid.

4 Marija Gimbutas, accessed on November 5, 2017. http://www.marijagimbutas.com/.

5 Manuela Dunn Mascetti and Peter Lorie, *Nostradamus: Prophecies for Women* (New York: Simon and Schuster, 1995), Chapter 1, page 47.

6 Joan Didion, *The Year of Magical Thinking* (New York: Vintage Penguin Books, 2007).

7 Rebecca Campbell, *Rise Sister Rise: A Guide to Unleashing the Wise, Wild Women Within* (Carlsbad, CA: Hay House, 2016).

8 Kavita N. Ramdas, Mount Holyoke, Commencement Address, "Dancing Our Revolution: Why We Need Uncommon Women Now," May 19, 2013, accessed on August 25, 2017. https://www.mtholyoke.edu/media/kavita-n-ramdas-85-citation-and-speech.

## CHAPTER 7: MOON EVOLUTION ESSENTIALS

1 Body Image Movement, accessed September 9, 2017. https://bodyimagemovement.com/.

2 Jessica Samakow, "This Woman Wants to Change How All of Us See Our Bodies," *The Huffington Post,* May 14, 2014, accessed on September 9, 2017. https://

www.huffingtonpost.com/2014/05/14/embrace
-taryn-brumfitt_n_5318178.html.

## CHAPTER 8: MOON MODALITIES

1 Miranda Grey, *Red Moon—Understanding and Using the Creative, Sexual and Spiritual Gifts of the Menstrual Cycle* (London, UK: Upfront Publishing, 2009), Chapter 4, pages 48–54.

2 Ibid.

3 "Meditation for Balancing the Moon Centers," 3HO: Healthy, Happy, Holy Organization, accessed on September 29, 2017. https://www.3ho.org/3ho -lifestyle/women/moon-centers/meditation -balancing-moon-centers.

## CHAPTER 10: WATER EVOLUTION ESSENTIALS

1 Doug Sundheim, "Good Leaders Get Emotional," *Harvard Business Review*, August 15, 2013. https://hbr .org/2013/08/good-leaders-get-emotional.

## CHAPTER 11: WATER MODALITIES

1 Dr. Vitale and Dr. Ihaleakala Hew Len, *Zero Limits*, news for the Soul Internet Radio, accessed on November 2, 2016. http://hooponoponoinsights .wordpress.com. Reprinted with permission.

## CHAPTER 12: EARTH MYTHOLOGY + POWERS

1 Jane Goodall and Phillip Berman, *Reason for Hope: A Spiritual Journey* (New York: Grand Central Publishing, 2000).

## CHAPTER 13: EARTH EVOLUTION ESSENTIALS

1 Amy Leigh-Mercree, *The Chakras and Crystals Cookbook: Juices, Sorbets, Smoothies, Salads, and Soups to Empower Your Energy Centers* (Allegria Entertainment, 2016), Chapter 1, "Chakras." Reprinted with permission.

## CHAPTER 14: EARTH MODALITIES

1 Amy Leigh-Mercree, *The Chakras and Crystals Cookbook: Juices, Sorbets, Smoothies, Salads, and Soups to Empower Your Energy Centers* (Allegria Entertainment, 2016), Chapter 1, "Chakras." Reprinted with permission.

2 April Holloway, "How Ancient People Marked the Equinox Around the World," *Ancient Origins*, March 20, 2014. http://www.ancient-origins.net/ancient -places/how-ancient-people-marked-equinox -around-world-001464.

3 Leigh-Mercree, *The Chakras and Crystals Cookbook.*

## CHAPTER 15: AIR MYTHOLOGY + POWERS

1 Scott Cunningham, *The Complete Book of Incense, Oils, and Brews* (Woodbury, MN: Llewellyn Worldwide, 2002), pages 27–44. Reprinted with permission of publisher.

## CHAPTER 16: AIR EVOLUTION ESSENTIALS

1 "Mission + History," WRISE, accessed on November 2, 2017. http://wrisenergy.org/about-wrise /mission/.

## CHAPTER 17: AIR MODALITIES

1 Siegfried Morenz, *Egyptian Religion* (Ithaca, NY: Cornell University Press, 1973), Chapter 5, pages 88–89.

2 Melissa Eisler, "Nadi Shodhana: How to Practice Alternate Nostril Breathing," The Chopra Center, accessed on September 26, 2017. http://www.chopra .com/articles/nadi-shodhana-how-to-practice -alternate-nostril-breathing.

3 Scott Cunningham, *The Complete Book of Incense, Oils, and Brews* (Woodbury, MN: Llewellyn Worldwide, 2002), pages 27–44. Reprinted with permission of publisher.

4 Anita Sanchez, *The Four Sacred Gifts: Indigenous Wisdom for Modern Times* (New York: Enliven Books/ Simon & Schuster, 2017).

5 Ibid.

## CHAPTER 18: SUN MYTHOLOGY + POWERS

1 Rachel Hunger, "Raging Unicorn," accessed on November 2, 2017. http://www.rachelhunter.com /blog/2017/6/29/anger-.

2 Skye Alexander, *The Modern Guide to Witchcraft: Your Complete Guide to Witches, Covens, and Spells* (Avon, MA: Adams Media, 2014), Chapter 6, "Gods and Goddesses," pages 75–76.

3 April Holloway, "How Ancient People Marked the Equinox Around the World," *Ancient Origins*, March 20, 2014. http://www.ancient-origins.net/ancient -places/how-ancient-people-marked-equinox -around-world-001464.

## CHAPTER 19: SUN EVOLUTION ESSENTIALS

1 Anne McGurk, "Powering Up: Meet the Women Electrifying China's Energy Transition," Greenpeace, accessed on November 17, 2017. http://www .greenpeace.org/eastasia/news/blog/powering-up -meet-the-women-electrifying-china/blog/58885/.

2 Ibid.

## CHAPTER 20: SUN MODALITIES

1 Kundalini, *Breath of Fire*. Reprinted with permission from The Kundalini Research Institute. For further information, contact www.kriteachings.org.

2 Ibid.

## ACTIVATING YOUR GODDESS POWERS

1 Skye Alexander, *The Modern Guide to Witchcraft: Your Complete Guide to Witches, Covens, and Spells* (Avon, MA: Adams Media, 2014), Chapter 6, "Gods and Goddesses," pages 75–76.

2 Ibid.

## AFTERWORD

1 Sandy Vaughn of Tonasket, Washington, "I Hear the Voices of the Grandmothers," from the CD *Home to the River of Love*. Reprinted with permission from artist.

2 Ibid.